DRUG WARS

Also by Tim Wells:

444 Days: The Hostages Remember

Also by William Triplett:

Flowering of the Bamboo

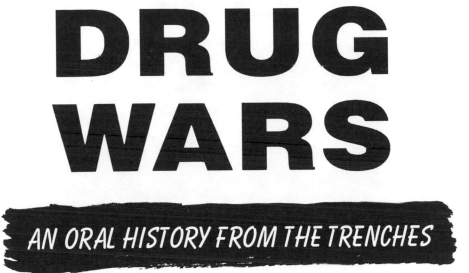

DRUG WARS

AN ORAL HISTORY FROM THE TRENCHES

TIM WELLS
AND
WILLIAM TRIPLETT

WILLIAM MORROW AND COMPANY, INC.
New York

Library of Congress Cataloging-in-Publication Data

Wells, Tim.
    Drug wars: an oral history from the trenches / by Tim Wells and William
Triplett.
      p.   cm.
    ISBN 0-688-09548-8
    1. Narcotics, Control of—United States. 2. Drug abuse—United
States. I. Triplett, William. II. Title.
HV5825.W3837 1992
363.4'5'0973—dc20

91-30465
CIP

Printed in the United States of America

First Edition

1 2 3 4 5 6 7 8 9 10

BOOK DESIGN BY PAUL CHEVANNES

This book is lovingly dedicated to

David Pursiano and Leni Wildflower
—whose wisdom and kindness provide a guiding light—

and to
Constant Roussel
—who showed the way, again and again.

CONTENTS

A NOTE ON
SOURCES

To draw the reader into the trenches of the drug war we have conducted over 250 interviews from which the text that follows is derived. All of these interviews have been tightly edited for thematic consistency, narrative control, and dramatic impact. On three occasions we relied on transcripts of sworn testimony delivered before the state of New Jersey Commission of Investigation into Cocaine in 1988. The quotes attributed to "Carlos" that appear on pages 43–44 and 99–100 are paraphrased from the testimony of a Colombian cocaine trafficker currently enrolled in the federal witness protection program. The quote from Dr. Mark Gold that appears on page 246 is taken from his testimony before the New Jersey Commission.

Due to the fact that a large number of individuals spoke only on the condition that their identity would be protected, we have employed pseudonyms to protect those who desire to remain anonymous. The book is constructed so that whenever a first name or

9

nickname is used to identify the source, that name is fictitious. Other significant details, such as city of residence and/or occupation, have also occasionally been altered at the request of the interviewee. In those instances where both a first and last name are used to identify a voice in the text, it is the real name of a person who agreed to speak on the record for direct attribution.

PREFACE

In June of 1971, Richard Nixon became the first American President to declare "war on drugs." His heavily publicized initiative was, he said, "designed to mount a frontal assault on our number one public enemy." Throughout the two decades that have followed President Nixon's declaration, the drug war has become a staple of contemporary political rhetoric, as a successive series of administrations have launched highly touted antidrug campaigns. President Bush has joined his predecessors in echoing Nixon's claim that the drug epidemic is "public enemy number one." Yet, the number of drug addicts living in our cities and towns has increased at geometric rates, and police officials routinely estimate that over 50 percent of all criminal activity is directly related to substance abuse.

Today, the United States government claims that 74,371,000 American citizens have used illicit drugs at some point in their lives, which represents 37 percent of the total population. For those under the age of thirty-five, the numbers are even more dramatic; it is estimated that a staggering 63 percent of all Americans born after 1955 have experimented with illegal drugs. The rise in addiction rates has been coupled with a steady rise in violent crime and drug-related fatalities. Since 1971, when President Nixon first declared war on drugs, the violent crimes most commonly associated with substance abuse (murder, robbery, and aggravated assault) have risen at a per capita rate of 67 percent, while arrests for violation of United States narcotics laws are up by a full 104 percent. If present trends continue, every citizen living in the United States has a fifty-fifty chance of becoming the victim of a drug-related crime at some point in the 1990s.

The only reasonable conclusion that can be drawn from these statistics is that the nation's drug enforcement policies have failed, and failed miserably. That failure has not, however, led to a systematic reevaluation of the problem, nor has it encouraged the emergence of innovative solutions that address the root causes of the epidemic. On the contrary, government officials and politicians have continued to deliver bombastic get-tough speeches that raise the decibel level of the debate, but fail to address the complexities of the problem in any meaningful way.

This problem has been compounded by the tendency of the nation's news media to deal only with the most sensational aspects of the drug crisis. It is impossible to turn on the evening news or open a newspaper without being confronted by stories of murder, violence, and tragedy. Such news bites offer brief, fleeting glimpses into the painful realities of the drug epidemic, but are too fragmented and narrow to offer any meaningful insight or comprehension.

Indeed, one of the ironies of the drug war is that we commonly hear the most from those who know the least. Lost have been the voices of those most intimately engaged on the front lines. Drug users, dealers, and addicts, as well as undercover cops, all struggle to maintain an invisible presence. Little is known about the circumstances of their daily lives. This oral history attempts to redress that imbalance. The authors have spent the past two years riding with undercover cops, and visiting jails, prisons, crack houses, public housing projects, rehab centers, emergency rooms, and precinct stations in numerous American cities to talk with a wide variety of law enforcement officials, drug users, addicts, dealers, and smugglers.

Our guiding concept has been to seek out those most intimately involved in the drug war, and provide them with an opportunity to describe their experiences in their own words. We have tried not to pass judgment or recommend solutions—only to listen and learn, with the hope that hidden truths will emerge.

What follows is the result of that effort.

*   *   *

This book could not have been written without the assistance of numerous individuals to whom we are deeply indebted. First and foremost are those people whose stories appear in this volume. They opened their hearts, gave freely of their time, and willingly shared what were frequently painful memories. A special word of thanks is due to Dr. Jaspar Ormond and Elin Jones of the Washington, D.C., Department of Corrections, and to the men and women enrolled in the pilot treatment program at the Lorton Penitentiary. Detectives John Brooks, Luis Fernandez, Mauricio Smith, and Jimmy White also deserve special recognition.

A number of people granted interviews that were not included in this volume, but they nonetheless provided significant insights that helped shape the book. Many others gave valuable leads and suggestions. We would therefore like to thank: Phil Arroyo, Ron Bancroft, Elizabeth Beauchesne, Dr. Art Behrmann, Jack Blum, Ted Bourke, Eric Butler, George Cadavid, Joan Caplan, Tom Cash, Scott Coffin, "Dan," Lieutenant John Diers, Lawrence Doman, Ron Dowdy, "Ed," Pablo Faria, Ron Flemmings, Dr. Ann Fletcher, Wanda Flores, Rosalyn Goldfarb, Jim Grange, Richard Gregoric, George Gunoe, Eva Harmon, Charlie Harrigan, Beverly Heinselman, Dr. Paul Hergenroeder, Vanessa Herring, "Jim," Jeffery M. Johnson, Margo Kail, Robert Kammer, Woody Kirk, Mark A. R. Kleiman, David Kruciger, George C. Larson, Loren Leadmon, Judge Alfred Lerner, Joe Lisi, Dr. Richard Lopez, Mike McQuillan, J. C. Mendez, Ken Morris, Frank Mullin, Patrick O'Brien, Bill Pappalardo, Mark Perry, "Phil," Robert Phillips, Eric Pomerantz, Jim Potter, Keith Powell, Janet Reno, Tim Resau, Richard Rider, "Robert," Judge Burton Roberts, Wayne Roberts, "Rose," Commander Richard Rothlein, Michael Russell, Russ Schuldt, Ted Sclavos, E. Elaine Shannon, Allen Sheperd, Dave Sherry, Edward Shohat, Gene Shook, Sergeant Fred Silber, David Skarwecki, Pat Slifka, Congressman Larry Smith, Andrew Sonner, Miles Sonnes, Louis J. Sperling, Gwendolyn C. Stewart, Donald Streater, Bill Thomas, Robbie Viator, and Joe Yacinski.

For their help and openness on the whole, thanks must also go to: the U.S. Border Patrol; U.S. Customs Service; U.S. Drug Enforcement Agency; City of Akron Police Department; City of Miami Police Department; Dade County Police Department; New York City

Police Department's narcotics unit; Prince George's County Police Department; Washington, D.C., Metro Police Department; and Washington Psychiatric Institute.

Our heartfelt gratitude is extended to our editor Liza Dawson, whose helping hand was indispensable, and to our agent Clyde Taylor, whose advice and encouragement proved as essential as it was steadfast. Thanks also to Stephanie Arts, who guided the manuscript through serial rights sales with consummate skill.

William Triplett would like to personally state: I am deeply indebted to Phil and Anna Menzies—truer, more loyal friends there never were. To my parents, Jacqueline and Ernie Triplett, I am grateful for the interest and encouragement they each showed. I also thank Marion Ness, my dear aunt, who never lets a visit go by without a strong word of support for my work. The same must be said for longtime family friends Bedford and Edith May, who never seemed to tire hearing about this book. Thanks, too, to my brother Jack, not only for his abiding interest but also for the room he gave me when I came to do interviews. And to my aunt and uncle Violette and Constant Roussel, I owe eternal thanks for the kind of love and generosity that is absolutely inspiring. Last, but most important, I thank my wife Ann Marie, whose love and support often sustained me when nothing else would. I am extremely fortunate for her wise counsel—accurate from first to last—and above all, for her presence in my life.

Tim Wells would like to personally state: Over years that are now stretching into decades, David Pursiano and Leni Wildflower, whose names appear on the dedication page of this book, have provided wisdom, friendship, and support that has enriched my life in ways that words could never adequately express. As always, Christopher Riggall provided more than friendship; throughout every stage of manuscript preparation his comments and suggestions were of great assistance. The gracious generosity of George Unthank significantly eased my burdens, and this book would be incomplete without noting his kindness. Eternal words of love and tribute are due to my parents, Robert and Phyllis Wells, who are always there no matter what the need, so that no son could ever ask for more. And finally, there is Patricia Davis, for it is her companionship that carries me, her smile that cheers me, her understanding that warms me, and her love that sustains me.

CHAPTER 1

RECREATIONAL USERS

"Drugs," the late Abbie Hoffman once observed, "are as American as apple pie. You know, 'sex, drugs, and rock and roll' formed a holy trinity. Millions of us have worshiped at that altar—even a good Jewish boy like me." Indeed, America's schoolchildren are introduced to illegal drugs at surprisingly young ages, and amid their peers they are forced to come to terms with the excitement of temptation, the powerful yearning for acceptance, and the beckoning of fun and laughter that "recreational" experimentation calls forth.

The progression from alcohol and marijuana use to hard-core drug addiction is frequently cited in antidrug campaigns and educational literature designed to get kids to "just say no." One of the myths of such campaigns is that people who use illegal drugs inevitably end up suffering. The truth, however, is much more subtle and complicated. The vast majority of people who experiment with drugs do not suffer adverse consequences, and many feel that their lives have been enriched by the pleasures afforded by drug and alcohol use.

A white-collar professional who frequently smokes marijuana and uses cocaine explains, "There's a tremendous difference between drug use and drug abuse. I can honestly say that cocaine has never interfered with my ability to function professionally, and it is certainly a lot less debilitating than alcohol. I hear a lot of horror stories on television, but most of my friends—I mean the people I party with—are users and not abusers. I've been doing coke for the better portion of a decade, and I've never encountered an addict or been close to a drug-related tragedy in my life."

This is a sentiment frequently voiced by those who came of age in the 1960s and 1970s. As recreational users, they cite pleasure and social acceptance as the motives that guide their indulgence. Hinting at hidden motives and unconscious desires, they also point to therapeutic qualities drugs possess. "I'm a shy person," says an architect who works for a prestigious firm. "At parties I tend to be quiet and withdrawn, unless I'm drinking or maybe doing a little coke. I really like cocaine. It's a terrific high. It makes me feel euphoric and chatty—like I have a great personality. Conversations become intensified. You get locked into whoever you're talking to, and everything you say is intense, meaningful, profound. You're wonderful and you think the people around you are wonderful. It's the only drug I know of that makes me fall totally in love with the world."

Whatever the motive, an undeniable fact of contemporary American society is that drug and alcohol use permeates every social and economic stratum of our national life. Illicit drugs are not confined to the ghetto or the schoolyard, but are commonly found in corporate offices and suburban homes. "I'm in the real estate business," says an attractive young broker with a confiding smile, "and I know a lot of mortgage bankers who are into coke, and I know a lot of attorneys who are into coke. There's a group of us who hang out at a local music club, and that group includes a state senator and a policeman—both of whom regularly come in and use coke. The thing about cocaine is anyone can be doing it, but with most people who do, you never know."

———

GAIL: When people talk about drug education and lecture kids to "just say no," the one thing they never mention is that doing narcotics is tremendously pleasurable. Getting high is a lot of fun. Not only do drugs provide you sensual pleasure, they make friendships seem much more intense. When you're using, you think of your friends as being very tight. It's like forming a secret society.

So, in a way, using drugs is a logical thing to do. It's quite natural to seek out pleasure.

SNAKE: All through elementary school and junior high school, I never got high. Then, in my first year of high school, when I was fifteen, one of my teachers asked, "How many of you have tried marijuana?" There were about twenty kids in that class, and everyone raised their hand except me. That made me feel funny. I figured I was missing something.

STEPHANIE: I was nine years old the first time I got high. I was the youngest of five children, and I knew my older sister smoked pot. She was sixteen years old at the time, and I kept pestering her. I'd say, "I want to get high. I want to know what it's like." So one night we went out for a walk and smoked a joint together. I felt like I was walking on air. I thought it was the neatest feeling in the world. I remember thinking, "I'm high! I can't believe I'm high!" For a nine-year-old girl that was a really big deal.

ANDREW: I was thirteen years old when I first started experimenting with drugs. I was in junior high school, and I had a fear of marijuana. That's because it was an illegal drug, and I'd heard all these things about how drugs can screw you up. I didn't know if I could handle it. The only reason I used marijuana was because of peer pressure, because of what all my friends were saying.

The first time I used it, there were nine of us, and we each put in seventy-five cents to buy a couple of joints. You know, we were spending our lunch money. Then we went out in the woods and smoked our joints. The only thing it did was make me laugh a lot. Everything seemed funny—what one of the guys said about our gym teacher, or about some ugly girl. We were all laughing and joking.

That took the fear away. When I got home that evening I said to myself, "Alright! You did it! You can handle it!"

After that, I became more confident experimenting with drugs. The more I experimented the more it built my ego. Pretty soon, I figured, "Hey, I can handle anything." And I became very aggressive in my drug use.

ERNIE: My father is in the military, and we lived overseas in Europe for a few years. When we came back to the States I was thirteen years old, and all the kids over here were into smoking dope. I remember the first time I tried pot, I didn't get off. I didn't feel anything. I told myself, "I'm not going to smoke anymore, because that stuff doesn't do anything for me." But a couple days later some of the guys on the football team asked me if I wanted to go get high. Of course, I said yes. I wanted to be accepted by these guys, so I went off and smoked with them. This time I got real high. I laughed a lot, and felt real good inside. It was like a light went on in my head. I thought, "Oh, so this is the feeling that everybody's always talking about. This is why people like to get high."

After that, I started smoking dope all the time. I figured it was a lot easier to smoke dope than it was to drink, because dope is easier to hide and it's a lot easier to get. There's no such thing as being "under age." You don't have to have an ID to buy pot or hash, and it's available everywhere—at school, at the shopping center, in the gym, at concerts, in the park. Everywhere. To score, all you have to do is hang out.

TOBY: I first started doing drugs when I was fourteen. Mostly, it was soft stuff—smoking dope, alcohol, and amphetamines. There was a group of seven or eight of us. We'd sit out on a bank behind the junior high school, smoke dope, drop pills, drink liquor, and talk about sex, music, and sports. That was a wonderful time of life.

At first I stayed away from hard drugs because I'd heard too many horror stories. I'd heard how PCP and acid can scramble your brain. I'd heard how addictive heroin and cocaine can be. But some of my friends were beginning to experiment with harder drugs, and it never brought them anything but pleasure. That was especially true of the psychedelics and cocaine. My friends would trip for a while, come down, and everything would be fine. I started to wonder, "If this stuff is so dangerous, how come everybody is having so much fun? How come we're all still alive?"

I figured all the horror stories I'd heard were just teachers and parents using scare tactics. So what do you believe? What you hear from someone who has zero experience? Or what you see with your own eyes?

I was curious. I wanted to know what cocaine and acid were like. So I started using heavier drugs. By this time I was sixteen, and pretty soon I was doing drugs five, six days a week, and getting away with it. None of my teachers knew anything was wrong, and I kept everything hidden from my parents.

My best friend was a guy named Tom, and he was pretty wild. He was doing drugs faster and harder than I was, and he knew how to play all the angles. Pretty soon, he started dealing, and that opened up a whole new world for both of us. He teamed up with this guy named Joseph, who was a graduate student at San Diego State, and a couple of times a month they'd make a cross-border run into Tijuana and bring back huge quantities of marijuana and cocaine. They were selling it to street dealers out of Joseph's apartment, and making a profit of about two hundred percent. They'd invest one thousand or two thousand dollars, and in a single afternoon would have four thousand or five thousand dollars in cash.

Now we not only had an abundance of drugs, we had lots of money too. Tom would stuff my pockets full of twenties and tell me to go spend it. The irony is that we were much more scared of our parents finding us with all that cash than we were of getting caught by the police. We *had* to spend everything. If our parents found that much money lying around, they'd know what was going on. I mean, how do two sixteen-year-old kids explain three thousand dollars' worth of pocket change? Mostly, we'd spend it on perishable items, because we couldn't bring hundreds of dollars' worth of clothes and stereo equipment into the house. So we'd buy Dom Pérignon by the case and huge quantities of cocaine, and then we'd throw parties under the railroad tracks at Torrey Pines. It's amazing how ten teenage kids can spend three thousand dollars in a single night, and have nothing to show for it except blistered nostrils and nasty hangovers.

ELIZABETH: I grew up in a traditional Christian home where my parents tried to teach me the morals and values of the Church. It was a very oppressive home full of Christian guilt.

When I was fourteen I started hitchhiking a lot. That was one of the ways I looked for drugs. I'd tell my parents that a friend was picking me up at the end of the driveway, then I'd walk up the street to this big intersection and stick out my thumb. When someone picked me up I'd always make a point of bringing drugs into the conversation. I'd say, "I want to see what's happening down at the park. I want to see if I can score some pot." It wasn't unusual for the person who picked me up to say, "I have some. Do you want to roll a joint?" Or, "I know where we can get some. Do you want to go to a party?" And I'd always say yes. For me, hitchhiking was a way of being wild. Every time I stuck out my thumb I was hoping to score some drugs, hoping to find some adventure.

The best times were when a cute guy would pick me up and we'd get high together and go to a party. At parties I'd be like this totally anonymous person, this waif who'd suddenly been found, getting to know other people—getting high and getting drunk, making new connections. I'd call my parents and lie to them, tell them that I was spending the night with a girlfriend, and I'd stay out all night. My main goal was not just to get drunk or get high, but to find people that I could forge a common bond with. The socializing that went along with drugs provided that link, that bond. It was like I was part of this underground community where we had our own secrets, our own language, our own culture, our own way of connecting.

A lot of times sex was a by-product of getting high. Belonging to this counterculture meant having sex with people that I didn't know very well—you know, the sixties' idea of "free love," the idea that you can connect with a stranger on a sexual level. Because of sex I got a lot of attention from older guys. That was flattering. It gave me a sense of self-esteem. Getting high and spending time with older guys alleviated the normal anxieties that every fourteen- or fifteen-year-old girl feels as she's entering adolescence—the fears and worries about whether you're going to be liked or disliked. The good thing about being stoned is you always feel like you belong.

PATRICK: For me, high school was a three-year party. All I was interested in was drinking and getting high—getting crazy with my buddies. There wasn't a day that would go by when we wasn't drinking. In the cafeteria at school, the first thing we'd do at lunch hour was go around and bum enough money to make a beer run. Often as not, we'd hook our afternoon classes. I very seldom picked up a book, and to this day I have trouble with reading and writing. At graduation, we was all sitting in the back row drinking and laughing.

I remember on my eighteenth birthday my mother asked me, "What are you going to do with yourself? What's your goal in life?" I told her, "Ma, I only got one goal: I want to drink a case of beer and walk." And I wasn't kidding. I thought being able to drink made me a man. I couldn't look beyond the next party. The only thing I cared about was getting drunk, getting high, and screwing different girls. My motto was "Live fast, die young, and leave a good-looking corpse."

ROBERT: I didn't get into drugs seriously until I went to Vietnam. I was a grunt in the Marine Corps—a machine-gunner, an automatic weapons specialist. I started messing with opium and uppers, and then took it from there. I was trying to cope with combat and that got me deeper and deeper into drugs.

I had buddies getting blown away and stepping on land mines. Any second you knew you might be dead, or maimed beyond recognition. And you knew there were going to be times when you'd have to kill another human being. The whole time I was over there, I was thinking, "Man, this war ain't right. We're fighting for all the wrong things." You try to deal with that straight, and you can't do it. You just can't do it.

Ninety percent of the grunts I marched into combat with were on drugs. Every time we went out on patrol we were high. We were smoking opium, popping pills, and shooting heroin because that was what we needed to cope. We needed drugs to help us keep our heads together so we could survive.

JOHN: I was a helicopter door gunner in Vietnam in 1966, and the opportunity to abuse drugs was always present. In Vietnam we had *tremendous* marijuana. We'd roll Thai sticks, which we called "all-day suckers," because one joint in the morning and we'd still be blasted at night.

As a door gunner, I had to go out on insertion missions all the time. Those were missions where we'd take a platoon up in a helicopter and drop them in a landing zone. There were many, many times when we returned to pull them out, and would find ourselves loading up guys who were missing arms and legs. Guys I'd spoken to in the morning were zipped up tight in body bags. Being forced to confront that kind of carnage day after day takes its toll. It works on your head. I was so jaded by combat that I thought the guys who got killed were the lucky ones.

I responded to all that death and destruction by smoking as much dope as I could and staying as numb as I could for as long as I could. I was always high when we went out on missions. One time our helicopter got shot down, and I was stoned to the hilt. We were in one hell of a firefight, taking all kinds of automatic weapons fire from the VC. The pilot was knocked out, and I pulled him to safety. Then

I yanked the door gun free and laid down covering fire until another chopper could get in and evacuate us. For that performance I was awarded the Bronze Star. Can you believe that? I was given this prestigious combat decoration for something I'd done when I was stoned off my ass!

ALLAN: After Vietnam the Marine Corps assigned me to White House duty. I guess that was because I'm a little over six feet tall and I wasn't disfigured from the war. President Nixon only wanted Vietnam veterans on guard duty at the White House. That was part of a master plan he had—he wanted to stand these healthy-looking Marines in front of the White House with all their medals on and have them tell people that the Vietnam effort was a good one.

The funny thing is, I was stoned the entire time I was on White House duty. I was drinking and smoking marijuana at all hours of the day and night. I remember standing at my post at the White House in a complete fog—completely bombed from dope.

Being on the honor guard also meant burying the dead soldiers coming in from Vietnam. At Arlington Cemetery we were burying five or six bodies a day. At night I'd go out drinking, whoring, and brawling. Then in the day, I'd drive out to the airport to pick up the parents of a dead soldier we were about to bury. I'd stand by the grave, totally bombed, and watch the parents receive their sons' posthumous awards.

DAVID: I didn't do any drugs until I joined the police department. I was working out of the downtown station, and after my shift one night I got into this little VW bug with three other cops. We were all in uniform. As we were driving home, one of these guys pulled a joint out and passed it around. They all hit on it, and when it came to me, I figured, "What the heck?" I went ahead and gave it a try.

I remember this was pretty late at night, because the city was all lit up. I worked the three-to-eleven shift, so it must've been about midnight, and we decided to drive around for a while and smoke a few more joints. The fact that we were police officers in uniform doing something that was illegal never even crossed my mind. A lot of the younger cops were into drugs, so it didn't seem like a big deal. We were never very serious about enforcing marijuana laws anyway. When you spend your workday dealing with robberies, rapes, muggings, and murders, it's hard to get excited about some guy sitting in the park with a bag of pot. As cops we all drank and a lot of us experimented with drugs. We're no different from anybody else.

I worked as a cop for five, six years, and loved every minute of it, but I left the force and ventured out into the business world because I wanted to make more money. Believe it or not, drug use is very common in the business community. It's no different from being a cop—once you fall in with a certain crowd of people, drugs and booze are always there in plentiful supply. It's the normal weekend thing to do. Over the years, I've tried lots of drugs, and I've never had any bad experiences with any of them. Cocaine, crystal meth, uppers, downers, psychedelics—they've all been good.

ROLFE: The other day I had lunch with a colleague. He's an attorney in his mid-fifties and we share some mutual clients. I've known him ever since I graduated from Wharton, so I guess that would be seven or eight years now. Somehow we got onto the topic of drugs and he made the comment: "I keep hearing about the astronomical sums of money involved in drug dealing, and how people spend thousands of dollars a year on cocaine. But I've never met anybody who uses drugs."

I almost choked. I was tempted to say, "Hey, Steve, you know me don't you?" But of course, I didn't. He got onto this kick about how the news media exaggerates and sensationalizes everything, and he didn't think drug trafficking was near as lucrative as the media would have us believe. He was talking like it was all a ghetto problem that left white working people untouched.

What made this rather amusing was that I'd been to a party at his law firm two weeks earlier, and I kept wandering back into the kitchen pantry area with some of the younger associates to do a line of coke. About a dozen people kept traipsing back there, and he knew every one of them. He was talking and laughing with these people while they were high.

They're people he works with every day; people he likes and respects. If I'd told him the truth he would have been shocked. It would've made him very, very sad.

JOHN: After graduating from college I worked on Capitol Hill for a while, and then got a job as a copywriter for a prestigious ad agency in New York. Madison Avenue was where I first discovered the joys of cocaine. One evening I walked into an agency party to celebrate a major new account we'd just landed. As soon as the senior execs split, people started pulling bags of cocaine out of their pockets. I was surprised, really shocked. In college I'd partied my brains out, but never had I seen anything like this. The stuff was coming out of the walls. People were walking around evaluating each others' stash, trading information about dealers, and showing off these expensive little spoons.

I'd never done cocaine before, but I sure as hell was eager to try. In that environment who wouldn't be? Everybody was snorting lines and talking like connoisseurs—they sounded exactly like our parents used to sound when somebody pulled out a rare bottle of fifteen-year-old Scotch. Everybody was talking about how this stuff was absolutely precious.

CATHERINE: Cocaine always gives me a happy feeling. When I do lines I feel this joyous emotion, this warmth surging through my chest. I say these profound and clever things that make everybody laugh.

On the weekends my boyfriend and I like to sit up and do coke all night. Sometimes we're alone, and sometimes we're with friends. When we're with friends we get a nice party atmosphere going. He's an investment banker, and is from a wealthy family. We can always afford to have plenty of coke around. In the summer we like to sit out by the swimming pool, get high, and watch the sun rise. That's the big ritual, staying up to watch the sun rise.

I remember one weekend last year we got this really good Peruvian flake. One line was all it would take to give you this wonderfully mellow high. We had a couple of friends over that weekend—one of my boyfriend's business partners and his girlfriend. We barbecued dinner, had a few drinks, then broke out this Peruvian coke.

That night I felt really in love with my boyfriend. Real close to him. At some point we all went skinny-dipping, then jumped into the Jacuzzi. The night was a little cool, so the hot water felt good. Talking and laughing, all four of us were perfectly tuned into each other. We'd hold hands and sing country songs, pop out of the Jacuzzi to do a line, then jump right back in and let the bubbly water wash over our bodies.

Now that was a perfect night. A perfect high.

BOB: One of the great things about getting high is that without even being conscious of it you're finding thrills beyond what the drug itself can provide. You're breaking down inhibitions, getting loose, letting yourself go wild.

I remember one time during my freshman year in college I was at this dorm party, and this girl was there who'd gone to my high school. She was the girl that every guy in school dreamed about—you know, long blond hair, really beautiful, a cheerleader, all that shit. I knew who she was, but I'd never talked to her except to say hello in passing. That night we were partying pretty hard. Everybody was drinking and dancing, and there was this small group of us that kept sneaking off to do some cocaine.

Sometime during the night I struck up a conversation with this girl. She remembered me from high school and she was real friendly. So we were talking and laughing and dancing, and I asked her if she wanted to do some 'caine. Her face lit up, and she said, "Do you have some?" I had a couple grams stashed in my dorm room, and the next time we ran off to do a few lines, I brought her along with us. And she loved it. Which surprised me, because I didn't think she was into drugs. But she'd obviously done it before; she knew exactly what to do.

When we went back out to the party she started getting real cozy, real happy. We were laughing and dancing and partying, and pretty soon she said, "Do you have any more 'caine?" Well, I had a lot more. This time, instead of going back to my dorm room, where we'd have a bunch of people around, we snuck off to her room. I'd always heard that cocaine and sex go hand in hand, and that's the night I learned the truth of that statement.

This girl put on some music and sat right beside me on her bed. We did a few more lines, and she was hanging on my arm, rubbing my back, kissing me and stuff. I was in awe of her—almost to the point where I was afraid to move. Afraid to do anything that would break the spell. While we were sitting there making out, she scooped up some 'caine and put it on the tip of her tongue, then wiggled her tongue at me, indicating I was supposed to lick it off. Which I did. Then she put some 'caine on the tip of my tongue, and kissed me like I couldn't believe. The next thing I know, she's unbuttoning my shirt and rubbing my stomach and chest.

Pretty soon, we're both naked. She's snorting 'caine off my chest and I'm sucking it off her nipples.

When you're high like that, you feel like you can do everything better—especially sex. You've got this euphoria burning inside you, and your senses are totally alive. You feel every little touch. And I mean to tell you, that was a night to remember—a night of pure cocaine heaven.

JOHN: New Orleans is a city awash in a sea of cocaine. The music boys discovered coke a long, long time ago, and it is big. It comes in fresh off the boat and is very pure.

I worked for a consulting firm in New Orleans that had several Latin American countries as clients, and everybody I worked with was doing coke. We were all making a lot of money, and we had an absolute blast traveling through Latin America, sampling all the native beers and rums and snorting cocaine. I was spending between a thousand and two thousand dollars a week on coke, and never thought much about it because I was running in a circle where my friends were all doing the same thing.

The ethic we lived by was work hard and party hard—and sometimes it was difficult to distinguish between the two. On one occasion a group of us got together to invest in a real estate venture, and we brought our dealer in on the action. Every investor put up ten thousand dollars per share, except the dealer. He paid in trade. He kept a running total of the cocaine we consumed, and as soon as it reached ten thousand dollars we issued him a certificate for his share of the investment.

WAYNE: I didn't have a drug of choice. Cocaine, acid, speed, Quaaludes—I loved 'em all. I'd do anything that didn't involve a needle. I loved acid, and I *really* loved cocaine. I spent fifteen years drinking and drugging to excess, and in retrospect I'd say that I used drugs to help me deal with things that I didn't want to deal with—you know, things like feelings of low self-esteem, or because I was mad about not having someone special in my life. If I was lonely or depressed, cocaine gave me an instant sense of euphoria. It would take away all of the negative feelings and problems that were dragging me down.

At night I particularly liked to go to clubs and discos. When you go out dancing, cocaine not only gives you a sense of euphoria and well-being, it heightens your senses. The lights are brighter, the music sounds better, the people you're with are prettier. It's easier to get lost in the crowd and meet new people because you feel so *good*. You're having this wonderful time, and you're giving off these wonderful vibes.

During my years of heavy cocaine use, I was working as a bartender at an after-hours club. It was a very busy, high-traffic place, and I never had to buy coke because that's the way I was tipped. All night long, people would come up to the bar and give me cocaine. In return, I'd give them free drinks or I'd pour extra-strong drinks. Every time I'd get a "tip," I'd run back to the walk-in cooler and do a hit of coke. Then I'd return to the bar and sling some cocktails and some attitude, get more coke, go back to the cooler, do more hits, go out and sling more cocktails and more attitude. All night long I'd be trekking back to the cooler to get high. The place was always jumping, and I thought it was great. The rule I worked by was that the people who gave me the best drugs got the best service. If there was a crowd at the bar, they'd never have to wait. They'd get served as soon as they came up.

I remember one night in particular when it seemed like every coke addict in town was at my bar. All night long I kept getting these *wonderful* drugs. And I was doing them behind the bar. I mean I was buzzing! When my shift ended I went out dancing with a group of friends. We danced nonstop until six A.M., and I was absolutely drenched with sweat. We walked outside and were amazed to discover that the sun had already been up for an hour, and we decided to go out for breakfast. I remember sitting at the table laughing and joking, having a great time, still blitzed on coke.

Looking back, that's what most of my drug experiences were like—lots of partying, laughter, and fun. Throughout the course of fifteen years of excessive drug use, I'd have to say that the vast majority of my drug experiences were good. I've always associated drugs with good times. As a matter of fact, for a long time the only way I knew how to have a good time was to go out drinking and drugging.

DORIS: When I was a child growing up, my father was an alcoholic. My mother never drinked or used any drugs, but my father was a drunk. When I was an infant child, he got angry and threw me out of a window into some bushes. He had six children, and he used to whip us with belts. He'd get drunk and demand things, and there'd be this anger, this forcefulness in his voice. I can't say that I come from a happy family.

As a child, I grew up going to church. My father didn't believe in God, and he never went to church, but my mother went, and she wanted her children to come up being Christians. I was involved in lots of things—Sunday school, choir, bake sales, rummage sales, rehearsals. Every Saturday and Sunday I was at the church. The pastor who preached the Sunday sermon was real nice to me. He took a special interest in me, and sometimes he'd pick me up at my house and take me out of town to go to other churches. Me being so young, I'm not knowing anything about sex. I didn't know that this man was looking at me in ways he shouldn't be doing. Then one day when I was ten years old, I was at the church helping out. I was in the basement, and he came in and threw me down and started pulling my clothes off. I was hollering and screaming, but nobody could hear me. He was sticking his penis inside me, getting off on me. I was crying and screaming, telling him to stop, that he was hurting me, but he wouldn't stop. He was holding me down, raping me. When he was finished, I be all wet in between my legs. This pastor, he gave me some candy, and was telling me how much more candy he was going to give me, like that was my treat for letting him do those dirty things to me. He was telling me not to say anything to anyone, not to tell my mother.

I went home, and I told my mother. I said, "Something is wrong. This man is doing this he don't have no business doing." I told her what the preacher had done, but my mother didn't believe me. She got upset and said, "Doris, don't say things like that! You know that man didn't do nothing like that to you!" She was in denial, and because she was not accepting what I was saying, she never checked me out like she should have done.

I got to the point where I wanted to stop going to church. I didn't want to be around this man. He was supposed to be teaching me things about God, and here he was, doing these things to me. He raped me three times, and he never got caught. I was hating this man. Being that my mother couldn't believe what I was saying, that was hurting me inside. It hurt me that she put her trust in this preacher before taking the word of her own flesh and blood child.

I think all this had a lot to do with why I started using drugs. My father being an alcoholic, and this preacher raping me, all that meant I had a lot of stuff I didn't want to think about. I had this pain inside me, and I didn't want to deal with it. I learned that getting high took the pain away. I learned that there were chemicals out there that could make me feel good. I started out by smoking marijuana and stuff, and when I reached high school I was smoking Love Boat, which is marijuana laced with PCP. I thought Boat was the best high there ever was. I loved it, absolutely loved it. I smoked Boat for breakfast, lunch, and dinner, and I smoked in between times too. My middle name was "Smokey." My Lovey gave me this sensational feeling, it made me feel that I could do whatever I wanted to do. Getting high on Boat blocked out all of the bad things, all of the negative feelings I believed about myself, and replaced them with a feeling of strength.

After I graduated high school, I got a job downtown working for the Drug Enforcement Agency. That's right, I went to work for DEA. I was a statistical clerk. I was stamping numbers on files, doing clerical work, and inputting information into computers. I liked the job, but it was getting to me because I was smoking my Lovey every day. I never smoked inside the Drug Enforcement building, but I'd go outside for lunch, get high, and go back to work. On my break, I'd run outside, smoke some Boat, and go back to my computer. I mean, I was smoking all the time. Here I was sitting there with all these law enforcement people, high on PCP. That was making me paranoid. So I resigned that job and went to work for the Department of Education. I was still working on computers. And it was at the Department of Education that I was introduced to rock cocaine.

What happened is I had this girlfriend named LaDonna that worked there with me. She came in and said, "Let's take a break." She had some rocks, and I was right there with her. We went into a little storage room, closed the door, and LaDonna pulled out her pipe and her cocaine. She lit it up and said, "Take a hit on this." I said, "Alright." And I won't tell you no lie. I took that hit, and I heard bells ring and I felt this tingling sensation all over my body. That first hit gave me the best high I have ever known. I set there thinking, "This is better than a PCP high!" I never thought I'd find a high that was better than Love Boat, but rock cocaine was better—it's the best drug ever invented.

I automatically got to smoking rock whenever I could. I'd smoke all day and all night. Rock cocaine was the most important thing in my life. I've always been a good worker, and my work never slacked, but I got to the point where I was smoking on my job. I had me a homemade pipe, and if nobody was around I'd sizzle up some coke right there at my desk. I really liked the high. The more I smoked, the more I wanted. Every dime I could make working overtime, I made it. That's because I never had enough money, I never had enough coke. The high was out of this world. As long as I was high, I felt good. I didn't have to think about no rapes or beatings. I didn't have no anxiety or guilt or emotional distress—PCP and rock cocaine set me free from all that.

SLICK: I had a job working in a bakery. I was making two hundred fifty bucks a week cleaning pots and pans. There was a baker there, and me and him would buy cocaine together. One payday the two of us went out, cashed our checks, and bought a hundred-dollar bag of cocaine. Then we went up to my place. I was ready to do a few lines, and this guy says, "Watch this."

He takes the cocaine, pours it into a bottle, and mixes it up with some baking soda. I said, "Hey, what are you doing man? Are you crazy? You're wasting our 'caine!"

I was pissed off. But he said, "Relax, man. Just watch what I'm doing."

Then he poured *water* into it. I couldn't believe it. I said, "Man, you are really messed up."

He said, "I know what I'm doing." And he cooked this mixture up into a nice square rock. Then he cut off a piece of the rock, put it into a little glass pipe, and lit up. He handed it to me and said, "Check this out."

I took one pull on the pipe, and that was it, man. I was *gone*. It was a great feeling. I felt that cocaine euphoria like I'd never felt it before.

We spent the rest of the night running down to the street corner, buying more cocaine, and cooking it up into crack. We'd smoke a rock and feel so good that we just *had* to have more.

JEROME: Crack cocaine really does what people say it can do. When you first smoke it, it's a rush that goes straight to your brain. God A'mighty, I can only describe it to a degree. It's like when you're making love, when you're inside a woman right at the point of arousal. When you got that tingly feeling right in the very instant before you come. A crack high gives you that kind of feeling—a rush of sensual pleasure. It hits the nervous system in a way that really turns you on. It hits you with the force of religious revelation.

DOUGLAS: When you're using drugs, there ain't nobody who's doin' it that can say they ain't enjoying it. At least, that's true when you first start up.

The good thing about abusing drugs is you've always got something to do. If you're not busy gettin' sick or gettin' high, then you're busy thinking about how you're going to get high. You're out robbin' and stealin'. You're having you some adventure. You get you some money, and you buy some drugs and some pussy. Man, don't let nobody tell you that kind of wild life ain't fun. When you're young and strong, it's fun. It's a lot of fun.

PATRICK: A few years back, my cousin Rebecca introduced me to something called Purple Microdot, which is just another name for acid. I started taking it, and pretty soon I discovered that when I did a hit of acid I could drink whiskey all night long. The whiskey'd taste like water, and I'd never black out. I thought, "Hey, this is great!"

I was always partying like a wild man, doing every kind of drug imaginable, but my drug of choice was acid combined with alcohol. I'd hallucinate and stuff, but never to the point where I couldn't function. Back then, my nickname was Dr. Love—that's because the acid made me so fuckin' happy. I've always been a happy-go-lucky drunk, and acid made me even happier. You could smack me in the face, and I'd just smile at you.

I was doing a lot of crazy stuff. After I'd discovered acid, I started drinking pure grain alcohol, which is one hundred ninety proof. You're supposed to mix it with punch, but I was drinking it straight. You take a gulp of one hundred ninety and I guarantee your lips and your mouth will go numb. I'd get all numb in the throat, and feel great, because I knew that grain was taking me where I wanted to go.

I heard all kinds of horror stories about drinking pure grain. Everybody was telling me, "That shit will make you go blind." When I heard that I'd just laugh and say, "Give me a break! This shit might make me see *double*, but I know it ain't gonna make me go blind!"

I remember one night a buddy who was in the Marine Corps with me drank a whole half gallon of Canadian whiskey, and he went into a coma. When I heard that, I was really disgusted. I was thinking, "Shit, man, that wimp can't drink!"

I was proud of the fact that I never met no man who could out-drink me. Because of my tolerance, I had a reputation where people would bet on how much I could drink. My friends would know when I was doing acid, and they'd make bets with other people in bars and stuff. They'd bet that I could take a pint of whiskey and drink the whole thing down nonstop. People who didn't know me would say, "No way, man. Nobody can do that." They'd put their money on the bar, and I'd take a pint and drink it down without ever letting the bottle leave my lips. I'd set the empty bottle on the bar, and say, "Well, gentlemen, is that what you wanted to see?" Then I'd take bets on another pint.

I was living wild, and there was a couple times when I got arrested and the judge threw my ass in jail. You know, for fighting and re-sisting arrest and shit like that. Nothing really serious. I'd spend a week or ten days in jail, and the whole time I was there my only goal would be to hurry up and get out so I could pick up right where I left off. They always let you out at one minute after midnight, and my girlfriend and my sister would always be there to pick me up. They'd be waiting in the parking lot with a case of beer iced down in the car. I'd get out, guzzle a beer, and we'd roar off into the night.

AARON: LSD has always been my drug of choice. I've always been really into music, and when I first began smoking pot I discovered that it seemed to bring my records alive. I'd get high and listen to the Rolling Stones, Santana, Miles Davis, and think, "Man, what great stuff!" I was thinking, "Wow, if pot is this good, maybe there's even more fun to be had out there with harder drugs."

I fell into a small circle of guys that did a lot of LSD, and they'd tell me about their experiences on Orange Sunshine. These guys were a couple years older than me, and they'd talk about how great acid is. How it expands your levels of consciousness and stuff like that. I'd listen to the Grateful Dead, smoke pot, and wonder what it would be like to listen to the Dead on LSD. I talked with some of my friends about it, and they thought I was crazy. They said, "Don't be stupid! Acid screws with your mind. It makes you nuts. It'll put you in an insane asylum."

I'd heard the same kind of nonsense about marijuana, so I didn't have that much fear. I knew all these older guys, and they were normal people. They were having a damn good time. So I decided to try it. The first time I only did half a tab, and it made me feel good, but I never got off like I'd expected. I was expecting to see dragons and things melting and disappearing—you know, Alice in Wonderland. I was expecting to hallucinate and see the rabbit and talk to the flowers. But that didn't happen. What happened was it made me feel good.

After that I started taking it in bigger doses, and I just loved it. I'd have hallucinations where the walls would breathe, and colors would become intensified, and people's faces would change and blend together the way they do in a dream. For twelve hours I'd be in tune with the entire universe; there'd be nothing that had any control over me. I could sit in my bedroom doing absolutely nothing, and feel enlightened by this astronomical force, this powerful intelligence. Or I could sit in the yard and spend four or five hours marveling at a single blade of grass. It would be like this blade of grass was an awesome miracle, a beautiful part of nature that was intimately tied to the miracle of existence. I felt like my insight was magnified beyond belief.

To me, LSD is like a window that gives you a different view of the world. It's sort of like Adam and Eve eating from the tree of knowledge. The question is, Can you handle the knowledge? I loved it. Over the course of the past twelve years I've done a lot of LSD, and there have been a lot of good experiences and I've met a lot of good people along the way.

In doing LSD, I was always looking to form a bond with people, with music, with nature. I was looking for a spiritual awakening, and every time I'd find it I'd think it was beautiful. It was the reason I got into LSD to begin with, and it was what kept me doing it for a long, long time.

ERNIE: In high school I was an acid and PCP freak. During my senior year, I didn't have any idea what I wanted to do after I graduated, so I took the entrance exams for the military. I figured I'd become an airplane mechanic or something. My test scores were real high, and recruiters from the Air Force, the Army, and the Navy all called me. They all said they wanted me to enlist. I thought, "Great! I'll enlist and get some training. I'll become a jet engine mechanic."

I went down to talk to the Air Force recruiter, and the interview went really well until he asked me, "Have you ever smoked dope?"

I said, "Yeah, I've smoked a little bit."

"How much is a little bit?"

"Oh," I said, "about an ounce a week." Which was on the light side. I was smoking a lot more than that, and didn't think it was a big deal. Everybody was smoking dope. All of the guys I knew who had enlisted in the military were into pot. So I didn't think anything of it.

But this recruiter almost fell out of his chair. He said, "You smoke *an ounce a week!*"

I just shrugged and said, "Yeah, about that."

Then he asked, "Have you ever done any other drugs?"

"I've experimented a little."

"How about LSD? Have you ever done LSD?"

"Yeah, I've done LSD."

"How much?"

"Oh," I said, "maybe a hundred fifty hits." Again, I was coming in on the light side. I was thinking that one hundred fifty hits wasn't very much. For me, LSD was a fun time. I liked the hallucinations and the trails. I liked walking on the far side, and getting outside of reality.

But this Air Force recruiter couldn't relate. He was looking at me like I was absolutely crazy. He didn't ask me any more questions. He just told me I could leave. I was denied enlistment. Which wasn't any big deal. I was a lot more interested in getting high and having a good time than I was in becoming a jet engine mechanic anyway.

SNAKE: I was down at the roller rink hanging out with my friends when this guy we knew showed up with some Angel Dust. I'd never smoked Dust before, but I sure had heard about it. So we smoked a couple joints, and I honestly can't tell you how incredible the high was. I felt like there was nothing in the world that could hurt me. Like I had this incredible power.

That night, I fell down two flights of stairs. I was all bruised and banged up, but all I did was lie there and laugh. Like it was real funny.

Dust was the best high I'd ever had, so I kept on smoking it. I was getting PCP in liquid form, and I'd take a joint, dip it, and then smoke it. It was great—I felt like the ruler of the world. Didn't care about anything, I was the ruler.

I was going into Manhattan clubs—Fun House, Studio Fifty-four, all those places—and every place I went in I was dealing. I got banned from just about every club in New York City. But it was easy dealing in the clubs. I'd pay off the bouncer when I could, and I'd have people inside lining up to buy from me.

One night we were smoking and this bouncer came over and told us to put it out, but as soon as he walked away we lit back up. The bouncer came back and said, "I told you to put it out. You light up one more time and we're not going to be polite about it anymore." My friend put it out and I went to the bar to get a drink. When I turned around I saw a whole crowd of people around my friend, and this bouncer is beating him up. I was trying to pull my friend away when somebody spun me around and hit me in the mouth with brass knuckles. Six of my front teeth were knocked out, my lip was totally destroyed, blood all over the place. I had to be driven to the hospital. Twenty-five stitches.

I was in terrible pain. As soon as I got outside the hospital, the only thing I wanted to do was smoke some Dust. I knew I had open sores in my mouth, but I didn't care. I just wanted to get high. And that's what I did.

When I got home I snuck in my bedroom. I got into bed and put a pillow over my head so my mother wouldn't come in my room and see my mouth. When I woke up in the morning the pillow was stuck to my mouth. I had to rip it off, and when I did that I ripped all the stitches out. They had to take me to a dentist right away, and the dentist had to restructure my whole mouth. But I didn't care. It didn't stop me. I kept on smoking Dust. I kept on loving that high.

GAIL: When I first started contemplating heroin, there was something really romantic, really glamorous about it. Those of us in the drug culture respected the fact that heroin is as hard as you can go. It's sort of like pushing the accelerator to the floor to see how fast your car can go.

RON: I was born in 1953 and I grew up on Capitol Hill in Washington, D.C. I was ten years old when John Kennedy died, twelve when Malcolm X was murdered, and fifteen when Martin Luther King and Robert Kennedy were gunned down. These were all people who were important to me. They were people who made their mark in the black community at a time when I was learning to stand up for what was right.

I was at the Lincoln Memorial when Martin Luther King delivered his "I have a dream" speech in 1963. It was a hot, hot day, and I climbed up into a tree to hear this man. I sat in that tree for ten hours, and when I left I felt something. I felt the world changing. I felt I knew what it was to be right. Then I turn around and John Kennedy is dead. I turn around again and Malcolm X is dead. Martin Luther King and Bobby Kennedy dead. All of them snubbed out. Erased from the page.

I never knew Martin personally, but I'd seen him. I'd listened to him, and he'd made sense. Then when he was gone, I missed him. I remember watching his funeral on TV and I knew something was seriously wrong because it made my parents cry. There was a feeling of sadness wherever you went, as if the whole world was at half-mast. The stores were closed. The schools were closed. But the churches were open and full. I remember seeing the black veils and gloves, and listening to the speeches. I knew that something terrible had happened, but I didn't understand the full significance of it. Inside, I was hurt and angry. But I didn't know how to deal with tragedy. I just knew that Martin's casket had been lowered into the ground.

That was the summer of 1968 and black militants were springing up like mushrooms. I listened to them, and I shared their anger and their rage, but I still felt empty and hollow. I'd walk by the tree I'd climbed into to hear Martin Luther King speak, and I could feel his absence.

A couple months after Martin died I started to run with this girl. Her brother was into selling heroin. I'd never done heroin before, and she told me it was nice, that I should try it. I said, "No, I'm not going to do that. I'll catch you later." And I ran off.

The next week I saw her again. I was bent out of shape, depressed and angry. I was saying, "Hey, white folks are the enemy. Anytime somebody rises up to make a mark in the black community, white folks gun him down. Look what happened to Malcolm X, Martin Luther King, and Bobby Kennedy. They got murdered in cold blood for standing up and saying what was right."

She had some heroin and she was saying, "Come on, try this. It'll make you feel better."

I gave it a try, telling myself, "I'm only going to do it this once. Just to know what it's all about." I can't even begin to describe the high. I thought heroin was the best thing I'd ever done. It knocked out all of the pain and confusion I was feeling. It pushed reality out of my mind. I didn't need to worry about politics, and assassinations, and doing what was right, because heroin was making the sun shine.

That girl and I got close, and I started using with her regularly. Even though I was headed down the path of self-destruction, I didn't know it. I'd come home from school and my love would be there waiting for me. My love was heroin, and my love would make the birds sing. Inside I was an emotionally scarred person. A damaged person. But on the outside, as long as I had my love, I was happy as a lark.

NAP: I started drinking wine and smoking cigarettes when I was in junior high school. It was the same story—be with the cool people, be with the girls, look like a man, that old shit. There was a group of us like this, wearing nice clothes, keeping the shoes shined, wearing big hats cocked ace-deuce on your head, smoking and drinking. Going to parties and turning the lights down low, rubbing up against the girls. All that kind of shit.

There was a lot of conflict for me, though, because I came from a strict Baptist upbringing. I was born in 1931 in a little coal-mining town in West Virginia. My father was a miner. I'd been taught that the music we were listening to at parties was the devil's music, and drinking and smoking were the devil's ways. When I was sixteen or so I was the secretary in the church Sunday school, and I had to make a decision. Did I want to stay with the teachings of my upbringing? Or, was I going to be a musician like I'd always wanted? The two didn't go together. I decided I was going to be a musician. I quit paying much attention to the church stuff, and I was living on the fast track.

I had some buddies I hung out with on Saturday nights. We'd go to dances together and check out the girls. One Sunday after we'd been together all weekend we decided to go hear some music. Count Basie's band was in town, and we were in the audience all hung over from the night before. This guy came up to us and said, "What's wrong with y'all?"

"Man, we are hung over! We're fucked up."

"Man, don't be silly! Smoke some of this reefer, and y'all feel better. No hangovers, no headaches, no pukin', none of that shit."

It was one of those situations where we all wanted to be a little macho. Everybody else was doing reefer, and contrary to what we heard about it making you crazy, it wasn't like that at all. It was a nice woozy high. Your senses were sharp—your hearing got amplified, and the colors and lights were nice. A smooth high.

This was about the time I was first trying to play music. My first instrument was made from a big stick, a rope, and a fat old syrup can. A homemade bass. We'd moved from West Virginia to Washington, D.C., and I was hanging around the clubs. I was too young to get inside them, but this was back in the days before air conditioning, so the club doors would be open and the windows up. You could stand on the sidewalk and hear the music. There were a couple of places where I could climb up on the fire escape and look in through the windows—see the musicians, and see the dancing girls all half-naked. I was fascinated by it, man. That whole life-style completely fascinated me. I wanted to be part of it.

It was in my second year of high school that I tried heroin for the first time. I was hanging out with some musicians one night, and we were in front of a club down on Seventh and T streets. This cab was parked by the curb, and the driver and this white boy were in there talking. We got in with them and rode around a little and smoked some reefer. Then the white boy came up with the horse and asked if we wanted to do it. I had mixed feelings about it. I knew about junkies, but part of me was saying, "What the hell? It won't hurt to try it just once to see what it's like. I ain't going to get hooked. I ain't going to become no junkie." So my friend and me snorted some heroin. At first, it made me sick to my stomach. But after I got over the nausea, I got extremely high. A real nice mellow high. That was the grooviest feeling I'd ever had up to then, and I must've stayed high two or three days. For two or three weeks after that, I didn't mess around with nothing, but gradually I started snorting heroin on a regular basis.

It was right about this time that I got my first real bass, and that put me in another class altogether. I was already wearing nice clothes all the time—I had a beautiful camel hair, half-belt overcoat with a big thick collar. I'd turn up the collar and I was always wearing Dobbs hats and shit like that. I'd break the brim down over my eyes, put on a pair of dark glasses, then take my mother's eyebrow pencil and work in the mustache a tad. Then with my bass, whenever I walked up to a club looking like that I got immediate entree. They knew I was coming in to play—wasn't interested in no whiskey, wasn't even interested in the money. I just wanted to play.

I was leaving behind the guys I'd grown up with, gone to school with. I found a whole new group of friends in the music scene. They was all musicians and into the nightlife and hustling and that kind of shit. It was fascinating and exciting. I was eighteen—getting a chance to ball chicks twenty-five, twenty-six, hang out all night, being around top-flight players and snorting heroin with them. That shit always felt good. The whole scene was exciting, man. I was having a whole lotta fun, a whole lotta adventure. There's nothing better in the world than being young and irresponsible. Getting involved in dope and jazz is very, very exciting.

A lot of the musicians, once they found out you were a young aspiring musician, they would tell you right out, "Don't mess with drugs. Stay away from them, man." I remember once I went to see Charlie Parker in his hotel room at the Dunbar Hotel. It was the hottest place in Washington. My friend Earl and me were visiting Bird together. Earl was an alto sax player too, and he was talking to Bird about playing. Bird asked to see Earl's saxophone, so Earl gave it to him. The reed was really ragged, but it was the best one Earl had. Bird took the reed off, took two quarters from his pocket, put the reed between the quarters, and pulled it down to where the ragged part was. Then he lit a match and and burned the ragged part off. That way the reed would vibrate evenly. In the process of doing this Bird was talking to us about drug abuse. He was very explicit in saying, contrary to what you heard, using drugs did *not* make you sound better when you played. If anything it made you sound worse. He was going on and on. I was getting real uncomfortable listening to him. I knew *he* was a drug addict—so what was going on? When Earl and me left we decided Bird just wanted all the dope for himself. His whole lecture became a big joke to us.

All this time I was snorting heroin. Doing it most every day, but I didn't think I was an addict. There's a class system in heroin. People who snort look down on people who shoot, and I thought it was the people using the needle that were crazy. They were the ones who had the problem, not me.

I hooked up with this band, and we went on the road. We were playing a nice little roadhouse club in Norfolk for a while. Getting paid decent. It was really good. The piano player and I shared a room in a house that this family lived in. They rented us this room for three dollars a week.

By this time I'd gotten real slick. On Sunday mornings I'd be sure and wake up around breakfast time, and I'd go downstairs. Now, on Sunday mornings, I don't care who you are, southern black people are going to offer you something to eat, even if it ain't included in your rent. Then if you wanted something for the afternoon and eve-

ning, you went to church. At some point in the service they'd invite
you up front of everybody, and you'd have to make a little speech,
say hello, that type of thing. All you had to do was say you were a
jazz musician on the road, but that you just *had* to go to church
every Sunday morning because you promised your family back home
you would. That you *need* spiritual replenishment, and that you
hoped the church would pray for you because you realized you were
in a job where danger and the devil existed. Amen! When the service
was over you'd be sure to leave real slow, because one of them sisters
was going to come up and invite you over for Sunday dinner. If you
were real lucky and played your hand right, you might even get some
pussy too.

By this time I'd been using drugs for three or four years. But
like I said, in my mind I was not hooked. I was not a junkie.
Then one morning I woke up and I didn't have any money. I
was having chills. I was sick, man. I went out on the street and
I was wearing a coat in the middle of summertime—sweating and
chilling. A junkie I knew walked up and said, "Hey, what's wrong
with you?"

"I don't know. I just feel bad."

"You need some dope, don't you? You need some stuff."

"No I don't. I ain't hooked. I ain't going to mess with it no more."

"Sheeeyit. You are sick, man. But for a buck, you can get well."

I had a buck on me, and that was all. This junkie said he'd take
me 'round to John Frye's joint back up the alley. Frye's joint was
really weird, because it was like this holy-sanctified church in the
front part of the joint, but back where the kitchen was supposed to
be, they'd closed it off and made a shooting gallery. Church up front,
shooting gallery in the back. The cat that was running the gallery
was a guitar player named Happy, and Happy had this stuff we called
"glue." It was a heroinlike substance that gave you a similar feeling,
but when you cooked it up it got all syrupy and gave you a nasty
taste in your mouth when you shot it. This was the first time I'd shot
anything.

The dude that took me in did the shooting. He told me, "Man,
you sick and you need this, but when you snort the shit you just
wasting the dope. You can get high on maybe a third or a half of
what you been snorting if you shoot it. You can get blind-high shooting just a little of what you been snorting.

I had my eyes closed, scared to death. He hit the vein. The second he started to push the dope into my arm, I felt my stomach growl. I could *taste* the dope. And I was high—instantly. The sweat stopped. The cramps stopped. The runny nose stopped. All that shit ceased immediately. I felt good again.

I had been terrified of sticking the needle in my arm, but after three or four days I got over that terror real fast.

CHAPTER 2

BORDER WARS

Every year illegal drugs manufactured in more than fifty foreign countries are smuggled across United States borders for distribution and sale in the United States. In trying to stop the flow, the federal government has pumped hundreds of millions of dollars into high-speed boats, airplanes, helicopters, and sophisticated communications and radar equipment. Every day millions more are being spent as thousands of officials from the Drug Enforcement Agency, the Coast Guard, the Central Intelligence Agency, the Customs Service, the FBI, and local police jurisdictions patrol our borders in the hunt for smugglers. Law enforcement agencies routinely hold press conferences to announce major seizures and display multimillion-dollar caches of cocaine. But those seizures rarely impact on the availability of drugs on our city streets, and law enforcement officials candidly confess that they are interdicting less than 10 percent of the illegal drugs that are pouring into the United States.

"As an undercover agent there are times when I know I'm being watched," says a federal narcotics officer. "Drug runners are very sophisticated. They have all our radio call numbers, and they know all of our call signs. They listen in on all of our conversations. It's

the sort of thing that leaves you with a mighty naked, vu'
feeling. Most drug runners know more about what we're doi...
our superiors do. I'd love to tell you that we're making great progress
in the war on drugs, but the truth is, we're not."

There is one point on which both law enforcement agents and
drug smugglers agree: Those responsible for securing United States
borders have been given a Herculean task. "DEA, Customs, and the
Border Patrol all suffer from limited resources and bureaucratic rigid-
ity," says a smuggler with close ties to the Medellín cartel. "They're
stretched very thin, and they're very predictable. At worst, they're a
nuisance. They might interdict some of our loads and send some of
our people to jail, but they'll *never* be able to stop drugs from entering the States. To understand the enormity of the problem all you've
got to do is look at a map of the United States and contemplate the
number of transport methods available to us. Looking at geography,
you'd think that God is on the side of the cartels."

———

The Export Underground

CARLOS: In Colombia my family was a political family. My father
had political problems, and my parents put me in the trust of a family friend. They were worried for my safety. The family friend was a
member of the cartel, and he took me to a camp located in the
interior of Colombia. In the beginning, I thought it was a rebel camp
because of the armed guards. But then I found out it was a camp
where cocaine was processed. It had huts, armed guards, and a large
tent which was used for processing. There was also a big radio tower
for communicating with the United States.

At first, I didn't do nothing. I just watched what they were doing.
I watched them process the cocaine. I stayed there. That camp is
where I lived.

I was fourteen when I was recruited. I was sent to this school—assassination school. It was located in a cave. You had to travel in a
boat to get to it. You got to the cave, you had to go down underground. When we first got there, there were people learning how to
make bombs. My protector explained to me this school taught different methods of assassination. The main purpose of our school was

to learn how to kill people who are against the cartel—judges, prosecutors, witnesses. You have to learn how to kill. We kill people so
we can sell cocaine.

It's a situation where the cartel wants to get rid of certain people
in the Colombian government. They want to put their own people
in there so they don't have problems operating the cocaine business.

PABLO: The street is a teacher—it teaches you tears. I moved a lot
of kilos. I've seen a lot of shit. You can't fuck with people in the
drug world, man. Guys get killed for fucking around. That's why I
always did the right thing. I never cheated nobody. I never stole from
nobody.

I've seen all kinds of violence. I've seen people get beat, and I've
seen people get killed. One time I was sitting in a bar in New York,
and three Colombians walked in and killed these three Puerto Rican
guys. They gunned them down with a machine gun—all because of
a sour deal. I was sitting there watching it happen.

When you deal with the Colombians you deal with some very bad
people. Very violent men. The Colombians send a lot of coke to
Mexico and stash it there. That's because the police are very corrupt.
The Mexican police love to do business with the Colombians. One
time I was working a load, and I crossed the border into Mexico. We
go to meet this cartel guy at his farm. He takes us aside and says,
"This is where I keep my enemies." He's pointing at a cemetery in
his yard! Little wooden crosses at the head of each grave. I was there.
I saw it. The guy had people buried in his yard! This was a big load,
more than two hundred keys, and he didn't want to lose it. He was
a very bad guy. He's had lots of people killed. He was telling us that
if we fuck him up, he bury us in the yard.

GUSTAVO: I grew up in a small town in Colombia and attended
university at Bogotá. My degree is in physics. After I graduated from
college, I got into the drug business. I started smuggling drugs into
the United States because I needed some money so I could start a
legal business. Everybody's got the same idea. Everyone says, "I'll
just do this for a little while. I'll make enough money so that I can
start my own business, and then I'll get out."

In Colombia the drug trade is very easy to get into. It's very well
structured, so all you need is a contact. Because of the huge amount
of money that is changing hands, many members of the Colombian

government and military are involved. The structure is strong because the people are very powerful. No matter what the authorities do, the drug business is going to be very difficult to tear up and destroy. It's a business that is going to thrive for a long, long time.

The way I got into it was through a colonel in the Colombian military. This was back in 1980 before the cartels had been formed. Even though the cartels hadn't come into existence, the same individuals were running organizations that were very strong. This colonel worked for one of those organizations. He asked me if I wanted to coordinate transportation for a major load. I told him yes, I wanted to work for the organization.

Coordinating the shipment and getting it into the United States was very easy. All I had to do was fly down to Miami, make arrangements with a buyer, and then hire a pilot to pick the load up in Colombia and fly it back to the United States. My job was to hire the people who did the actual smuggling. I never got near the load myself. I never touched any drugs.

There's a weird phenomenon that takes control of everyone that ever gets into this business. You start out with a plan to make some money so that you can do something legal. You tell yourself, "I'm only going to do this for a short time." But once you get in, you *can't* get out. Something forces you to keep going. The money, the excitement, the feel of incredible wealth—all of that comes into play. The business pulls you and pulls you. Once you start running major loads, there's no escape. It's exhilarating.

PETROCHELLI: I come from a wealthy family in Colombia, but I didn't want my family's money. I wanted my own money. That's why I got into drug smuggling.

When I first started I didn't have any moral qualms because I was mainly running marijuana. Even though marijuana is illegal, I didn't think it was bad. I've never thought of it as a dangerous narcotic. Back in the late seventies, when I got started, it was easy to smuggle marijuana into the United States. People were bringing in one-hundred-thousand-pound loads by boat and plane. No one in Colombia cared about it, and law enforcement in the United States wasn't as aggressive as it is now. You could smuggle without any real risk. For a long time, all I did was marijuana. That's because I could justify that to myself. I thought it was like Prohibition—that the laws were wrong, and someday they'd change.

I didn't feel that way about cocaine. I resisted getting into cocaine, because there's evil in cocaine. But in the United States cocaine is what everyone wants. In the mid-eighties the American government started hitting drug shipments harder and harder. They were going after smugglers, and beefing up their interdiction efforts. That made marijuana smuggling dangerous because a bale of marijuana is difficult to conceal. It's big and bulky. Because of its weight you need to lug it around. But cocaine is easy to conceal. It comes in small packages. And no one in the United States wanted marijuana anymore. The American public is demanding cocaine.

That forced me to move into the coke trade. As a businessman, I saw that I could quadruple my money at less risk. Millions of dollars was sitting there waiting to be had.

MOSE: I've been smuggling illegal narcotics into the United States for the past ten, twelve years or so, and of all the deals I've done, my first trip was the roughest. What happened was my partner and I purchased eighteen thousand pounds of marijuana in Colombia. We had a connection in Tijuana who was going to transport it across the border to Los Angeles, where we had a buyer. To make the deal work, we had to get the load from Colombia to Tijuana.

We flew it by private plane to a small town in Mexico. The Mexican military is very corrupt, and we'd made arrangements with them to bring the plane into the country, and we landed without any problems. It was only after we got on the ground that the problems began.

We'd hired a Mexican ground crew to unload the plane and take it to a warehouse. Then we were going to have it driven by truck to Tijuana. But the Mexican ground crew kept stealing our marijuana. We were fighting and arguing with them, and they kept stealing from us. Then the truckers that were supposed to pick the load up at the warehouse and take it to Tijuana also started stealing. They had lots of friends who were thieves, and instead of loading the marijuana onto the truck, these guys would grab a dozen bales, throw them into their own pickup trucks, and drive off. So we had more arguments and more fights. We were getting very nervous, because this was a small town, and the police were watching. To keep them from arresting us, we had to bribe them with marijuana. The Mexican police were stealing bales from us too.

The entire trip to Tijuana, we were fighting with the truckers and the police. Every time we'd stop or pass through a town, there'd be more thieves and police, more fights and arguments. Of course, the Colombian cartels would never let something like that happen. The cartels hold you to your word. If you promise to transport some dope, and start stealing, the cartels will kill you. But this was back in the days before the cartels, and we were too young to even think in those terms.

We finally got to Tijuana, but we only had three thousand pounds left. The other fifteen thousand had been stolen by the Mexicans. Of that three thousand pounds, only fifteen hundred made it to our buyer in L.A., because our Tijuana connection stole half of what was left.

My partner collected on the fifteen hundred pounds that did arrive, and when I requested my share of the money he shafted me too. He said, "No, that fifteen hundred pounds that got stolen were yours. The fifteen hundred that arrived, I worked those."

I didn't get paid a penny, and lost several thousand dollars. At the time it seemed like a major rip-off, but over the long haul it wasn't that big a deal. I've written it off as "tuition," because that was the beginning of my education—my drug smuggling education. Since then, I've learned a lot.

SANTA: I buy cocaine from guys in Colombia, Chile, and Peru, and sell it to guys in different cities—mostly New York and Philadelphia. These guys take the coke and sell it on the streets. They have people working for them, and they buy five or ten kilos at a time.

Right now, a kilo of coke costs thirty-four thousand dollars in New York, but in Colombia or Chile, two thousand. Sometimes less. What makes the coke so expensive in the U.S. is transportation. Pilots and transporters add thousands of dollars to the cost of a kilo. I don't fuck with those guys. I have my own connections in Colombia and Chile, and I have lots of ways of getting the coke into the U.S. Mostly I use mules. Sometimes I carry it myself. One time I bring five kilos of coke into the U.S. What I do is I comb my hair and dress up as a father, a priest. I got the five kilos under my robes. When I get off the airplane I pass through Customs. I'm wearing my cross and shit, and I say to the Customs inspector, "God bless you, my son. God bless you." He don't fuck with me. He just stamp my passport and wave me through.

Other times I send a woman to pick up the cocaine. She fly down to Chile, and what the guys in Chile do is hide the coke in wine bottles. They put it inside the bottle, fill the bottle up with wine, and seal it. The bottle is wrapped in wicker, and looks just like red wine. You can't see the coke inside. I pick the woman up at the airport and she give me the bottles of wine—five kilos in five bottles.

I do that *lots* of times. I do regular business with these guys in Chile. Each time I send down a different mule to pick it up. Mostly I send womens. I make sure they dress nice so they look just like tourists. Nobody fuck with them. Even if Customs search their luggage, they no find the cocaine. They look right at the wine, and pass it through.

The womens give me the bottles, and I say, "Thank you very much." The kilos makes me rich.

ROD [U.S. Customs inspector]: Dealers in the States pay Colombian mules to smuggle cocaine in for them. The mules are frequently uneducated peasants who get two thousand dollars for making the trip. As a Customs inspector working the airport, I'm always looking out for these people. A lot of times they're pretty sloppy and are easy to spot.

Not too long ago we had a guy come off a flight from Bolivia, and I knew something wasn't right. In the first place, he looked like a peasant, and I have enough sense to know that most peasants can't afford international travel. I stopped him, and speaking in Spanish I asked, "Why are you here?"

He said, "I'm going to Disneyland."

I thought that was strange, and asked, "Do you have a wife?"

"Yes," he said.

"And do you have any children?"

He nodded yes, and said, "I have three children."

"Why didn't you bring your wife and children to Disneyland with you?"

He just shrugged. He didn't know what to say. It was obvious to me that someone had given him a passport and a plane ticket, and told him to say that he was going to Disneyland. I checked his bags, but couldn't find anything. So I took him to an interrogation room, did a full search, and came up empty. Even though I couldn't find any drugs, his story was bad. The lack of contraband didn't make the story any better.

I escorted him down to the county medical center where his abdomen was X-rayed. That X ray was one of the most amazing things I have ever seen. This guy had swallowed more than one hundred condom pellets of cocaine, and we could see every one of them on the X-ray screen. Right away, the doctor gave him a laxative to clean his insides out. Of course, we wouldn't let him go in a toilet. We made him squat over a pan. The laxative was pretty potent, and as soon as this guy pulled his pants down he was literally shitting cocaine.

LARRY [U.S. Customs inspector]: One of the methods drug couriers use to avoid detection is to package their cocaine inside condoms and then swallow the condoms. They can bring in a pound or two that way—which can have a street value of a hundred thousand dollars or more. Although these are very small shipments by cartel standards, it's a method that a lot of small-time operators like to use. At the airport, it's virtually impossible for Customs to detect the swallowers, and I'll bet that ninety-nine percent of them get through.

We know they're out there because every now and then an international flight will arrive at the airport with a dead passenger on board. Swallowing cocaine is very dangerous. If a condom breaks, it will kill you in fifteen to thirty seconds. Cocaine is assimilated through the stomach lining very quickly. That's not true for heroin. If a heroin balloon breaks, you'll live for a couple of hours, and might have a chance to go to the hospital and get pumped out. But with cocaine, if it breaks you're dead. The last swallower we pulled off an airplane was a woman five months pregnant. The bag had exploded in her stomach, and she died from cocaine poisoning.

PETROCHELLI: You want to know how I smuggle cocaine in the United States? Okay, I'll tell you. There are lots of techniques I've used to deceive law enforcement. I work as a transporter. My job is to serve as the link between Colombians who own the coke, and people in the United States who want to buy it. I'll organize the transportation, and oversee the delivery. Once the load is in the U.S., I have it delivered to a person who is in charge of distribution. I never touch the cargo myself. I hire people, I fire people, and I run people.

My favorite method is to bring the cocaine in by private plane. Planes travel faster than boats. For me, the important thing is to have good pilots. You need experienced pilots who know what they're doing, who know how to avoid radar. There's an area in West Palm

Beach, where if you fly a certain predetermined approach pattern, radar won't detect the incoming plane. It has to do with the nature of the geography in this area, and when our pilots were flying into West Palm Beach they knew the route to fly. They knew they could come and go without being detected. No one uses West Palm Beach anymore, because the U.S. government has found out about it. But there are other small airports and clandestine strips where the same technique can be used, where the geography is such that by flying a certain route you can avoid radar. Another method pilots use is to fly their plane in very low, very close to the water. What they're doing is flying under the radar.

What happens is the pilots will fly to a clandestine strip, and a ground crew will be waiting at the drop site. As soon as the pilot lands, the ground crew will unload the plane. In maybe five minutes at most, the pilot is back in the air with a phony flight plan.

I've run over a hundred plane loads, and have never had any trouble with Customs, DEA, or the police. I've never even had a close call. I don't want to say that it's easy to smuggle narcotics, but when you're in the business, and you know the proper techniques, the odds are that your loads are going to get in. As long as you've got good, intelligent pilots, you're going to have success.

While a lot of plane loads are still coming in, it's also true that the police have become strong against the drug trade in both the United States and Colombia. It's not as easy as it used to be. They've interrupted the smooth flow of the business. They've learned a lot, and have become very good at fighting narcotics traffic.

To keep up with them, we've had to change our tactics. We've adopted more and more innovative techniques. In moving loads from Medellín, one of the things we like to do is package the cocaine in legitimate cargo.

There are all kinds of ways to do that. I'll tell you some of the methods I've used. Colombia exports lots of flowers. Every day thousands and thousands of flowers arrive in Miami from Colombia. The flowers are perishable, and Customs can't hold them for long. They have to speed delivery. So I'll arrange to have the cocaine hidden in the bottom of these huge flower cartons. On top of the cocaine there's thousands of flowers. One time I shipped eight hundred kilos of cocaine in a single flower shipment. I've also used plantains and fish. The cocaine is hidden beneath the perishable items, because it guarantees quick delivery. If Customs is going to search the load, they have to do it right away.

One of the advantages of a product like cocaine is that it's very malleable. It can be sent as either paste or powder. Using paste, cocaine can be made to look just like chocolate. I've had paste packaged and shipped as candy. Powder can be made to look just like ground coffee. All we have to do is put a dark tint on it and send it in a legitimate coffee shipment. If a Customs official opens up the coffee and stumbles across some cocaine, he can't tell by looking at it, because the cocaine will look exactly the same as the coffee. It will be packaged in and around so much real coffee, it'll smell like coffee too.

There are many, many methods. When you're making cargo deliveries, the best way is to shotgun your approach, use lots of different commodities and package the loads in different ways. If I'm sending one hundred kilos, some of the load might be hidden in flowers, some of it in plantains, and some of it in coffee. I won't send the entire hundred kilos in one shipment, but will spread it around. By spreading it around, you don't lose the entire load. Most of it will get through. As a general rule, I've found that for every ten kilos shipped, nine of them will clear Customs. Absorbing that ten-percent loss is just part of the cost of doing business.

JIM [U.S. Customs inspector]: There are so many points of bureaucratic vulnerability that the cartels exploit. The federal government can be remarkably stupid. Just one example will illustrate how easy it is to import drugs into the United States. For a long time the Customs Service would inspect about five percent of the cargo that came into the Los Angeles Harbor. It was done on a random basis, with all incoming cargo subject to inspection. But the cargo wasn't inspected on the docks. Customs would have it trucked down to a central receiving station. Now here's the catch. The Customs Service didn't own the trucks used to transport the cargo. They hired that job out to private contractors. Now that's not the kind of thing that an independent dealer would necessarily know about, but the major drug cartels all knew! They put in the low bids on the government contracts, and were actually hiring the drivers to transport the cargo slated for inspection. That way if any of their shipments got tabbed by Customs, they could pull the trucks into a warehouse en route to the inspection station, off-load the drugs, and then send the cargo down to get inspected. For a long time no one knew what was going on except the cartel dealers. They had a foolproof point of entry into the United States.

CHRISTIAN: The Colombians have been trafficking narcotics for a long time, and they know what they're doing. As a boat pilot running loads out of the Bahamas, I have access to intelligence that facilitates the smooth flow of our smuggling operations. I always have airplanes overhead circling my approach route, so I'll know if any Coast Guard cutters are in the water. That makes it easy to circumvent their patrols. The farther north we go, the easier it is to lose law enforcement surveillance.

The major reason most drug smugglers don't get caught is the U.S. has such a huge coastline. There are lots of isolated inlets, bays, and levees where it's easy to bring a boat in. Along the Georgia and North and South Carolina coasts the only law enforcement people I need to worry about are the local police jurisdictions. The feds don't even have a presence in those areas.

In running loads, I always make a point of knowing how the local police authorities work. I know what time the shift changes take place, and how many officers they have on duty. In some of these remote areas there isn't any law enforcement after ten or eleven o'clock at night. You know, the local sheriff and his two deputies are in bed. To avoid detection, all I have to do is bring my boat in at night. I'll pull up into some little inlet, have a ground crew waiting to off-load into our transport vehicles, and then I'll sail back down the coast to Florida like I was on a pleasure cruise. As far as I'm concerned, law enforcement interdiction efforts aren't even a factor. I've run hundreds of loads and have never been caught—never even had a close call.

The only thing I worry about is having an informant infiltrate the organization. If someone were to get busted and cut a deal with the police, he could easily set us up. Which is why I try to be very careful in picking my crews. I only do business with people I trust.

WILLIE: Let's face it, drug pilots are gamblers. We're always banking on the odds.

I'd been flying loads for a long time when these two Mexicans came to me one day in El Paso and said they had an airplane, fuel, and a load to move. The airplane and the fuel were hidden away at a private strip outside El Paso, and the load was down in Mexico. I looked at the airplane and the amount of fuel it was carrying; I looked at the charts, the weight of the load, and the distance; and there was no question about it—that airplane was not going to make it on the fuel they had. I checked and rechecked—no way it was going to make it. I told them that and they offered me fifteen thousand. I said, "Look, the airplane doesn't fly on money. It flies on fuel."

These guys were desperate. The dope was already on location in Mexico, and if they wasted two or three hours trying to get more fuel it would queer their deal. They said, "We'll give you twenty thousand."

I said, "Don't you guys understand the problem?"

They said, "Twenty-five thousand."

I started to walk out, and they made their final offer. "You can have twenty-five thousand, and *keep the airplane!*"

I turned around and said, "Okay, I'll do it." I figured what the hell, maybe I'll get a lucky tail wind and make it back. I climbed into the plane, flew down to Mexico, got the load, and on the way back I ran out of fuel. I had to crash-land in the Mexican desert, and then hitchhike back to the border. I *knew* I wasn't going to make it back, but once they threw in the airplane, hell, I just couldn't pass it up. It was worth the gamble.

JOHN REDDEN [pilot, U.S. Customs Air Branch]: In air smuggling operations the ground crews are frequently the weak link in the chain. They're the lowest paid and they're the dumbest. To get a ground crew to unload a plane, a smuggler goes out into the dirt country and rounds up twenty unemployed illegal aliens. He'll give them fifty bucks each.

They go out to the landing site, where they'll smoke dope and drink liquor while they wait for the airplane to come in. Every clandestine strip I've seen is littered with huge piles of beer and whiskey bottles. The ground crews are usually drunk and stoned by the time the pilot arrives with the load, so there's no telling what's going to happen when he tries to land.

One time Customs was tracking an air smuggler who was flying in from Latin America, and he didn't have any fuel to spare. He was running right on the edge of his range limit, and the weather was bad. His ground crew was late getting out to the landing strip, and driving out there they decided to stop and get some hamburgers. They were in radio contact with the pilot, and they told him they were stopping. They still weren't anywhere near the strip. We were monitoring the transmissions, and we could hear the pilot screaming at them to get over to the strip and light it up. They kept saying, "Relax, man. We're on our way. We'll be there in a minute."

Well, when this pilot arrived he had to circle the landing area because it was pitch-black and he couldn't see the strip. There was nothing beneath him but darkness. While circling overhead waiting for the ground crew he ran out of gas. His engine coughed and died and the plane crashed. On his way down we could hear this poor guy screaming into his radio, "You sorry sons of bitches! You stupid motherfuckers!"

GUSTAVO: I've worked loads where everything has gone as planned, and others that have ended in death and disaster. The worst one involved a Cuban buyer in Miami who wanted me to transport over two hundred kilos of Colombian cocaine into the United States. I spoke with him in Miami and told him okay, I'd be willing to do it. Then I made all the arrangements, and had the cocaine moved to a jungle airstrip in Colombia.

An American pilot was supposed to fly down in a DC-six to pick the load up, and when we radioed the boss in Miami that everything was ready, the pilot took off from a small airport in West Palm Beach. A ground crew was waiting for him at the landing strip, but he never arrived because the DC-six had some mechanical difficulties. The pilot had to make an emergency landing in the Bahamas. By the time the plane was fixed, a series of tropical storms had set in, and there was no way he could fly into this remote jungle area at night. So we had to wait another several days for the storms to clear.

As it turned out, the American pilot was an alcoholic, and the whole time he was in the Bahamas waiting for the plane to get fixed and for the storms to clear, he'd been drinking. I mean this guy went on a binge like you couldn't believe. He stayed drunk that whole time. No sleep. No rest. Just drinking, drinking, drinking to the point where he couldn't even stand up.

On Monday, after six days of this, the weather started to clear, and the pilot says, "Okay, we'll go tomorrow." That night he finally quit drinking and went to bed. When he showed up at the airport the next day, he looked like shit. He was hung over, and his face was gray. When he reached for the steering wheel his hands were shaking like crazy. The guy had the dt's.

Of course, that drunk bastard never found the landing strip. There was more bad weather over Colombia—lots of low clouds and rain, and those guys couldn't see a thing. They flew around until they were low on fuel, and finally had to turn back and land in Aruba.

At that point I should've backed out of the deal. Everything that could possibly go wrong had gone wrong—from mechanical problems to bad weather to a drunk pilot. I should've said, "This one's a loser. I'm writing off the losses." But back in Miami, the Cuban boss was going crazy. The buyers he'd lined up were getting tired of waiting for the cocaine to come in. He was losing millions of dollars' worth of business because of all the delays. And the Colombian in Medellín who owned the cocaine had gone to the expense of having the coke moved to the landing strip. He wanted the deal to proceed. So I said okay, and the next day I arranged to have a small plane guide the drunk pilot in the DC-six to the landing strip so that he couldn't get lost.

Finally, after eight days of screwups, the DC-six arrived to pick up the load. I had a ground crew waiting at the landing strip, and they loaded two hundred-plus kilos of cocaine onto the plane. From Colombia, the DC-six was supposed to fly to Bimini, where the dope would be transferred to fast boats. I had that all set up. The speedboats were sitting in the water in pairs. They were ready to grab the merchandise and go.

Meanwhile down in Miami, the Cuban boss had a group of five guys who were going to fly to Bimini to meet the DC-six. They represented the buyers of the merchandise in the United States, and they were going to count and verify the load when it came in, and monitor the exchange. These guys had chartered a plane to fly to Bimini. From the landing strip in Colombia, we radioed that the DC-six was loaded and ready to go, and the Cubans took off from Miami. About an hour later, disaster struck. As the five Cubans were approaching Bimini, their chartered plane exploded. All five guys on board were killed.

In Colombia, we didn't know anything about this accident. The exchange with the speedboats was supposed to take place at five that morning, and the DC-six took off for Bimini on schedule. Meanwhile, the Nassau police were investigating the plane crash. They saw our speedboats in the water, and suspected that something was up. They thought maybe there was a connection between the plane crash and the boats. So they jumped on our boats and interrogated the crews. They grabbed one guy and started beating him in the ribs to make him talk. He broke down and told them that the boats were waiting for the DC-six, and that it was due in at five o'clock that morning.

When the DC-six arrived over Bimini, the Bahamian police were waiting at the airport. They were going to seize the load, and arrest everyone involved. But the police made a big mistake. I had arranged to have an airport official there when our plane came in. He'd been bribed to turn on the runway lights. When he saw all the police at the airport, he left. He didn't want to have anything to do with that. So when the DC-six came in over the airport, the runway lights never went on. The police should've known better. They should've had the sense to turn the damn lights on. The pilot circled the airport for a while, but he couldn't land in the dark. He sensed that something was wrong, and left. The DC-six never landed in Bimini. Because he'd flown all the way from Colombia and circled the airport for about twenty minutes, he was low on fuel. So he flew the DC-six to West Palm Beach, because that was the closest place he could land safely.

At West Palm he landed at the little private airport he'd originally taken off from eight days earlier. As soon as they touched down, the pilot and copilot got off the plane and got the hell out of the area. They left this DC-six sitting on the runway with over two hundred kilos of cocaine. They called the boss in Miami and told him, "Hey, your load has arrived. It's in West Palm Beach." That's when they learned about the earlier plane crash, and how the Bahamian police had been waiting for them in Bimini.

The owner of the two hundred-plus kilos was a big-time Colombian drug lord, and since the exchange had never been made it was still his dope. By this time I'd returned to Miami, and I called the owner of the cocaine in Medellín and told him everything that had happened. I said, "Your dope is sitting on the runway of a private airport in West Palm Beach." He listened to everything I said, then told me, "Whatever you do, leave the dope alone. Just forget about it. I'll take the loss. If somebody tries to retrieve it, they'll get arrested. Five people are already dead, and that's enough." When the airport authorities went out and boarded the abandoned plane later that morning, they found this huge load of cocaine.

I laid low for a long time after that. When you're involved in a disaster it works on your head. It makes you paranoid. The fact that five people died haunted me. They were people I knew, and I felt real spooky about that—very wary. I was slow getting back into the business. I let several months pass before I started running loads again.

JOHN REDDEN [Pilot, U.S. Customs Air Branch]: Even after I catch most pilots, and they're sitting on the ground with handcuffs on, I can relate to them as pilots. The ground crews and the dealers are scum, but the pilots are usually a cut above them. Except for the fact that what they're doing is against the law, a lot of them are really pretty good guys.

I remember one time I was tailing a guy who was heading into Mexico to pick up a load, and right near El Paso he landed at a small airport to refuel. I touched down behind him and pulled up to the fuel station. He's got no reason to think I'm anything other than another private pilot—I'm flying a Cessna Two-ten with no Customs markings on it and I'm dressed in civilian clothes. At the fuel station the two of us start shooting the breeze. He's a young guy in his early thirties, and he feeds me this cock-and-bull story about how he's flying down to Austin. He's really a very friendly guy, and we have this nice little pilot-to-pilot chat. We just keep shooting the bull until our planes are full, then we pay for our gas, he takes off, and I take off right behind him.

Of course, he's not flying to Austin. He heads straight into Mexico, right into the badlands of Chihuahua. This is real mountainous, rugged country. It's beautiful on the ground, but a nasty, terrible place to fly—especially if you don't know what the hell you're doing. The wind drafts can be tricky amid all the ravines, and the clandestine landing strips are all very short. Well, this guy overloads his plane with dope and fuel, and when he tries to take off, his plane skids off the strip, flips over, and then explodes. He was burned to death in the crash.

That made me feel bad. One of the things he told me on the ground in El Paso was that he was getting married in a few days. You could see he was excited about that, and now there he was a burned-up corpse in the Chihuahua mountains. The Mexican ground crew dug a very shallow grave, and tossed him in it. Even though what he was doing was wrong, I couldn't help but feel for the guy. He seemed like a nice guy fresh out of the military who was short on money. On a personal level, I couldn't help but empathize.

Interdiction

MAURICIO SMITH [narcotics detective]: Even though I'm a cop in the United States, I was born in Colombia. I lived there, and I still go back. People in the United States have a hard time understanding how much poverty there is in South and Central America, and how that impacts the drug trade.

In Colombia if you go into a small pueblo and walk the streets, you'll see people living in miserable shacks. There's no indoor plumbing, no running water. You see people who are starving to death. People who are emaciated from lack of food. You'll also see lots of children, because there's no birth control.

When a man gets up in the morning, he's got nothing to look forward to. But he's got children, and he has to feed them. For breakfast he might have some crackers and a little bit of milk—whatever he could get from begging the day before. He'll take his little bit of milk and divide it among his five children. Each of them will get a quarter glass of milk. But that's not enough to fill their stomachs. So he takes the glass and fills the rest of it with water, and that's what he gives them. For these children, that's breakfast.

The irony of the situation is that most of the people I arrest here in the United States—the mules bringing cocaine across the border—are just poor homeless peasants that come from these impoverished backgrounds. I talk to them all the time. I know what their lives are like. There's no food stamp program in Colombia. No welfare. It's a world where people starve to death every day, and you survive any way you can. So when a major doper comes into one of these pueblos and starts spending money, everybody wants to work for him. They don't care that he's a doper or a murderer. They don't say, "Hey, this guy is a criminal, I'm going to stay away from him." They say, "I want to feed my children. What do you want me to do? Carry a package from here to there? Okay, I'll do it for my children. Now my children can eat instead of starve."

So these poor peasants get sent to the United States to carry around a few keys of coke. When he comes here this poor peasant, this mule, isn't thinking, "What I'm doing is against the law. If I get caught I'll go to prison for fifteen years." He's thinking, "For carrying these two packages I get five hundred dollars. My wife and children are eating now." For five hundred dollars he can feed his family for six months.

The majority of times, it's the mules that get arrested because they're the ones who actually handle the coke. The big-time dopers, the guys who are making all the money, never get near the dope. They never touch it.

When I catch one of these poor mules from Colombia with five kilos of coke, yes, I place him under arrest. And when I got to court, yes, I testify against him so that he's got to go to jail. But I don't hate him. I understand the guy. I can empathize with what he's doing. If I was in that position, living in that miserable poverty, I think I'd do whatever was necessary to feed my children too. As a matter of fact, I'm sure I would. I'd risk fifteen years so that my children could eat.

TOM WALTERS [agent, U.S. Border Patrol]: We went down to Bolivia in 1986 to help the Bolivian government get rid of the cocaine production problem, and we went down with such certainty in our beliefs. Our overland interdiction operations were designed to stop the influx of precursor chemicals—sulfuric acid, ether, and the like—into the jungle labs where they're used in cocaine processing. When I looked at the overland problem, I saw what I thought was a perfect setup for enforcement. If this area was in the United States, there'd be no trouble controlling it. We were working in the Chipari, which is a giant bowl where a lot of coca is grown. The Chipari is surrounded by mountains and rivers on four sides with only one major highway going in and out of the bowl. All the chemicals we were looking for were being smuggled in by that one highway. All we had to do was shut them off at the highway, and we'd have it under control. So it looked like an ideal setup.

We built a static traffic checkpoint that was manned by both *umapar* troops and American Border Patrol or DEA agents. On Saturdays and Sundays we'd have traffic backed up for two or three miles, because we were checking everybody that came through. We'd even check the buses. Everybody would get off the bus, and if they were carrying bags or containers that they could hide stuff in, we'd have a look. So it was a major inconvenience for the Bolivian people, but by the same token we were consistently finding people who were trying to smuggle large amounts of ether, sulfuric acid, and hydrochloric acid into the processing labs.

According to Bolivian law, possession of small amounts of these chemicals is not illegal. Hydrochloric acid and sulfuric acid have a

lot of chemical uses, but of course there's no legitimate use for them
that far out in the Bolivian Chipari. Their sole purpose is to leech
coca leaf to make coca paste. There was no real punishment involved
for the smugglers. We weren't out there putting hundreds of people
in jail.

We'd catch people smuggling in fifty or one hundred liters of
chemicals, and when we'd confiscate it they'd look at us like, "Jesus,
I can't believe you're doing this!" Most of them were poor *campesinos*
just trying to smuggle enough to get by. They didn't think they were
doing anything wrong, and they'd get incredibly angry and indignant.
They'd say, "What are you gringos doing down here? You're taking
this stuff off my truck, and I only make two or three *bolivianos* off
it. Why are you picking on me? The traffickers make all kinds of
money, but you never do anything to them."

Some of the peasant women, the *cholas*, were the worst. They'd
be smuggling a large amount of chemicals, and when we'd pull it
off their slat-board truck they'd hang on us and beg us not to take it
away. If we took it off one side of the truck, they'd run around and
put it back on the other side. It was like the Keystone Kops. We'd
run around and take it back off, and they'd put it back on. Or they'd
just sit on the stuff and refuse to move. Some of these *cholas* weigh
close to two hundred pounds, and they'd sit there with their arms
crossed and flat out refuse to move. The *umapars* would get a good
laugh out of that, but for us Americans it became a matter of honor.
We wouldn't quit. We'd refuse to let the load go.

We'd try to give them our speech: "You don't understand the damage this stuff does to people in the United States. It's destroying lives,
destroying children." And every single seizure it was the same thing.
They'd say, "Look, I've got to make some money. I've got a grand-
mother that's sick. I've got five hungry kids. My husband ran away
from home, and I've got to feed my kids. Why are you picking on
me?" That was the sort of thing that would go on for hours. Eventually, they'd realize that we were serious, that they weren't going to
get their chemicals back, and that they had no choice but to go away.

While I was in Bolivia, dealing with these people on a day-to-day
basis, my perception of the problem changed dramatically. Prior to
going down there, I saw it as something that could have a solely law
enforcement solution. I thought that if we worked hard, we'd plug
the holes and get the job done. But I don't feel that way anymore.
For one thing, I never saw the *cholas* and the *campesinos* who were

smuggling the precursor chemicals into the labs as "bad" people. Ninety percent of the *campesinos* in that region make their living from the coca plantations. There's this huge number of people, and they're all in the dope trade. It's their economy. The fact that they are living in extreme poverty makes the problem all the more intractable. No amount of law enforcement can remove poverty. We were fighting what they perceived as their "right" to a job that provided them with their only opportunity to feed themselves and their kids.

JOSEPH R. GOULET [marine supervisor, U.S. Customs Service]: I was working in the Bahamas, and at five in the morning an officer came into my stateroom saying he just heard on the radio that there's a boat being pursued. I tell him, "Fine, go prep the catamaran."

While he preps I get the communications center on the radio and say, "Alright, I need the suspect's origin, and I need his course heading." Basic stuff, nothing more than that. They give me the origin and a course of zero ninety at forty knots. Very easy to plot—he's headed for Bimini. So we head for Bimini.

At about six-fifteen, six-twenty, we arrive. We check the beaches and the entrance of Bimini Harbor, but don't see anything. So we pull the boat off to the side of the harbor entrance, figuring that we're too late and the dope is on land by now. We're just sitting there, engines off, sort of drifting, then all of a sudden I see one of these fucking Coast Guard Dolphin helicopters really low on the deck of the horizon. He's getting bigger and bigger! Then I see one of our boats with a flashing blue light chasing a go-fast. I jump up and start the engines.

We're near the opening of Bimini Harbor and as I'm watching the action come toward me, I see the doper boat suddenly swing south. "Shit," I think. My boat is slow compared to his, and we'd be history in a chase. Then, all of a sudden, the doper swings back toward the entrance of the harbor. He's coming right at us! I can't believe my luck! I'm thinking, "What is this, fucking Christmas?"

I tell my officer to get into the harbor and to lay us at an angle so we can cut this guy off. While he's getting us in place, I get the long-gun—which is a rock-and-roll weapon, a big heavy weapon that fires fully automatic.

The doper is racing in with the Customs boat and the helicopter chasing him. It's a pretty impressive sight—lots of gunsmoke and bullshit. As soon as the bad guy comes in, we close nice and tight.

I tell my officer that he's got to hit the doper boat. Absolutely has to hit him! Because I can't fire my gun unless we hit him. When you bang gunwales—no matter how it starts—that's use of deadly force against a federal agent. That gives me cause to fire. I keep yelling, "Hit him! Hit him!" And I'm also yelling at the bad guy, telling him he's got to stop or I'll blow his fucking head off. But he doesn't go for that shit. He's yelling at me, "Fuck you! I'm going into that fucking harbor!" I can't even shoot the guy's engines out unless we ram him.

The next thing I know, we're in a crash—but not with the doper boat. The bad guy hauls ass right on by, while my horizon tips upside down. I don't know what the fuck's going on. I can hear a lot of screaming, and somebody yelling, "Man overboard! Man overboard!" Well, I see my officer is still on the boat, and I know I'm on the boat, so who's overboard?

What happened was a little whaler had deliberately come out to get in our way. My officer tried to avoid the collision, but the whaler kept coming right at us in a civilian blocking-action for the doper. They rammed us before we could ram the bad guy.

Great, isn't it? The "innocent" people are on the dopers' side. Down there, *we're* the bad guys.

DAVE KUNZ [undercover pilot, DEA]: There's no doubt about the fact that working undercover is dangerous, and when you work south of the border in the countries like Mexico, Bolivia, and Colombia, the risk is infinitely greater. You can trust *no* one in Latin America. Everybody has a price. In the States, if drug dealers become suspicious of you, they clear out and try to keep their distance. But in the Latin American countries they will kill you.

On my first undercover assignment I was nervous as hell. I was working as an undercover pilot for DEA, and our agents had some inside information on a Los Angeles drug ring. We knew that this smuggling ring was looking for a pilot. So I went undercover and met with them. Sure enough, they hired me to fly five hundred kilos of marijuana out of Mexico.

I took off in the direction of southeast Mexico, and eventually saw my signal—two tires burning on the ground. I landed the plane in this dried-up lakebed, and when I got out there were about twenty Mexican *banditos* standing there with rifles. Being surrounded by all those guns made me uneasy, but I learned right away that as a pilot you are very important to them. Without you, they can't move their goods. As long as they don't have any reason to be suspicious they're going to take very good care of you. My trick was to pretend that I couldn't speak a word of Spanish. I wanted them to think that I was just a dumb gringo pilot.

These guys had five hundred bricks of marijuana wrapped up in butcher paper, which they loaded on the airplane. They also had a truck full of aviation fuel, which they used to refuel me. After that was all done, I flew out of there to a small private strip in Nevada where the guys from L.A. were waiting to receive the load. As soon as I touched down they came running out and loaded all of the marijuana onto a couple of trucks. I was given instructions to fly the plane to Las Vegas and to check into a hotel where I was told that I'd receive a phone call.

Sure enough, about seven that evening the phone rings, and this guy tells me there's a gentleman who wants to see me at the bar. I go down to the bar and this guy that I've never met before walks up and hands me a briefcase with thirty thousand dollars in cash inside. That was my pay for smuggling one little load.

Of course, DEA was running surveillance from the moment my plane touched down in Nevada, and had agents trailing everyone involved. As soon I walked out of that bar, they started making arrests.

That was a very successful operation, but I was nervous every step of the way—especially down at that lakebed strip in Mexico when all those *banditos* were standing around with their rifles. But once it was over, I thought, "Hey, this is easy." As long as the bad guys believe I'm who I say I am, then everything slides along. All I've got to do is act like a dumb cowboy eager to make thirty thousand bucks.

BRAXTON MOHLER [agent, U.S. Border Patrol]: Catching a load of dope will make you identify with a narcotics abuser. You get an adrenaline rush so strong it's almost addictive. Have you ever been so scared you just about wet your pants? It happens in this job. When you're out in the desert working the border, and you detect a group of smugglers coming in and you know that the bad guys have guns, but you and your partner go ahead and take them down. Just the two of you. At the time you do it you're scared to death. But you get a big rush. It's fun—if you survive.

One night my partner, Rodney, and I were working near Penitas,

Texas, along the Mexican border. We were on the west side of town, and at about two o'clock in the morning we saw some aliens cross the river wheeling a load. We followed them into an abandoned gravel quarry, and then they came up to this aluminum gate about four miles north of the river. Then they just sat.

Rodney and I were three quarters of a mile away, and we covered our car with blankets so the moonlight wouldn't reflect off it, and we kept an eye on them with a pair of binoculars. These guys sat there for three hours. Then finally a GMC pickup truck arrives. The aliens jump up and load all the dope onto the pickup truck, right there on the highway.

We waited until the dope was all loaded, then Rodney fired up the engine, I yanked the blankets off the car, we went after the truck. They had a three-quarter mile lead on us so Rodney had to push it. The pickup had a hot-rod engine, and the bad guy was tooling along at about eighty. We ended up hitting one thirty-five just to make contact with the guy. Rodney pulled in tight behind him, threw on the lights, and all hell broke loose.

The bad guy floors it, and off we go on a chase. Both of us are flying down the road. Rodney swings into the left lane and punches it to get alongside the truck. I'm hanging out the window with the wind damn near tearing me apart, waving my shotgun at the guy trying to get him to pull over. Instead, he tries to ram us.

We got on the radio and called for help, but it's five A.M., and every law enforcement officer in south Texas is asleep. Nobody but Rodney and me working for seventy miles. We blow through one city and go tearing around city hall with tires squealing and horns blaring, but there's nobody there. The whole place is dead asleep.

Finally, when we start getting near McAllen, the police department there responds. They set up a roadblock by pulling two vehicles nose to nose across the road. The pickup heads for the shoulder and hits it at one hundred-plus, a dirt rooster-tail goes flying eighty feet in the air behind, and he slides broadside, but manages to straighten out and keep on going—with us right on his butt.

He's still flying as he heads into a four-way Stop that's got a concrete island in the middle of the intersection. We head around on the inside, trying to cut him off, but he gets around us. The McAllen police have a souped-up car, and we can see them moving up fast behind us. So we move over to give them a shot. They go busting past us like ninety-to-nothing and tear right up alongside the pickup.

As soon as they're even with him, he slams on the brakes, and the police go flying off the left-hand side of the road into a water ditch.

The pickup makes a right-hand turn off the road and goes tearing into a grapefruit orchard. He's hauling ass between the rows. I looked at our speedometer and saw we were hitting sixty trying to catch this jerk. The trees were so big that the branches overlapped, and big old ruby red grapefruits were flying everywhere. At that speed his windshield got busted out, and the little camper he had in his pickup bed got beat all apart. Then he ran smack into a tree.

Finally, after chasing him for over forty miles at speeds in excess of one hundred miles per hour, we got him. A chase like that is scary as hell, but boy is it fun. Once it's all over and you've got the guy in handcuffs and have confiscated the dope, you sit back and say to yourself, "Damn, that was fun!"

JERRY YOUNG [pilot, U.S. Customs Air Branch]: You do your best all the time. You try to look professional, but sometimes stuff just happens and you don't know where the hell it came from. The reports will always say, "Of course, this was the result of a carefully planned six-month investigation," and so on, when the fact is you stumbled onto something the night before.

A few years back we identified an airplane—a DC-seven—that was being used by a drug smuggling organization, and we managed to get a tracking device on it. Well, one day the airplane flies down to South America and is seized in Colombia by the authorities down there. Our case goes down the tubes, and we go on with other work.

A couple years pass, then out of the blue we get a call at about one in the morning from NORAD [North America Radar Air Defense] and they're saying, "Hey, we've picked up one of your tracking devices on our radar." We jump into two airplanes, and take off. We're up there locked into the radar and we're all wondering the same thing—"We don't have any airplanes wired, so what the hell is going on?"

We can see that this plane is doing one hundred eighty knots, and we're all trying to figure out what kind of plane it is, who it could possibly belong to, where it's coming from, and how this is happening. Eventually, we get an infrared picture, and we can see that it's a four-engine plane with one engine shut down. We're looking at each other, saying, "We don't have anybody working any four-engine planes. How come it's got our tracking device on it?"

What the hell? We decide to keep following it and see what happens. Eventually, the thing ends up landing in Middle of Nowhere, Utah. We call the Utah State Police, and continue orbiting overhead while they converge on the area. Once they've moved in on the ground, we touch down—and what happens? We wind up catching almost twenty-five thousand pounds of marijuana, and arresting over a dozen people. All of them were Miami people moving west. And just like that, we've made one of the biggest airplane cases in history.

What had happened was this Miami organization had bought the DC-seven out of seizure in Colombia, but they obviously didn't know we had wired it two years earlier. They just loaded it up, and we make this huge seizure by total accident.

LARRY CAVER [agent, U.S. Border Patrol]: On detail once to the thriving metropolis of Hebbronville, Texas, I was operating a traffic check with a couple of our younger agents. A real good-looking lady pulled up wearing short shorts and a tank top. My colleagues were sitting by the chase vehicle, and I thought they ought to have the opportunity to handle the usual inquiries with this young lady. So instead of just waving her through, I stopped her, and called the young guys over. They asked the normal questions. "Are you a U.S. citizen?" She said yes. Then they asked, "Would you mind stepping out and opening the trunk?"—not because they thought they'd find anything, but because they wanted to get a better eye-load on her.

Immediately, she started shaking. "It's not my car," she said. "I don't know what's in there."

Of course, that triggers bells and alarms. One of the agents reaches inside the car, turns off the ignition, and grabs the keys. When they opened the trunk they found several hundred pounds of marijuana. Had the girl not been so attractive, and dressed in such skimpy clothes, she never would have been asked to get out and open the trunk. If she'd have been one of these one-hundred-ninety-pound *mamacitas* we see all the time, I'd have just waved her through.

Another time, my partner and I had just left a coffee shop late one night and drove out into the middle of the boonies. Of course, when you're working out in the Texas brush you get rid of processed coffee right there on the spot. We pulled up on a river levee and got out to take a leak. We were standing there taking care of business, when all of a sudden a bunch of people jump up and start running like hell. They were mules who'd been hiding in the bush. When they saw us, they panicked and got the hell out of there. We looked down and found a bunch of marijuana in the bushes where these guys had been hiding. We seized forty bags of pot just because we'd stopped to take a leak.

HANK HAYS [agent, U.S. Border Patrol]: The last load of dope I caught was pretty much a matter of dumb luck. I just happened to be in the right place at the right time. I'd been flying supplies into New Mexico State Police outposts that had been stranded by floods, and I'd been up in my helicopter for about eight hours. I touched down in Deming, New Mexico. The Border Patrol was in the middle of a shift change and there wasn't a unit on the line. A ground sensor popped about a mile away. I heard a radio call go out for a Demming unit to respond, but Demming replied that because of the shift change nobody was within thirty miles. So I got on the radio and said I'd take a look.

I took my helicopter up, got a little altitude, and sure enough, I see this Mazda pickup truck with North Carolina plates that had just come across the border. He was racing along a dirt cow trail, and eventually turned onto a graded dirt road heading toward El Paso. I radio for an El Paso Sand Hills unit to make the stop, but they didn't have any units available. So I said, "Alright, I'm going to take this guy down."

I was keeping enough altitude so that he didn't know I was trailing him. He ran east along the border fence for quite a ways. Then suddenly, I swooped down out of the sky and got right on his tail. He couldn't believe it. A helicopter is a very intimidating machine. You stir up a lot of dust and wind, and it frightens people to have this big, huge machine hovering over them. I hit the siren and was low enough so that he couldn't back up without taking one of my landing skis through his rear windshield.

I got on my loudspeaker and told him to get out of his truck and to keep his hands above his head. I put my helicopter down, and had a weapon trained on him as I walked over to where he was standing. I placed him under arrest, and handcuffed him to the bumper. Sure enough, he had a big load of dope on board his truck.

As it turned out, this guy had been raised right near there, so he knew the area really well. He'd since moved to North Carolina, and his brother was in jail for drug trafficking. So this was obviously a family operation. I'm sure they had been running drugs for some time.

It was about forty-five minutes before a backup unit arrived to take him to jail, and the two of us were just standing there with him handcuffed to the bumper. He was really shocked. I remember he asked me, "How fast does that helicopter go?" He wanted to know if he could outrun me in his pickup. I just laughed, and said, "Even if you could outrun my helicopter, you never could have outrun my radio."

TOM [pilot, U.S. Customs Air Branch]: The craziest chase I was ever involved in began out over the Gulf of Mexico, where one of our Citation radar planes picked up a suspicious incoming target. I was flying the Blackhawk [helicopter] that day, and flew out to fall in behind our Citation as he was tailing this guy. It was strange because this was a beautiful day. There wasn't a cloud in the sky. Normally, if some guy is going to try to sneak in under our radar, he's going to do it at night under cover of darkness. But here was this guy flying real low out over the Gulf of Mexico in broad daylight.

At some point after this doper crossed inland, he realized we were there, because he started kicking his rudder real hard and banking his airplane. He tried losing us, but when that didn't work he started throwing the dope out. There were two guys in the plane, and every now and then the pilot would go into a bank and his partner would drop a few bales.

We'd mark the spot where the dope was thrown out, and radio the information down so that local police authorities could retrieve it. The pilot was smart. Instead of trying to outrun us, he had his throttle pulled way back and was flying real slow, trying to run us out of gas.

We pulled up alongside the plane so we could get a good look at the two guys, but when we tried to look into the cockpit the pilot put a map up in the window and hid his face. We swung around to the passenger side of the plane, and saw a Colombian sitting there. We got a good look at him. The Colombian didn't try to hide; all he did was flip us the bird.

That pissed me off. I dropped back behind the plane, and crept up on the tail; then very slowly I brought the helicopter rotors in and shaved about two inches out of his rudder. Then I gave him a little bump. We pulled back up alongside the passenger side, and I could see the Colombian screaming at the pilot, telling him to land the plane. He was scared shitless—obviously afraid that we were going to chew them right out of the damn sky. Boy, he was sweating. Every time they'd fly over a farm or a field the Colombian would point down at the ground showing the pilot where he could land, but the pilot kept on going. Every now and then he'd go into another hard bank, and they'd drop more cocaine. We had people on the ground picking up kilos of cocaine that day all the way from Arkansas through Alabama and on into Tennessee.

Unfortunately, after several hours in the air I was running out of gas. This guy was flying with illegal fuel tanks, so he was able to keep on going. We radioed one of our ground stations and had a Citation radar plane come in behind us to take the handoff, and I broke off to refuel. While we were on the ground we received word over the radio that this smuggler had managed to give the Citation the slip. He dropped down way low, and got away. When we heard that, everyone of us on the helicopter crew damn near started crying. When you get beat like that it hurts—it hurts bad.

ROGER "MAD DOG" GARLAND [pilot, U.S. Customs Air Branch]: I remember one time we spotted a low-flying target coming in over the western Gulf of Mexico. We trailed him up into central Florida, where he was going to put down on a small landing strip. As he was making his approach the guy saw that we were tailing him, and instead of taking his plane down, he climbed up to ten thousand feet and parachuted out.

On that mission we had the Blackhawk out working with us, and the helicopter crew saw this guy's parachute open up and come down through the clouds. They closed right in, and as he was descending the helicopter pilot could see this guy's face—he could see how pissed the guy was. When that doper saw the helicopter he knew he wasn't going to be able to run away. And sure enough, when his feet hit the ground the helicopter was right on top of him. The crew jumped out and placed him under arrest.

Meanwhile, this guy's plane and all of his dope are still up in the air. Before he jumped he flipped on the autopilot. I was flying a Cessna Four-oh-four, and I took off after his plane. I pulled up alongside it, looked into the cockpit, and was able to confirm that there was nobody there. That plane passed over Tampa at ten thousand feet—without a pilot. At that point, it was just an unguided missile. There was no telling when or where it was going to crash. If it was low on fuel, it could easily have crashed in a densely populated area and killed a bunch of people on the ground.

Fortunately, it drifted out over the ocean, where it lost an engine and went down. I watched it hit the water and explode; then the next thing I saw was all these bales of cocaine come popping to the surface. I radioed to have a Coast Guard cutter called into the area to retrieve the dope.

HANK HAYS: If you look at a map of the U.S. border with Mexico, you'll see how vast it is. There's nothing out there. It's a very sparsely populated region that is full of wide-open spaces. Before I was transferred to El Paso, I worked Border Patrol in southern New Mexico for nine years, and the closest town to my station was a hundred miles away. And it was a small town with a population of about four thousand.

Drug smugglers know how to take advantage of that much territory. They know we don't have enough manpower, airplanes, or ground vehicles to keep up with them. A lot of dope is getting through.

In Arizona and New Mexico the mountain ranges all run north to south. The geography is such that you'll have a ridgeline, a valley, and another ridgeline. The smugglers use those valleys to great advantage. Once they're down in there, it's very hard to detect them from the air. That's particularly true at night. They can do quite well under cover of darkness. Along the border with Mexico, there are areas where the terrain is too rugged for vehicles, so the drug runners will cross over on foot or on horseback, and they'll bring their narcotics in on a train of pack mules. About the only way you can catch them is to be right on top of them when they cross the border. Otherwise, they'll just disappear into the landscape, and work their way up to a drop-off point from which the drugs can be transported out by truck or van.

JOHN FRANCE [agent, U.S. Border Patrol]: I transferred to the Tucson sector because I loved the mountains and canyons, and preferred working in them to working the flatlands of Texas. When I arrived at Tucson I started scouting around the border area where the deep canyons and mountains run. This is extremely rugged country, and no one had been working this particular area because it's so labor-intensive. Cutting around, I found some deep-cut horse trails that were worn down from generations of traffic. Hell, they'd probably been there since Prohibition. They were littered with tequila bot-

tles and beer cans and cigarette butts, which made it obvious that
not only was tons of stuff getting through, but that the *banditos* running the horse trains weren't the least bit concerned about getting
caught. By cutting sign [reading clues on the ground], I found that
three horse trains had passed through on one trail in a single week
with at least six horses in each train. "God," I thought, "that's at
least a thousand pounds of dope per load!" Which meant that more
than three thousand pounds had been smuggled into the U.S. in one
week on that one trail.

So I set out to get the horses. This was my big chance. No one
else was working the area. It was virgin territory. I had my own unit
and freedom to run operations. Some of the old heads in Tucson
were very skeptical. They thought I was wasting my time. They'd tell
me, "Even if you find the horse trains, what are you going to do?
You can't catch horses in that kind of rugged terrain." Of course, the
irony of the situation is here is this multimillion-dollar smuggling
business, and we've got all this high-tech equipment, but what it
boils down to is horses. In terrain where it's too rugged to get a vehicle in, how the hell do you stop a guy on horseback?

When we went into the canyons, our agents would be on foot,
and I knew there was no way we could catch or outrun the *banditos*
on horseback. No one had ever dealt with stopping horse trains before, and I had to think of a way to grab these guys. I briefly considered things like nets and tranquilizer guns, but couldn't come up
with anything that would be effective until I hit upon the idea of
using flash-bang grenades. Flash-bangs emit a blinding light flash
and have a tremendous explosive sound. The idea was to frighten
the horses so they'd buck like crazy, but wouldn't get physically hurt.
Even the best rider would have to use all his energy trying to stay
on the horse, so he couldn't fight us or get his horse to run in any
particular direction. I figured the shock value of the flash-bangs
would be devastating, particularly if they were used at night on a
lonely trail.

After two weeks of humping up mountains and down into
canyons, I found the best hill to lay-in on, and I took a small team
to the hill's ridge and laid an ambush. This was Thanksgiving Day
1988. I knew a horse train was going to come through because of
the frequency of use the tracks showed. Since it was a holiday, I also
knew the bastards would think that we weren't working. So we set
up very carefully, and put in some sensors along a trail they'd been
using.

Unfortunately, a horrible storm blew in. The gully washes can be terrible in the canyons, and here we are standing around with shotguns as though they were lightning rods. Even though it was prime time for movement, we figured the bad guys had probably decided to forget it because of the lousy weather. There were four of us, and I told two agents to pack up, while another agent and I went down to pick up the sensors.

If I'd waited another sixty seconds, we would've ambushed a horse train. As we were heading down the trail, we literally walked right into a group of smugglers coming north. For about two seconds everybody froze. Then the bandits kicked their horses into a full gallop and got the hell out of there.

When I got back to the office I was really pissed off. They'd come within fifteen minutes of when I'd expected them, and they'd come up the exact trail we were laying-in on. All of my planning and intelligence had been perfect. I'd never been more right in my life, and I'd never fucked up so badly. All the guys in the office were laughing about it. It was like, "Ha, ha, France. You fuck-up!"

I was more determined than ever. I was going to catch those bastards, or die trying. About two weeks after the Thanksgiving fiasco, we went back to work the trails late one night. The area we were working had two parallel trails that dropped into a canyon, and then merged into a single trail on the north side of the canyon. I placed two agents where the trails merged for the sole purpose of forcing the *banditos* back into the canyon. I figured that when our agents stepped out on the trail, the bad guys would naturally turn around and ride back into the canyon, where we'd have another team of agents waiting for them.

On this particular night, we had a three-quarter moon in the sky and a lot of cattle were roaming the hills. I was lying along the ridgeline talking with another agent when I heard the cadence of horse feet. I said, "Chris, you hear that? Horses!"

"Bullshit," he said. "That's cows."

"No, no, it's horses!" I grab the binoculars, and sure enough, I can barely make out a horse train heading through the canyon on the lower trail—the exact trail on which we'd run into them on Thanksgiving Day. I radioed the guys on the other side of the canyon to let them know the train was coming, then we started moving along the ridgeline to get into position. The ridge was so narrow that all of us kept slipping down it as we were trying to run, and I'm racing along like a goddamn cheerleader: "C'mon, c'mon, you sons a bitches! Gotta move! Gotta move!"

On the north side of the canyon, our agents step out and challenge the horse train. Just like we'd expected, the *banditos* turn and gallop back into the canyon. I'd never seen anything like it—it was like the charge of the Light Brigade. The horsemanship was incredible. They charged down the trail back into the canyon and started back up the other side. Huffing and puffing we got into position on this steep, narrow trail to cut the *banditos* off. I had my shotgun, and one of the agents with me had a flash-bang grenade. The idea was to have him throw the flash-bang and spook the horses, and then we'd move in to seize the dope and arrest the riders. But what happened was this young agent who had the flash-bang failed to straighten the cotter pin on the grenade. The horsemen are hauling ass toward us, because they're in a hurry to get back to Mexico, and I'm telling the agent, "Throw the grenade! Throw the son of a bitch!" He's dancing around pulling as hard as he can, but he can't pull the pin because the cotter pin acts as a safety. In the meantime, I'm picking up the horses in my sights. "Throw it! Throw it!" Well, he pulled so hard that the fuse came right out of the grenade, rendering the damn thing useless. By that time, the horses were practically on top of us. I shouted for the riders to stop. But they refused. They just kept coming right at us, and there was no place for us to go.

When you're at close range like that, there's no point in shooting the rider, because the horse will keep coming and run you over. If you shoot the horse in the chest, it will still keep coming. Its momentum will propel it forward. Either way you're screwed. The only thing you can do is shoot the horses' legs out from underneath them. At a distance of about ten yards we opened up and shot the shit out of those poor horses. That was a mess. The lead horses went down, *banditos* were bouncing off of rocks, dirt and dope were flying all over the damn place, and the horses were screaming something terrible.

It was an ugly, bloody scene. We seized over five hundred pounds of marijuana, but the riders got away. They were able to crawl into the bush and disappear, while the horses we didn't shoot yip-yapped their way back to Mexico. The horses that were lying on the ground had to be put out of their misery.

This was not something I enjoyed. It made me sick. I hated shooting those horses. I still thought the flash-bangs were the answer, it was just a matter of getting them to work. Subsequent to that night, we've had numerous flash-bang ambushes that have been successful and haven't resulted in injury to the animals. We've made huge cocaine and marijuana seizures, and have put a lot of people in jail. When these flash-bangs go off it's a sight to see. There's an incredible boom and a brilliant flash. We'll be out in a remote area, and when the horse train gets close, the flash-bang will scare the holy bejesus out of the horses and riders. It comes as a hell of a surprise.

We've also used shotgun-propelled rounds that work in a similar fashion. There are two types of shotgun rounds. One is called a star flash, which shoots thousands of sparks in a blinding flash, and the other is called a star burst, which is like a miniflash-bang that travels out about forty meters before it explodes.

The first night we used those shotgun-propelled rounds was really hilarious. What happened was a horse train tripped one of our sensors coming across the border, so I assembled an ambush team to cut them off near the end of the trail. When we got to the ambush site, I did a quick recon of the area, and then started assigning positions. "Okay, you get behind that bush, you take the ridge," and so forth. But before anyone had a chance to move, I heard horses. We'd only been there a few minutes, and the train is already coming. We were standing on a levee, and all we could do was lie down so that the horsemen coming up the trail won't see us. The reason they got there so fast was because there were only three horses—two riders and a pack horse.

The riders are cantering along, talking to each other in Spanish. Unlike a military ambush, where you only have to get close enough to shoot the enemy, we're law enforcement people, we're supposed to catch them. We've got to get close enough to arrest them. So I initiate ambushes at a range of five to ten yards. When these horsemen got to the base of the levee, I rolled a flash-bang down the bank. It exploded at the feet of the lead horse. KA-BANGGG! The horse went skyward, just straight up in the air. I couldn't believe it, because the damn rider somehow managed to stay on the horse. Another agent threw a second grenade. BOOM! The horses are rearing up and whinnying like crazy, but the riders managed to stay on.

It was like something out of a World War I movie—five Border Patrol agents come busting off this levee just like we were charging out of the damn trenches, and we're screaming bloody murder.

The riders turn, and the guy with the shotgun rounds is blasting away. His first three rounds are star flashes, so we've got umpteen million sparks exploding in the air, but all that does is make the horses run off in the opposite direction. I'm counting rounds, because I know the fourth round is going to be a star burst. The agent fires, and I can see this meteor travel out toward the *bandito*, and right when it gets alongside him—BOOM! The damn thing goes off, nightblinding both the horse and rider. The horse races into a barbed wire fence, and the barbed wire rips through the saddle cinch, so that the saddle, the rider, and the dope all go flying. The poor bastard lands right on top of his saddle on the ground, and he's so shell-shocked by all of the explosions he doesn't know what the hell's going on. He's just sitting there on the ground, grabbing his saddle horn, screaming, "*No mi mata! No mi mata!*" ["Don't kill me! Don't kill me!"] Oh God, it was funny. That big bad drug smuggler had been reduced to a whimpering fool.

The other horseman got away, but we seized all the dope. We found his bags with the dope in them about a hundred yards away, and we seized the pack horse as well. So that was a nice cocaine seizure.

Overall, I'd have to say the flash-bangs have proven to be the perfect weapon for this kind of terrain. Just a couple weeks ago, we had a record seizure where the Border Patrol grabbed over thirty horses and forty-three hundred pounds of cocaine. So we're hitting them hard. Those guys had been running tons and tons of dope through that area unchecked for God knows how long, and now we've pretty much shut them down. In the last year, only three horse-trains have come through the area, because the dopers are scared of the flash-bangs. We've come a long way from the days when agents were telling me that we'd never catch anybody on horseback.

I can honestly say, I've never had as much fun as I have working the horse trails. It gives me a good feeling to know that if any smugglers try to cross the border into Arizona, their assholes are going to be puckered. But I don't fool myself. I know that as long as there's a demand for cocaine in the United States, it's going to get in. No one down here in the Border Patrol believes we're going to stop it. When we shut 'em down in one area, I know the dopers will just move someplace else. Well, fine. When we find out where that is, we'll move in and kick their butts again.

A friend once asked me, "Don't you think your job is a joke? I mean you catch these guys, and throw them in jail, but ultimately there's really nothing you can do to keep drugs from coming into the United States." Well, to some degree the job is a joke. Every law enforcement officer in the world knows that we can't win the war unless we eliminate the demand for dope. But by going out and doing our jobs we can make it better. All I said to my friend was, "How much worse do you think it would be if I wasn't out there?"

HANK HAYS: It used to be that drug smugglers *never* shot at federal law enforcement officers. They carried weapons, but that was primarily to make sure they weren't ripped off by other smugglers.

Then, about four or five years ago the size of the loads they were bringing into the United States started to increase dramatically. In the early eighties the largest loads we saw ranged from five hundred to a thousand pounds. But these days cocaine shipments are being measured by the ton. Obviously, a ton of cocaine is worth millions of dollars, and with the monetary stakes rising, smugglers have begun shooting at federal agents. In the past sixty days we've had five shootings in El Paso alone. Near Tucson, a band of smugglers tried to bring a mule train across the border, and those pack mules were guarded by seven armed bandits carrying AK-forty-sevens. Two of our Border Patrol agents were tracking them, and when the smugglers realized what was happening they opened up with their AK-forty-sevens. Our guys were only carrying sidearms, and here they were caught in a shootout against assault rifles. The smugglers had our agents pinned down and outgunned. The agents were lucky to get out of there without getting killed.

We're seeing more and more of that kind of thing. The southern border with Mexico is really heating up. In 1988 we had two hundred ninety armed encounters with drug smugglers along the southern border, and in 1989 we were up over three hundred seventy. Those numbers are still rising. So we're in a situation right now where we're averaging more than one shooting incident every day. Gun battles have become commonplace, and they're getting worse all the time.

LARRY DAVIDSON [pilot, U.S. Customs Air Branch]: On my first day at Homestead, I walked in to report for work and was standing around looking for someone to introduce myself to. The first person I saw walked up, handed me a shotgun, and told me to go board an aircraft. One of our pilots was involved in a chase, and needed a bust crew. I ran out and jumped into a Beech Baron that was just starting up. I climbed into the copilot's seat with my shotgun and we took off to join the chase. I hadn't even been on the job ten minutes. I was sitting there with my shotgun, thinking, "This is going to be one hell of a great job! You don't get an orientation like this on any other job!"

When we showed up over the target area, the guy in the trail plane was right on the smuggler's tail and was following him down toward a landing strip. Right about the same time we arrived, a Marine Corps OV-ten observation plane showed up to see if he could help out. The smuggler must have seen all of the air activity behind him, because instead of taking his plane down he climbed in altitude, veered east, flew out over the Atlantic, and dumped bale after bale of dope into the ocean. Then he flew back in over the mainland and touched down at a small airport.

We went down and arrested him, but he didn't have any dope on his plane. He'd done a very thorough job of cleaning that sucker out. Consequently, this guy was never prosecuted on any drug or smuggling charges. We didn't have any evidence. He had to pay a small fine for violation of FAA regulations due to his failure to file a flight plan. That was the best we could do. It was like hitting him with a traffic ticket.

I remember thinking to myself, "Goddamn, this ain't no way to win a war." In an eerie sort of way it reminded me of Vietnam. Over in Vietnam it seemed to me that we were making a lot of smoke and noise, but I always had this nagging sense of frustration that we weren't doing everything that needed to be done. It was like we were fighting a war without being willing to do what was necessary to win it. I felt the same sense of frustration when I realized that we had apprehended this guy who was obviously trying to smuggle drugs into the United States, and yet, we couldn't prosecute him. After six years of flying for Customs that sense of frustration hasn't gone away. It's with me every day.

CHAPTER 3

DEALERS

The engine that drives the nation's drug trade is money—billions of dollars of it. One of the more telling yet rarely observed facts of the drug war is that you can make up just about any statistic and people will believe it. Some experts say Americans spend between $10 billion and $20 billion on illegal narcotics annually. Others have said $50 billion. Still others point to a total world market that approaches $200 billion. No one really knows what the precise figures are, but everyone agrees that an enormous amount of money is being spent.

Much of that money is changing hands in America's inner cities, where drug dealing has become a curbside business. No longer intimidated by the police, dealers hawk their wares openly, calling out to potential customers like barkers at a carnival. These "open-air markets" have spread to every major city in the United States. "We call it hand-to-hand combat," explains a young teenage dealer. "We go out in the street and sell hand-to-hand, because that's where the money is. A lot of people is afraid. They read about all the murder and violence and shit in the newspaper. They'll drive into the strip, but they won't go inside no project. You can't get no turnover if you is sitting inside an apartment. The turnover is on the street. Cars be lining up to buy drugs, and you got to be jiving with them dudes because that's what all the other hustlers is doing. You got to show 'em what you got. That's the only way you gonna be turning cash. Dealing drugs is a very competitive business."

———

SANTA: I come to Miami from Cuba. I didn't have no family, and I start fucking around. I start selling drugs. One day I sell ten ounces of coke to an undercover agent, and I get five years. I do forty-four months in prison, and when I get out I'm worse than before because I meet a lot of heavy-duty people in prison. When I come out I get with a group of Puerto Rican guys, the Puerto Rican mafia. Believe me, they knows the drug business. They love any kind of drugs, and the business very good.

They send me up to New York, and I live on One Hundred Seventy-eighth Street in Spanish Harlem. All the Cubans hang around there. And I start to move drugs. I never move no heroin. I move cocaine. This is the late sixties, early seventies. Remember, in those times there was no crack. You do cocaine by the nose. That was some of the best coke I ever saw in my life. It was packaged in soft paper, and when you opened the package it was bright, shiny. Like butter. That's because the cook was a professional. It's not like now where they cook the coke all over Colombia, Bolivia, and Peru. Back then, only the best guys would cook.

I was moving twenty kilos a week in Harlem. What we'd do is the Puerto Rican guys would bring the coke from Peru to Brazil, and from Brazil to the United States. At each stage, we'd move it by mule. We'd send five people—three guys and two womens carrying it on the body. They'd have a special rubber band around the body, and each of them could carry four kilos under their clothes. We'd send all five mules down to Brazil at the same time, but each one would return to a different place—Baltimore, Philadelphia, Boston, New Haven. Wherever. Then someone else would pick up the cocaine and bring it to me in New York.

In Harlem, I'd only work with the black guys. There was a lot of entertainers doing coke. I don't want to talk bad about nobody, but I had a guy that used to sell to Sammy Davis, Jr. Back then, I'd sell him a quarter kilo of cocaine for twenty-five hundred dollars. Not directly, I'd always have a black guy send it. I'd also send it to

Richard Pryor. Lots of famous people was doing coke, and I was their copa.

Every day I'd sell to the pimps. I'd sell to all the bad guys because my coke was so good. The black guys would always hit the coke three times. My coke was so pure, they could put three hits on it—they'd take one kilo and make three. They'd sell the coke in little capsules, and they'd sell a lot. I had one guy working for me that was selling five kilos a week.

Like I tell you, the drug business was very good. I was moving lots of cocaine. Back then, nobody fuck with you. The bad guys don't rip you off. Maybe some people be jealous, but they don't kill you. They just leave you alone. The police is the only people who fuck with you. And in New York the police was corrupt. You could buy them off.

ESTELLE: I used to work for this guy that had one of the biggest cocaine distribution networks in this city. He was big, man. Bigger than most of the people you hear about on the news. He had bunches of people working for him—runners, sellers, lookouts, body-guards, drivers. All that. Me and him used to run together. We was tight. He saw the way I could handle myself on the street, and he started liking me—not liking me the way a man likes a woman, but liking the way I carried myself, liking the way I handled my customers on the street.

He was bringing drugs into the city, and then distributing them to his sellers on the street. He had an L.A. connection, some people there that had access to cocaine coming into the U.S. from Colombia. They could get him however many kilos he wanted, and he was buying twenty, thirty kilos a week. This one girl used to fly out to L.A., pick up the cocaine, and then fly back to the East Coast with however many kilos she was supposed to carry. She was a friend of mine, and she got paid good for doing that. This guy always used women to fly out to the West Coast to get the cocaine. He had women constantly going back and forth, back and forth. His business was expanding like crazy, and every day he had more kilos coming in.

I used to do a lot of driving. He'd pay me to drive out to the airport, pick up the cocaine, then drive back into the city. I'd sit there with him when the transactions were being made. I'd count the money, weigh the cocaine, and test the drugs. Because he trusted me, I was doing a lot of counting. I was seeing more money than your eyes can imagine. Every day there'd be thousands of dollars turning on my fingers. I'd count so much I'd get tired. I was tired of even *seeing* money. I didn't want to look at it no more.

The runners would come in, and they'd be bringing money from the hustlers working the street. They'd drop the money off and go back out. That meant there'd be another twenty thousand or thirty thousand dollars sitting there that had to be counted. That's the name of the drug game— money, money, money. When you're moving kilos, and running street hustlers, you're counting lots of cash.

CHARLIE FERNANDEZ [detective]: In the past few years I've seen a big change in the way drug dealers conduct business. In the mid-1980s I was working with SWAT, and back then drug dealing was an indoor business. People would sell from a house or an apartment where they couldn't be seen. Our police tactic was to send an undercover cop or an informant inside to make a buy. Then we'd get a search warrant and send a SWAT team in to execute the warrant. Those operations were very successful. In one year we served over five hundred warrants. We were busting down a couple of doors every day, and it seemed like every time we executed a warrant we would get a trafficking amount. We were pulling in a lot of cocaine, a lot of heroin, and a lot of marijuana. Kilo-size seizures were not uncommon, they were routine.

That tactic forced dealers out on the street. That's why you see so many open-air markets today. The dealers adjusted to our undercover operations by sending sellers out to work in the open. They deal on the street where everybody can see them, but the catch is the sellers keep a very small stash on their person. You know, the supplier will give a guy a few rocks, and when he's done selling that he'll be given a few more. Even though the sellers have moved outside, the stash that is used to supply them is being kept hidden in a house or an apartment that nobody sells from—which makes it very difficult for us to get a warrant, because no one can make an undercover buy. It's difficult to locate the stash houses where you'd find the trafficking weight.

When we bust a guy on the street corner, it's very rare to find trafficking weight. Even though we're making more arrests, the stashes are a lot smaller. So having the drug business come outdoors in the open, where we can see what's going on, has actually made it more difficult for the police. What we are getting is a lot of small arrests that don't amount to shit.

CHARLIE: I've only had me two real jobs in my entire life. The first was mopping floors and cleaning toilets at the airport, and the second was shining shoes in the men's room at the airport. Do you know what it's like to be working in the shithouse all day, man? People in there be groanin' and fartin'. Some of 'em stink so bad you can smell it coming through the door. It's degrading, man. Degrading. After a while, I quit going to work.

Why should I be standin' in the shithouse, when I can make ten times as much on the street? Working don't make no sense, man. I ain't got no education. Never even passed the fifth grade. I can't get me no *good* job.

When I'm on the street, ain't nobody askin' how much schoolin' I got. And there ain't nobody telling me to put on clean clothes. All they doing is givin' me rock, sayin', "Sell 'em, man. Sell 'em."

SHIRLEY: I was seven months pregnant when I was arrested. The cop who arrested me kept asking, "What are you doing selling crack when you're carrying a baby? What do you think that baby is going to be like?"

I told him I didn't do no drugs. I don't smoke crack. I just sell it. Hell, I don't even smoke marijuana. Just cigarettes, that's all. But the policeman kept being mean about the baby. He kept saying, "What's that baby going to be like?" Tellin' me I wasn't cut out to be a mother.

Hell, you can't hurt a baby by *selling* drugs. The baby don't know. It ain't even been born yet.

SNAKE: When I was in the tenth grade I met some older guys who wanted me to sell pot for them at my high school. They told me I could keep twenty-five percent of everything I sold. I thought that was pretty good, so I started selling nickel bags at the bottom of this outdoor stairwell. I always had a few friends nearby, and they'd warn me if a teacher started coming down the stairs.

I never had any trouble with the authorities at school, but I did get into a couple of fistfights with guys who tried to rip me off. But it was never that big a deal. The only real trouble I had was with this black guy who came after me because I was selling pot to his little sister. He told me he didn't want his sister getting messed up with drugs. At first, I ignored him. I figured that if his sister wanted to buy some pot that was her business. Then he came after me with a gun. He put the gun to my head and threatened me.

The funny thing is, that didn't scare me that much. To tell you the truth, I thought it was exciting. It made me feel tough.

JEROME: My mother had eight kids. I'm the next to the oldest, and my father died when I was in the third grade. So it was a strain on my mother, trying to bring up eight kids. When I was fifteen, sixteen years old, I took a stand. I tried to help my mother out by buying all my own clothes and all my own food. I didn't want her to have to worry about me.

I knew all the dudes on the street selling drugs, and this one guy took me in. He wanted me to go to work for him. He gave me fifty quarters of heroin and told me to bring him back a thousand dollars. But before I tried selling it, I wanted to see how good the dope was. So I took a bag and snorted it up, and it was good. It was real good. I went out on the street and sold my fifty quarters in a couple of hours. I took the dude his thousand dollars and he gave me another fifty quarters and I went back on the street. Now at that time a quarter was selling for forty dollars. So if I sold all fifty quarters I'd pay him back his thousand dollars and keep a thousand for myself. Every day I was doing that, and I was making a lot of money.

I had a regular routine. I'd be out on the street at seven in the morning. I'd get my dope the night before and I'd be out there selling to people who had jobs. They'd get their dope on their way to work. You'd be surprised at the people who line up to get drugs—there'd be mailmen, secretaries, school kids, construction workers, truck drivers, and dudes wearing coats and ties. A lot of 'em were white people. At first, I didn't trust them. I was suspicious. I thought maybe they was policemen. They'd come up asking for dope and I'd say, "Man, I ain't selling no drugs." Then one day this black dude that I used to run with introduced me to this guy named David and this girl named Laura. They was white and they was real cool. The brother told me, "These people are alright. I know them." So I shook hands with 'em and sold 'em some dope. After that they'd come up to me every day—sometimes they'd come up to me two or three times a day. They was spending a *lot* of money. And I was knowing more and more white people, and selling to them too. After I got over my fear, white people was some of my best customers.

In this particular area where I was working, you could buy heroin, cocaine, marijuana, PCP—whatever you wanted you could buy. And you never even had to get out of your car because we'd walk right up and sell it to you. Every morning by being out there from seven until about ten I'd gross anywhere from fifteen hundred to two thousand dollars. During this time I got more and more acquainted with how to manipulate sales. How to make people buy drugs from me instead of some other dude. The most important thing was I'd always sell 'em good dope. I'd never step on my drugs. I'd always keep it pure. And I'd always be real friendly to my customers. Like they was my best friends. If I had a regular customer who was short on money, I'd break up a quarter and give him half. I'd tell him, "Go ahead and take this. It'll be enough to keep the illness off." That would keep him from getting cramps and chills and all that, and he'd see that I was a good person. So when he got some money together he'd come back to me. That's how I built my clientele up.

As time went by, my clientele got to be big. Sometimes I'd sell five hundred quarters in a single day. That meant I'd be grossing fifteen thousand or twenty thousand dollars a day, and I'd be keeping half of what I took in. After paying the dude who supplied me, the rest of the cash went straight into my pocket. I was liking that.

Now the main thing about hustling is you've got to make sure your dope is selling itself. You may think you're selling the dope, but you're not. Good dope always sells itself. So the dope you take on the street has got to be pure. Once one person shoots it or snorts it, everyone is going to know about it. It's like a chain reaction thing. Everybody that's messing with dope is going to know, "Hey, Jerome's got the good dope." The word will be spreading like wildfire. "Jerome's got the bomb." People will be telling each other, "Jerome's got the bomb." Good dope gets a lot of money coming in quick.

TUBBS: When I was dealing heroin I never worked the open-air markets, man. I wasn't standing out on no street. I wasn't fuckin' with no hand-to-hand. Mostly, I worked jazz clubs and nightclubs. I'd deal straight from a table in the club. Everybody knew who I was, and among people who was using, the word spread that I was holding.

What I'd do was go into a club, sit down at a table, and I'd have a beer on the table with me. People would come up to me one at a time, and I'd rap with them. Say, "Hey, man, what's going on?" I'd be sitting there drinking a beer and having a conversation. I'd make the sale, the person would leave, and the next dude would come sit down at my table. Everybody knew the rules: no standing in line and only one customer at a time. That way we wouldn't be drawing no attention to what was going on. If the police came in the club, everything would look cool.

All the club owners knew who I was, and what I was doing, but they didn't care. As long as I didn't make it obvious, they wasn't gonna worry. They wanted the people in the clubs to be happy, so they was always good to me.

DERRICK Money is like a drug. Once you get a little taste of it you want more. And when you start getting a whole lot of it you still want more. It's like a fever. An addiction. There ain't no such thing as enough. You look at all these guys who've been arrested on Wall Street—Ivan Boesky and Michael Milken, they've got *hundreds of millions* of dollars, but that still ain't enough. They want more. And they're willing to break the law to get it. That's because they've got the fever. The addiction.

That's the way it is for a drug dealer. They've got the same fever.

I first started selling drugs when I was thirteen. I was working for this guy that drove a flashy Corvette. He was my role model, and he got me into the business. By the time I was fifteen, I was doing ten thousand dollars' worth of business every day selling cocaine, heroin, BAM, and Dust. Out of that ten thousand my take would be twenty-five hundred. That's a lot of money for a little teenage boy to be bringing in every day.

I rented my own two-bedroom apartment that I used to deal drugs out of, and I bought a brand-new Lincoln Town Car. I put nine thousand dollars down in cash, and then paid the rest off in cash installments. I wasn't old enough to have a driver's license, so I had to have my mother cosign for the car. There I was, driving this big fancy car and buying things that my mother had never been able to buy for me.

I wasn't a drug user. I was just a dealer. Which gave me power over the users. The same faces would come to me day after day needing their drugs. The thing about people who are addicted is you can tell them to do things and they'll do them regardless of the consequences, because the only thing they're thinking about is getting their drugs. Like I had a problem with this one lady who called the police to say there was a lot of traffic in and out of my apartment. That pissed me off. She was trying to put the heat on me. I knew she had just bought a brand-new big-screen TV, so I told a dude to break into her apartment and steal it. I didn't want the TV, but I wanted her to know not to be messin' with me. And the dude did it because he wanted his drugs. He stole that woman's TV knowing that I'd give him some 'caine."

I'd prey on drug users the same way a lion preys on other animals in the jungle. I was strong and they were weak. A lot of times the drug business gets rough. There's a lot of violence on the street. But I never had to do violent things, because I could get other people to do them for me. I'd tell a drug user, "Hey, you know Billy Rae?" And he'd say, "Yeah, man, I know Billy Rae." I'd tell him, "Billy Rae has been fucking up. He's taking shorts. Why don't you go get my money for me?" And the dude would do whatever was necessary to get my money. He'd beat Billy Rae up or he'd shoot him. Whatever it took. He'd figure, "If I do this to Billy Rae, then Derrick will remember what I done for him. He'll take care of me because I went out and got his money."

It's a mind-boggling thing for a teenage kid to have that kind of power. I knew I could tell a grown adult to do something, and my orders would be obeyed. These people like Nancy Reagan, who come up with slogans like "Just say no," they don't have any insight into what's happening. To really understand what's going on, you got to live the life and play the game. You got to *feel* the power. You got to *feel* thousands of dollars of cash sitting in the palm of your hand.

The thing that makes it seem right is I'd always go home and give money to my mother. She was working, but she wasn't making a whole lot of money. She couldn't afford to buy nice things. She couldn't afford to take care of the family, and buy my brothers and sisters food and clothes. Life for her was a struggle. A lot of times you'll hear these young kids dealing drugs say, "Man, my mother needs help." And that's the truth. That's how it goes. To me, that made what I was doing acceptable. My family never had nothing, and I was taking care of them. Nobody could say that what I was doing was wrong.

DARYL: Getting a job selling drugs is just like answering an ad in the newspaper, man. All you got to do is show up and ask the dude, "Hey, man, you need any help? You want me to sell coke for you today?"

I used to do a lot of jobs cooking coke for hustlers, because a lot of them was young—seventeen, eighteen years old—and they didn't know nothing about how to cook it up. All they knew how to do was sell it and make money. They didn't know the right way to cut it, mix it, and cook it. My services was always in demand, because I had this skill. I was a cook.

There was this one guy, he wasn't but nineteen years old, and he used to come get me with nine or ten keys of coke. That amazed me, man. This dude would travel around with a quarter million dollars' worth of cocaine. He had a Porsche and two other cars. He had a gang to control his territory. Everywhere he went he had bodyguards and machine guns. That was his life-style.

He'd come get me to cook his keys. I would work from eleven o'clock at night 'til six o'clock in the morning, just cooking coke. I'd tell him, "I can't work unless I'm high." And he'd let me smoke as much as I wanted, 'cause they didn't have no one else to cook.

I might cook three or four keys in a single night, and the dude would give me three hundred dollars and an ounce of cocaine. If I took that ounce, cooked it up into crack, and tried to sell it on the street, I could've made a nice piece of money. I could've made two thousand easy, because when you cook it you stretch the coke and make a profit. But I never done that. I smoked up everything I got.

A lot of these younger dudes who's in control are not on drugs. They move keys, but they ain't smoking. That's the way you get ahead in the drug game, man. You stay clean and don't smoke up none of your money. Otherwise you just making yourself available to be used.

JEROME: The dude that took me in, he could see that I was doing real good selling on the street. I was moving lots of heroin and never coming up short. So he took me aside and he showed me how to cut up dope. Until this time I'd never seen no raw heroin. He showed me how to mix quinine and bonita in with the raw dope and how to measure it out. If you don't put no bonita in, the heroin will go bad. It won't last for more than a couple days. The bonita will preserve it so you can sell it longer, and the quinine is to give the dope its initial rush. It shoots the dope straight to the brain. This dude showed me how to mix it up, and he told me to practice while he was sitting there watching. I took the bonita and the quinine and I mixed it in real good. You don't mix it up all at once. You tap in a little bit at a time. Then he showed me how to measure it out and break it into quarters, spoons, and dippers. I did all that in front of him, and when he saw that I could do it right he started selling me raw heroin.

I wasn't buying quarters no more. I was buying ounces and mixing up my own dope. I could make it as potent as I wanted, or I could stretch it as much as I wanted. I thought to myself, "There ain't no sense in stretching this dope. I'm going to keep it potent." Because the thing about hustling is quick turnover. If the dope is hitting you can sell it, run back and get some more, and some more after that. That's how you keep the money coming in.

Out on the street, people got all kinds of names for their dope. There's dope called First Degree, there's dope called Good Time, and there's dope called MG. All kinds of names. When they're standing on the corner they'll be calling out to the customers, "I got First Degree! I got First Degree!" Or, "I got MG! I got MG!" The majority of the dope that's out there is good, but some of it is stretched more because a dude might be trying to make a higher percentage of profit. So you might buy a quarter of MG, and you'll find that all that first quarter will do is take your illness off. But a dude who's into shooting heroin isn't spending his money just to keep his illness off. He wants to get twisted. He might do a second quarter of MG and then a third quarter, and that will make him jive a little, but he still won't be high like he wants to be. Because his tolerance has built up, he'll have to do *four* quarters to get to where he's feeling really good. A person like that will go to whoever is selling the most potent dope. That's why I had a lot of people coming up to me. A dude that had been shooting dope for twenty years knew that he'd never have to buy more than two quarters from me. No matter how much tolerance they had, two quarters would always get them twisted.

I called my dope Kneeknocker. After I mixed it up I'd always make a little test before I'd put it out on the street. I'd find a person that had abscesses and tracks all over their arms and give them some, because I knew if they could get high then it'd be good for everybody. The first time I tried that, I found this dude that had been shooting dope for twenty-five years. I gave him the dope I'd mixed up. He shot it—and *boom!* When he stood up his knees knocked. I mean, he couldn't stand straight. I saw that and I said to myself, "I'm calling this dope Kneeknocker." That's because it was so potent it'd make your knees knock.

When I was out selling I'd always tell the customer, "This is good dope. Be careful with it. Don't try and do it all at once. Just put a little in. Take your time with it." That was my advice to every person I sold to, because if you're not careful with potent dope you can OD.

As time went by I graduated from selling drugs on the street to selling drugs to people who was selling on the street. I'd have my own people out there standing on the corner selling for me. That's how I was making my money. And making money was the only thing I cared about. I wasn't worried about my girlfriend, and I wasn't worried about school. I wanted money. Lots of money. And selling drugs was an easy way to make money. You know, if you work a job you might have to wait two or three weeks before you get your pay- check, but by selling drugs I'd have money coming in every day. I was at a point where I could make thirty thousand or forty thousand dollars in no time.

ISSAC: I got involved selling heroin at the age of thirteen. It was 'cause of my uncle. He was a distributor. He'd buy raw heroin and pass it around to the neighborhood sellers—you know, keep them supplied in dope. He had a big old house, and a big old car. But he was always tellin' me not to mess with drugs. He was sayin', "Drugs is a dirty game. I don't want to see you on the street. You go to school and get you an education." You know, he loved me like a son.

One day me and my cousin was out at my uncle's house, and we stole some heroin from him. He had so much of it hidden he didn't even know what little we took was missin'. At the time, I didn't know it was raw. There's a difference between scrambled, bone, and raw. Scrambled has two different cuts on it, bone has one, and raw has none. I ain't aware of the difference at that time. It was kind of funny though, because I was snorting, and I'd take a little match-head of this dope and stay high all day. Normally, it would take me three caps to last all day. I never thought about why it affected me that way, until this young lady bought some heroin from me and she OD'd. She went into a coma. She was in a coma for six, seven months, and to tell you the truth I don't know if she ever died or not. I lost track of what happened to her. But when she OD'd it scared me. I checked it out with an older guy, a guy named Larry. He was a seller. I showed him what I had, and he said, "Man, this is raw dope!" He showed me how to cut it and mix it, and from there on I wasn't turning back. I was selling. I was making money.

My uncle drove by saw me on the street one day, and I tried to run away. I didn't want him to see me out there, but he did. He didn't get mad or nothin'. He just said, "If you is gonna be in the game, you might as well work for me." After that, I was gettin' all my narcotics from him. Me, my cousin, and my uncle—we had us a little family business.

FAST FREDDIE: I was selling marijuana, Delaudin, and PCP. Then my connection got busted and was incarcerated. He needed fifteen thousand dollars to make bond. So I paid the fifteen thousand.

To pay me back he came over to my house and gave me a kilo of cocaine. He said, "This is for the fifteen thousand that I owe you."

I was more interested in cash, and I said, "What am I supposed to do with that?"

He said, "I know you can move it, man. You can move anything you put your hands on. I'm giving you a chance to double or triple your money."

At the time crack was just beginning to become popular. He took me into the kitchen and taught me how to cook up crack. The method I used was to mix water and baking soda with the cocaine. The baking soda makes it draw together and adds potency. When the mixture dries up, the cocaine is in its pure form. To cook it right, you have to have an eye for it. You have to have precise timing. I learned to cook mine quick, and I wouldn't add much water. If you put too much water in, the crack comes out soft. My crack is always hard and crisp. The other thing is I never use yeast or blowup to stretch the cocaine. I always keep it pure. I don't cheat nobody.

Anyway, this brother taught me to cook it up, and I can't even express the feeling that I got when I hit on it. It made me feel great. I knew that if it carried me like that, there were a whole lot of people who would line up to buy it. So I went into the crack business. I formed my own little organization. A friend of mine was my lieutenant, and he hired sellers to work hand-to-hand combat in the street.

I'd cook up the crack, give it to him, and he'd distribute the rocks and collect the money. Right away, I learned that when people hit on my crack they'd come back for more. I did tremendous sales and made a tremendous amount of money.

The way I operated was I'd buy the cocaine and cook up the crack myself, but none of the people that were working for me knew that I was the man. That way I could walk out on the street and watch my sellers work. I could see with my own eyes who was moving it, and who was sneaking off to hit the pipe. If my lieutenant came back and told me that somebody messed up and didn't have their money, I'd know whether or not they was one of the ones sneaking off. They'll always blame it on the stickup boys. They'll always say that they got robbed.

If anyone messed up they had to come in for a little talk. I hired another guy to take care of that. His job was to portray me. I'd give him two thousand dollars a week, and the sellers all thought that he was the man. I'd given him a weapon and he used that to make sure everybody paid their debts. He didn't listen to excuses, and he didn't let nobody mess up a second time.

MICHAEL: Cocaine is deadlier than heroin. If you do heroin and OD, there's a chance you'll survive. I seen people be gone for an hour on heroin before they come back, but death comes quick in cocaine. I seen people hit the crack pipe, fall on the ground, and die. I mean just drop dead.

Back in '88 I was moving heroin and grass, but the product wasn't as good as what I'd been getting. That put a sting in things. Not only was demand down, I had street sellers running out on me. They wanted to be where the money was hitting. My buddy, Billy, suggested that I buy some 'caine and start selling rock. I said, "Naw, man, I don't mess with that shit."

He said, "You don't have to mess with it. You just got to move it. Crack 'caine is what sells. That's where the money's at."

"No," I said. "I don't want to mess with that shit. I don't like the clientele. Pipeheads are crazy. Unpredictable."

Billy says, "Look, Chief, the money's fast. I seen people go to work all damn week, get their paycheck, and then smoke up their entire week's pay in two, three hours. They smoke it up fast. There's never enough crack 'caine."

Well, we went back and forth, and eventually Billy talked me into it. We bought some powder, this really pure cocaine, and Billy cooked it up into crack. He put a big batch of it on a plate, set it down on the table, and said, "You watch. You gonna move that shit. People go through heaven and hell for that shit sitting right there."

He cut off a small piece, smoked it, and said, "Man, this is the best I ever had!" Billy was really excited, 'cause what we had was so pure. He tried to get me to smoke some, but I don't mess with 'caine. I told him to get the pipe away from my face. He says, "I want Sleepy Jake to try this. He ain't gonna believe this shit. He's down there on the street working, and I'm gonna get him to try this."

I told him, "That's fine with me, but I don't want Jake up here in the apartment. If you want to smoke with him, go do it in the park."

Billy went downstairs and got Jake, and the two of them went over to the park. I walked down to the supermarket, and then went over to where they was standing in the park. They was standing right by a bench. As I was walking up, I seen Jake hit the pipe—then all of a sudden he started shaking. He was real weird, man. He was shaking so crazy I thought he was joking. Then he flat hit the ground.

I got over there and said, "Jake, man, don't play around like that."

Billy said, "I don't think he's playing, man."

"What do you mean he ain't playing?"

I bent over, put my hand under his nose, and didn't feel no breath. I put my hand on the side of his neck, and didn't feel no pulse.

I says to Billy, "He's dead, man. It's time to leave." You know, if the police came around I didn't want to get stuck on no murder rap.

Me and Billy got the hell out of there. We called nine one one from a pay phone and told 'em that some dude had passed out in the park; then we went back up to the apartment. All that crack was still sitting there on the kitchen table. I told Billy, "Don't smoke anymore of that 'caine, man. It's too potent. I'm gonna cut it down."

But when Billy seen what it did to Jake, he knew it was *pure*. So he kept smoking what we had. He'd been doing drugs for years, and he figured he had tolerance in his system. He said, "Don't worry 'bout me, man. I can handle it. I can handle it." And he kept on hitting the pipe.

I took that 'caine and cut it with blowup. I stretched it so it wouldn't be so potent when we sold it on the street.

FAST FREDDIE: In New York and Washington, D.C., the crack scene is very competitive. There are lots of people selling on the streets. So what I decided to do was branch out into the western states—Utah, Idaho, and Wyoming.

I have some friends out there and they said they could move it. So I got in my van and drove a kilo out to Utah. I was treating that cocaine like it was ninety-eight percent pure, even though I stepped on it. Because crack was foreign to them, I knew I could cheat 'em and make an extra ten or fifteen thousand dollars on every key they moved.

Now when you're coming into someone else's city, you're going to come in strapped. I always had my gun strapped on. Whenever I was confined in a room with the dudes who were going to move the cocaine, I wanted to get the point across that I was a dangerous black man. I'd let them know that I was strapped. The dude that told me to come on out there had been in the Job Corps with me. He was a white guy and he knew that I got kicked out of the Job Corps for trying to kill another dude—for trying to break his neck. So these white guys were all saying, "That's a dangerous black motherfucker, man. He ain't to be messed with."

They also knew that I had access to drugs. Lots of drugs. I showed them how to cook the cocaine into crack and they started moving it. They formed their own little organization using me as their supplier. By taking three or four days to drive out west I'd make thirty or thirty-five thousand dollars. That's what I was making per trip, and I didn't have to worry about all the violence associated with the cocaine trade here in New York and D.C.

HANDJOB: It ain't hard to spot police. Any educated person like me can do it. Like just a few minutes ago, I seen a guy in a black shirt coming down the street and it was obvious the guy was a police officer. He was clean and he had all those big muscles. I can't explain it exactly, but I know what happens in the street. I got the instinct I need to survive.

Wanna know how to make a bust? Okay, this is how. The police can't be sending in all these big healthy-looking guys all the time. They got to send in a guy that looks like he's addicted. You got to see it in his eyes. They got to send in a guy who looks like he wants the pipe so bad he'll get down on his knees and suck some dick to get it. Send in a little skinny guy and throw some dirt on him. Make him stink. I never seen a cop that had any stink on him. Sure, they got some clean basers out there, but they's executive basers. Every time they come in, they buy two hundred dollars' worth of rock. If you a cop and you just want to make a little ten-dollar buy, come in dirty with some stink on you. That's how to make a bust.

JOHN: I went to Mayfair Paradise Apartments looking for work. There was a big open-air market there, and I thought it would be a good place to find a job. This one guy named Sammy took me in. He was the dealer, and I worked the street as his runner.

Sammy stayed inside one of the apartments, and I'd go out on the street. I'd call out to potential customers that we had product for sale. Our product was crack cocaine. If somebody wanted to make a buy, I'd take them inside the project and tell them which door to knock on. There had been a lot of rip-offs, and Sammy always held his crack in one hand and his gun in the other.

When I was calling out to customers, I never had any drugs on me. If the jump-out boys showed up, they couldn't arrest me. If they searched me, I'd come up clean. Sammy moved around between four different apartments, so that he was never in the same location for more than an hour or two. That made it hard for the police. If an informant or an undercover cop made a buy, and the police tried to come back with a search warrant, Sammy wouldn't be there anymore. The police would waste their time searching an apartment that didn't have any drugs in it.

REX: Undercover cops are out there, and they try to make a lot of buys. So you got to be careful who you messing with. If I'm selling on the street and I don't know you, then I'm not going to serve you. First, I got to get to know you.

If some white person I've never seen before drives up and wants to buy a rock, the first thing I do is I'll hand him a little piece and tell him, "Smoke it in my face." A cop can't do that. A cop can't smoke crack. If you smoke it in my face, I'll serve you. After you do that two or three times, I'll get to know you. I won't make you smoke it in front of me no more.

THOMAS: The jump-out squad has arrested me three times for selling crack, and that's the worst feeling in the world, man. After sellin' to an undercover, the jump-out squad swarms right down on you.

They put you in handcuffs, knee you in the back, rub your nose in the dirt, and leave you lying on the ground. The neighbors all gather round and stand there looking down at you. It makes you feel real stupid. You're thinking, "Damn, how could I let this happen?"

But there's really not very much you can do to protect yourself if you're working the open-air markets. Customers are coming up to you so fast that you can't screen them. Getting busted is just part of doing business. You've got to go through the routine of being taken down to the station, getting booked, and then sitting in a holding cell for three or four hours until one of your buddies comes along to bail you out.

DOUGLAS: When I'm hustling, the last thing I worry about is the police. Every now and then the jump-out squad will make a bust, but I don't worry about them too much. I never keep enough on me for anything but a misdemeanor possession charge, and as long as you don't give 'em no guff, jump-out boys ain't gonna shoot you or beat you.

What I worry about the most is the stickup boys. They come at you with their guns drawn; if they get upset they'll shoot. A lot of 'em are junkies and crackheads and they're not thinking too clear. If they think you're hiding money from 'em, even if you're not, they'd just as soon shoot you as argue with you.

The second thing I worry about is rival drug dealers. You may be hustling for some organization thinking they're in control of the territory, only to find some other group is trying to move in. You'll be standing on the corner thinking everything is cool; then all of a sudden a van full of dudes will drive by and start shooting. I've been caught in the middle of two drive-by shootings, and all you can do is hit the pavement and say your prayers.

Then the third thing I worry about is my customers. There are a lotta people out there who have been busted, and you won't know about it. To keep from going to jail, they tell the police they'll work off their beef. Then one day a dude you been selling to for two, three years will make a buy wearing a body mike. Sometimes your best customers, your best friends, will turn you in. And they're the guys you'll sell felony weight to, because you trust them. You've sold 'em felony weight a hundred times before.

If the jump-out squad was all I had to concern myself with, then my job would be easy. I'd never get shot at. I'd never get robbed.

And I'd never get hit with anything other than a misdemeanor possession charge. All I'd need would be a little emergency bail
money—and in this business bail money ain't squat.

DARYL: The police busted me for selling rock, and they held me in
the car about three hours. They was tryin' to use me as an informant.
They was saying, "Hey motherfucker, you tell us who your man is,
and we'll let you go. What time you supposed to meet your man?
Where's he live at? What kind of car does he drive?"

Instead of taking me to the police station, they was driving me all
over, tryin' to get me to flip. I said, "Fuck this shit. I ain't talking
to you, man." They kept asking me questions, and I told 'em, "It's
time for me to take a little rest." Then I laid down on the backseat
and went to sleep. So they gave up and put me in jail.

A lotta crackheads will tell. They don't want to sit in jail, 'cause
the only thing they're thinking of is getting more 'caine. So they tell.

The worst ones is the women. These female crackheads, man,
after they flip and start working for the police, they'll have sex with
you. They'll screw you real good and be finding out information at
the same time. A lot of dudes get busted like that. They'll trust the
woman 'cause she's givin' him a piece of pussy. The dude'll think
she's alright, but she'll be looking around seeing where he's hiding
all his coke and listening to everything about how his operation runs.
Then as soon as she gets her panties back on she'll run and tell the
police.

A woman like that gets off two ways, man. She done got a good
fuck, and she don't have to do no time.

DONNELL: Most of the people that are using drugs have never been
to jail. So when they get busted, they get scared. You take a man
that has never done any time, and has a wife and kids, and you put
him in handcuffs and let him sit for a couple of hours, he's going
to talk. The police will do everything they can to scare him. They'll
total up the maximum time he might have to serve, and they'll tell
him they're going to put him away for that long. Then the DA will
come walking in the door and give him a choice. The DA will say,
"You can go to jail or you can give up your connection. Tell me
where you're getting your drugs, and then help the police set him
up, and you won't have to do any time."

People who use drugs don't want to go to jail. They don't want to pay the price. So a lot of 'em turn. They'll help the police to save their own skins.

The police have been trying to get me to turn all my life. Ever since I started going back and forth to jail, they been trying to get me to talk. But the first thing I learned when I started using drugs is that's a no-no. You just don't talk to the police. It's a matter of honor. A matter of trust. There's a code, and that code says you don't tell on nobody. If you do, there's a good chance something will happen to you. Word gets around. You might get hurt, or your son or daughter might get hurt. You might even get killed. Drug dealing is the dirtiest game ever. It's very dangerous, and it's very violent. If you create enemies you're not going to live long.

Just because you don't have to go to jail doesn't mean you can walk around feeling free. There are gonna be people out there who know what you done. You're gonna have to pay a price. You're gonna be looking over your shoulder.

FRANK [detective]: There's no doubt that the increase in drug violence has impacted on the ability of the police to cultivate informants. Five or six years ago we could arrest a guy and threaten him with a long jail sentence to extract information. But very seldom does that work today. Street sellers are much more afraid of retaliation from within their organizations than they are of the police. Jail doesn't frighten them. They know that because of crowded conditions it's unlikely that they'll have to do much time, and that a competent attorney can cop a plea. The ingrained code of the street says: "If you talk to the police, you die."

REX: A lot of hustlers is scared of white people. They's afraid white people is the police. But when I was selling PCP juice, white people coming in from the suburbs was my main customers. I wouldn't sell a bottle of water [liquid PCP] to no black man. Black people is like a time bomb. They sneaky. If you give them any, they come back around and try to be sneaky. They lie to you. They rob you.

A white person will come up, do what he's got to do, and be gone. He ain't going to play games, and he ain't going to pull a pistol on you. A white man comes in and wants a bottle of water, he'll pay you and be gone. I used to give white people my beeper number. They were my daily customers. They'd beep me and I'd meet them to serve them.

THOMAS: Back when I first started dealing we'd never even heard of the jump-out squad, and the stickup boys didn't come around. Selling drugs wasn't dangerous. You could relax and work at an easy pace.

But these days, when you go out there hustling, there are a thousand forces working against you. There's the jump-out squad, undercover police task forces, stickup boys, and all kinds of snitches who will tell on you if they get busted. Hustling isn't easy anymore. It's hard.

What I do is I try to make my money a lot more quickly. I'll go out there for two or three days, make me five thousand or six thousand dollars, and then step back off the street. I'll take me a nice little vacation, and won't expose myself to the risk of getting arrested or getting shot. I won't work again until I've run out of money. I'm not trying to get rich, or driving to be a big-time dealer. I'm just trying to support my habit and survive.

DARYL: You got crooked cops out there. I know for a fact, 'cause they've ripped me off a couple times when I was sellin' hand-to-hand. Both times it happened the same way. They drive up outta nowhere, jump out, throw me down on the ground, and handcuff me. They're calling me all kinds of dirty names, saying, "Shut the fuck up, scumbag! You ain't nothing but a stinkin' dope fiend. Shut the fuck up and get in the car!"

Then they'd drive about three blocks away, take me out, and shake me down. They keep my money, and tell me, "Get the fuck out of here! We don't want to see you out on the street again, motherfucker!" Then they drive off. They took fifteen hundred dollars off me that way.

That's the only time you don't get beat for coming up short. Everybody on the street will see the police get you. The dude you sellin' for will understand. He'll say, "Yeah, man, I know you got jumped out on. Don't worry about it, man. That's the cost of doing business."

DONNELL: In this city certain narcotics officers are assigned to certain districts. The same officers are working the same districts every day. If you're selling narcotics, you're going to rub elbows with them. You're going to know who they are, and they're going to know what you're doing.

I was working in this one section of town for about eleven years. I was selling heroin and the narcotics cops knew what I was doing. This was the part of town where all the white people would come in from the city, buy their drugs, and then go right back across the bridge into the suburbs. They didn't want to risk going into some of the tougher neighborhoods, where there was a lot of violence and rip-offs. They'd come into the neighborhood where I was working because they knew they could make a buy without getting ripped off.

The police knew what was going on, but they never could arrest me because I was careful how I operated. I never made a sale on the street. I had runners doing that for me. And I never let anybody bring a stranger to me. If one of my runners brought a stranger with him, I wouldn't let the guy in the house. I didn't want any of that going on.

There was this narcotics officer who started putting the heat on me. Even though he couldn't arrest me, he'd pull me over and search me. He was hassling me, and making it tough for me to move around. He'd say, "You want me to stop fucking with you? Then act like it, man. You got to act like it." That was his way of telling me he wanted some money.

So I gave him some money. I gave him three hundred dollars. Then he came around the next week, and the week after that. He had a regular payday. Every week I'd give him three hundred dollars. In return I got protection. I knew he wasn't going to hassle me, and I knew he wasn't going to arrest me. Given the amount of money I was making, three hundred dollars was nothing. I was happy to pay it.

CARLOS: I started by working for another dealer. I was making about twelve thousand dollars a week, but I realized I was doing all the work and he was making all the money. So I told him, "Look, I don't want to be a worker. I want to be a partner. You stay at home, let me run the business, and we'll split the money."

He took me in, and we expanded our territory. It turned into a twenty-four-hour, seven-day-a-week operation. I got beepers for all my people on the street, and I pushed them to work every hour of every day. We had all our markets covered, and were selling two, three kilos of cocaine a day. I had about fifty people working for me, and kept on expanding the business. I took over my territory completely. I called it a corporation. I was the president. I was the owner.

I was buying cocaine from the Colombians at a good price—seventeen thousand dollars a kilo. On the street it was worth thirty thousand a kilo. So if we stepped on it, we could easily make more than a hundred-percent profit. On the average, I was bringing in three hundred fifty thousand dollars a week.

The way my corporation worked was I'd give the cocaine to the dealers, and the dealer would have to give me the money when he was finished selling it. If he needs anything, I help him. I'm his superior. Whatever he does, he's got to tell me. He's got to let me know what he's doing. And I always protect him.

One of the ways I protect my dealers is I purchased some apartment buildings, and used them as a base of operation. That way I could move my people in as tenants. I'd have people that worked for me living there. I could put the cocaine in one apartment one day, and move it into some other apartment the next day. The day after that I'd have it in the basement. That's to confuse the police, so they don't know who's selling the cocaine. It's always coming out of a different apartment. Then the next week we'll move it over to some other building.

Cops were never really a problem. One time they came into my house with a search warrant. They found me with a lot of money—two hundred thousand dollars on the table, cash. I was counting it, putting it in bundles so I could change it at the bank. They walked in and asked me, "Where did you get the money?" I didn't answer. They asked me, "How would you like it if we brought the IRS in? We'll let them ask you where you got it." Again, I didn't answer. So they took the money and left. No receipt, no nothing. They just took off and left me sitting there. I was never placed under arrest.

Another time, I got pulled over by two cops. They found a lot of cash on me, but no drugs. I never have drugs on me. The cops know where the money's coming from. They know I'm a big drug dealer, but they don't have any proof. So they just take the money and let me walk. I'm happy because I can't afford to spend time in jail. I'm making too much money.

JACK BLUM [U.S. Senate investigator]: The amount of money involved in the cocaine trade tempts everyone who encounters it. The mind just cannot deal with that much money.

Down in Miami I was sitting with a smuggler in Coconut Grove.

He told me, "One night after we'd gotten several loads in we brought in all these duffel bags full of money. We started dumping them on the floor, and pretty soon the entire floor in the living room—wall to wall—was covered with money. We were standing knee-deep in twenty-dollar bills."

This was a big living room. We're talking about millions of dollars of cash lying on the floor. Most people can't even imagine what it's like to be standing knee-deep in a couple of million dollars. How many times can you expose yourself to that and not give in to temptation?

That's why there is so much corruption among law enforcement people involved in the drug war. Cops will bust a place, and one of them will find thousands of dollars stashed away in a back room. He'll grab a handful and stuff it in his pocket. He knows that what he grabs in that one handful will be more than his salary for the entire month. He also knows that nobody will be doing any counting until he turns the money in.

JOSE: Let me explain to you, there's two kinds of drug users—the bums and the good people. I never mess with the bums. I don't hustle on the corner. I have regular customers. When I go to a restaurant I have beautiful women with me, beautiful women who are working for me. I buy Dom Pérignon, and surround myself with people who have money.

I never deliver the coke, and I never collect the money. Other people do that. The guy that delivers the coke rents a limousine, and he rides around Beverly Hills, Bel Air, Santa Monica, and Malibu making deliveries from the limo. They'll pull into a driveway, and he'll take a package to the door, just like he's delivering a present. A lot of times, I send roses with the cocaine. The little packages that come with the roses will look like candy from a sweetheart.

Sometimes, at a party where I know people like to use, I'll put the coke in a bowl on the table. If somebody likes your blow, you got a new customer right there. When I go out, I got beautiful women working for me. If you go to an upscale restaurant and some guy likes the women, he'll buy some coke to keep 'em happy. He don't know they're working. He just wants a little pussy, so he buys some cocaine. He thinks he's impressing the women. She says she wants coke, he buys coke. He don't know he's being used.

When you surround yourself with beautiful women, and travel in circles where people have money, you can afford the roses. You can afford the Dom Pérignon. Every cocaine user loves his connection. Why hang out on the street corner when you can go to the top?

ADAM: I got into dealing by accident. When I first started I was just rocking along, going to work, smoking pot on a recreational basis, and occasionally dabbling in cocaine.

That was a couple years ago, and I had the same job then that I've got right now—working as an engineer for a property management company. To score my drugs I'd go into one of the black neighborhoods nearby where they've got hustlers out on the street. A lot of people who know me on a professional basis know that I use, and they do too, but they're leery of going into the black neighborhoods. I was fortunate in that I had a regular contact, a guy that I bought from on a regular basis. If I was tied up, all I had to do was make a phone call, and he'd deliver to me. Because I was such a good customer, he'd send some kid over on a bicycle.

Some of my friends were hinting around about how they wanted to score, so I started buying dope for them. I wasn't making any money at it. I was just doing it as a favor. You know, I had my contacts and knew my way around, so it was no big deal. But word gets around. Pretty soon friends of my friends were coming in asking me to score for them too. By and large, they were all people who either work in this high-rise or work nearby. All of 'em professional people—lawyers, accountants, secretaries, real estate types. You know, white people who like to use, but are afraid to trek into the ghetto.

Well, trying to keep track of all these special orders got to be a hassle, so to make things easier I started buying in weight. My office is on the ground floor of a downtown high-rise, and without even realizing I was doing it I was dealing out of my office. I had a steady stream of people coming into my office to buy dope all day long. It was strictly a coat-and-tie crowd. Which was nice. I never had to haggle with them over money, and I wasn't worried about getting busted because most all of them were business associates. If they didn't know me directly, then they'd all been referred by friends of mine.

That proved to be a very convenient arrangement for everybody. I was generating four hundred or five hundred dollars a month in extra income to help me over the hump, and they could score quality dope without ever having to leave the building.

MIKE: I've been selling drugs for almost a decade now—mostly pot and cocaine, although if somebody wants some Quaaludes or some acid I'll get it for them. I'll go out and get anything my clients want. I have a regular clientele that I service, and most of them are pretty wealthy. I never have to go out and drum up new business. I deal with the same people over and over again, so my business pretty much comes to me.

If I had a nine-to-five job, I couldn't live the way I live now. I wouldn't have my Mercedes-Benz, and I wouldn't have season tickets to see the Rams. And most of all, I wouldn't have free time to just kick back and enjoy life. Money is freedom. It gives you the freedom to do what you want to do.

I bought two clothing stores, just so I'd have a cover to keep the IRS off my back. Those two stores make money, but I feel sorry for the people working there. The starting wage is four fifty an hour. Whereas the kids I put to work on the street can make four hundred dollars in an afternoon, easy.

I've had friends ask me if I feel guilty, and the answer is no. I don't feel the least bit guilty for what I do. I'm practicing capitalism in its most pure form. The way I look at it is, people want to have fun. I sell them something that provides them with pleasure. Why should I feel guilty about that? It's as innocent as selling tickets to Disneyland.

REX: There have been many times when I've come into the house and I'd say to myself, "I'm not hustling no more. I ain't going to do it no more. You get paranoid. Sometimes I got so much money on me I get paranoid that the stickup boys is going to pull a gun on me and rob me. A dope boy can't walk down the street straight ahead. He's always looking around. He's always afraid he's going to get robbed or arrested. The stickup boys know you're a dope boy.

I always tell myself I'm going to stop. But hustling is like a drug. It's addictive. When I wasn't selling drugs, I couldn't get many girls. But when they see me start selling they know I got money, and they try and be all about me. My buddy drives a brand-new Porsche, and we go out to the go-go and sit around outside talking and laughing. We mess with the girls. Once you get in that life, with the money and the cars and the girls, ain't nobody going to want to quit. You tell yourself you're going to quit, but it's the last thing in the world you're really going to do.

JEROME: I was making thirty thousand or forty thousand dollars a month, and I was spending that much too. Spending like crazy—buying clothes and cars and going to Las Vegas. That made me feel good. For once in my life, it made me feel like I was somebody.

I flew out to Las Vegas to see the Sugar Ray Leonard–Roberto Duran fight, and I seen the Michael Spinks–Mike Tyson fight. I was out there spending money in the casinos, looking good. At those fights there was lots of movie stars there. I seen Burt Reynolds, and I seen all these other movie stars. I was right there with 'em. I looked around and said, "Man, these people ain't got to worry about the stickup boys. They ain't got to worry about getting locked up. They ain't got to go out and stab or shoot nobody if somebody messes their money up." You know, they was making their money legally. That's something I've always wanted to do. I wanted to do all the right things. I wanted to stay off the street. I didn't grow up thinking I wanted to be a drug dealer. That wasn't my goal, my dream. It's just that drugs is where the opportunity came. I never had no chance to be a movie star.

DERRICK: Man, I've had women like you wouldn't believe. Women that I could never have gotten on my own would come to me because they knew I had drugs and money. The first thing a woman that's addicted uses as a negotiating tool is her body. When I first started dealing, I'd never had a sexual relationship with a white woman. But once I was in the business I had all kinds of women, and they'd do whatever I asked them to. I had this one white woman named Gloria. She was twenty-five years old, and everything you could ever dream of in a woman. She was pretty. She was sexy. And she had beautiful blond hair. She worked as a secretary for a colonel at the Pentagon. Every morning she'd get up and go to work for him, but if she needed drugs she'd be with me. As a teenage boy, I was fascinated by that kind of sex. I was fascinated by the things she would do with her body.

Sex was definitely one of the benefits. I could get laid or get a blow job anytime I wanted it. That's because addicts are desperate. One time this dude came by with his girlfriend, and he wanted some drugs but he didn't have enough money. He was a pipehead, and he was desperate. He wanted a rock. So I told him, "Tell your woman to suck my dick." And he told her to do it. This was his girlfriend! And she sucked my dick right in front of him. He just sat there watching. All he cared about was getting his dope.

Whenever I'd go to Atlantic City, I'd take two women to bed with me. When you're living like that, you're young, you've got money, power, and women, nobody can tell you, "Man, what you're doing is wrong." Because the life is a dream come true. Here I am, a high school dropout, and I'm making more money than my mother, father, and grandfather put together. I'm thinking, "This is the way life should be. This is going to last forever, because I want it to last forever."

JEROME: When you're dealing rock you get a lot of women, man. If I'm on the street and I see a woman that I might want to be with, I find out if she likes rock. If she does, I give her a proposition. I tell her, "Hey, baby, you give me some head, and I'll give you this here rock." And they do it, man. Really beautiful women, all races, they'll give you head for a little tiny rock.

A lot of hustlers like to go to bed with crack whores. Not me. I'd never put my penis in their vagina, because I'm thinking 'bout AIDS. A woman pipehead will spread her legs for *anybody* to get cocaine. These women out here, they'll be with ten, twelve, fifteen dudes a day. They stay on the streets where hustlers sell at, and they walk up to dudes and tell 'em, "Hey, honey, I'll give you whatever you want for that twenty-dollar rock." And because they be laying down with so many men, they carry a lot of diseases in their vagina.

Fortunately, I've got a good wife at home. I know there's gonna be times when she wants to make love. That's something I gotta do, and I don't want to be bringing no diseases home to my wife. So I don't go down on no crack whores. I only let 'em give me head.

DARYL: Hustlers like to mess with trick whores. They like to take advantage of 'em. A woman who sells her body for heroin might only do one trick a day. But cocaine—those women'll trick all day long.

I've seen one girl screw ten dudes because they promised her a rock. Ten dudes, man! One right after the other. They was hustlers and they was just messin' with her.

I've seen some cases even worse than that. One of these young hustlers out there, he was sixteen years old, and this girl come up to him and say, "I'll suck your dick for a rock."

He said, "No, bitch. I don't want you to suck my dick. I know how you carry your body. You want a rock? Then suck my dog's dick!"

And she went down on his dog, man. She put that dog's dick in her mouth, and he made her suck it real hard before he give her the rock. A bunch of us was watching—it was real funny.

CHAPTER 4

COPS

Undercover cops live in a world where murder, violence, and treachery are commonplace. Their job is to penetrate that world in unobtrusive ways, because to be successful they need to belong. "Going undercover," explains one detective, "gives you an opportunity to invent another self. You hang out in bars and explore the criminal side of your soul. It gives you an excuse to buy a Harley and strap on a pistol. You can act out all sorts of underworld fantasies. Your job, your duty, is to be macho and irreverent in a society full of assholes."

This is an attitude heard in precinct houses across the nation. It is also an attitude that causes concern among those responsible for the supervision of undercover operations. "My biggest problem as the commander of the narcotics unit," says a police supervisor, "is that my undercover officers are all gung-ho. They're young, and they like making cases. They're willing to do whatever is necessary. But I need to think about their safety. I don't want any of my officers getting hurt or killed just so we can take a few more kilos off the street. I know that no matter how many kilos we seize today, and no matter how many dealers we arrest, there are another hundred thousand kilos and hundreds of dealers coming in behind them. So in fighting this drug war, I go in for small victories. I work one case at a time, taking all the precautions I possibly can to protect the safety of my men. But no matter how many precautions I take, I know that danger is inherent in narcotics work. That's why my officers love it so fucking much. They thrive on the adrenaline."

———

MIKE YEE [agent, U.S. Customs Service]: I'm a bit of an oddball. I was born in California, but my father was a Chinese immigrant. Both of my grandfathers were smugglers—one a rumrunner and the other a heroin smuggler for a Chinese mob. I graduated Phi Beta Kappa from college, went to medical school for three years, became disenchanted with medicine, and decided I wanted to be a cop. The family wanted me to see a psychiatrist. They thought I was nuts.

When I came out of training I was real gung-ho. I'd gotten my badge and my gun, and I was ready. I went out and started gathering informants, because they're the lifeblood of narcotics investigations. You can work cases without informants, but it will take you longer and your success rate will diminish.

The fun part of the job is going out and fucking with informants. When you work informants you learn that no matter who the person is, a convicted felon or an upstanding member of society, they all have something they're afraid of. Everybody has something to hide. Everybody has a weak point that you can exploit. I've done things that would be called blackmail in any other context, but when you're wearing a badge you're doing it to uphold the law. You've been granted certain powers, and you use them.

Sydney was one informant that I worked. He was a big, dumb bar bouncer who was dealing drugs. I knew he had information that could help me, but I couldn't get him to budge. He absolutely refused to cooperate. So I started going to the bar where he worked, hanging around Sydney, letting everybody see the two of us together. Everybody knew I was a cop, and the more I hung around Sydney the more it looked like he was an informant. I knew that would bring the heat down on him, and eventually it did. One day he got the crap beat out of him by a local motorcycle gang. After that, he came to me and said, "Please, I'll give you any information you want so long as you quit hanging around at the bar. Just put the word out on the street that I'm *not* informing on anybody." And Sydney was as good as his word. He helped me out.

There have been other people that I've threatened with tax audits. That always gets results. And revenge is a good motive too. I had one guy I was investigating who'd gotten caught by the local police. He'd been convicted and was on his way to prison when I went in to talk to him. He didn't waste any time with me. He said, "Hey, I've been to prison before. I'm going on a solid conviction, and I know there's nothing that you can do to help me. So don't even bother. I'm not going to rat on anybody to help you make a case."

I talked to him for a little while, and told him that during the course of my investigation I'd been doing a surveillance on his house. Then I casually asked, "Hey, who's the guy that's fucking your old lady?"

All of a sudden he turns red-hot and he says, "That motherfucker!" He starts ratting on his supplier, spewing out every detail. I didn't know if his girlfriend was messing around or not, but he had his suspicions, and when I touched a raw nerve that was all it took.

T. J. WALKER [detective]: One time I got a tip on the phone about an apartment in Liberty City, where they were selling crack. The lady that called was really upset because people had been breaking into her place and stealing things so they could buy drugs. They even stole the clothes off her wash line.

I asked her, "If we send somebody to the door, will they sell to a stranger?"

She said, "Yes, but the person will have to look like a dope user."

I sat on it a couple of days and then decided I'd try to make a buy so we could get a warrant on the place. I put on my worst clothes—a dirty old housedress and sneakers, and stuffed a bunch of things into a bag so that they looked like my last possessions on earth.

About two blocks away from this place, my partner let me out of the car, and I walked toward the address. I remember feeling anxious, but I was also very determined to get the buy. Because all I had to do was make the buy right there at the door, I wasn't wearing a wire, which meant I couldn't communicate with my backup. It was all going to be on visual. This was in one of Liberty's public housing projects, and I had to dodge all the young kids who were out on the street corners selling drugs as I walked up to this place.

I found the apartment and knocked. A black male, late twenties, opened the door. "What do you want?"

"I want a dime."

"Come in."

I went inside; he closed the door behind me and locked it. My heart started beating fast. I was locked in with no way to communicate with my backup. There were ten or twelve people inside freebasing and the air was thick. I thought, "Oh no, he's going to make me smoke the stuff here." Very casually, I was looking around the place to see if there was anyone in there that knew me from the street. That's an undercover cop's biggest fear—that you'll get burned by someone you've arrested previously.

He looks at me and says, "Who sent you here?"

"Some boy down the street."

"What boy?"

"Some boy, I don't know. Says you got the good shit."

He starts calling out to everybody in the place, "Anybody seen her before?" Nobody says anything.

His next question is "You a cop?"

That scared me. I thought maybe he knew something. I had to think fast. I got this real mean tone up, got right in his face, screaming, "What the fuck you talking about? You must be fucking crazy! You think I'm a cop? I just come in here to buy some dope!"

I was carrying on like it was a big insult, and that must've convinced him, because the next thing I know he's giving me two nickel bags. I gave him ten dollars, and he says, "Next time you come you ask for me. You come straight to me, 'cause I got the good shit."

I say, "Sure, I'll ask for you." Then he unlocks the door and I go out. As I was walking down the street I let out this huge sigh of relief. I was really tense from the thing, and I decided I would never go into a crack joint like that again without wearing a wire. If someone in the room had identified me they would have jumped me. I think that's as frightened as I've ever been as a cop. But in the end it was worth it. We got our warrant and raided the place the next day.

LUIS FERNANDEZ [detective]: I've always said there's no drug deal worth getting killed over, and there's no suspect worth dying for. You never know what's going to happen in a drug deal, and all of them are dangerous. Every single one. But as long as I have a measure of control over the situation I won't let myself get into something that I can't get out of.

Once I set up a two-kilo deal with a guy who wanted me to get in his car—which is something you never do, because that's where you lose control. Once you get in the car, the drug dealer's in control. He's at the wheel, and he decides where you're going to go. What happened in this case is I met with this guy to set up the deal. He had the coke and I was posing as a buyer who had forty-four thousand dollars in cash. After setting the terms of the deal, we agreed to meet near the Orange Bowl, where we'd make the exchange.

The guy shows up right on time driving a beautiful four-door Cadillac with dark-tinted windows. He was a rip-off artist, and he wanted to make it look like he had a lot of money. He wanted to look like a big-time drug dealer so I wouldn't be suspicious.

He pulled into the parking lot, and I walked over to his car. He wanted me to go get the money, and told me I could test the coke in the backseat of his car while he counted the money. But I wasn't about to do that. I said, "Listen, I've got the money nearby, but I've got to see the coke before I get it. I've been ripped off before, and I'm not getting in the car with you until I see the coke." So the guy shows me two kilos, but he says he won't let me test them until I get the money. I say, "Fine." And I leave like I'm going to get the money. As I'm walking away, I give the bust signal, and our backup units move in and arrest this guy.

See, as undercover detective I don't have to actually make a buy. The guy can be arrested for trafficking in cocaine as soon as I see the two kilos. So once the guy shows me the two kilos, why keep playing? The only thing I wanted to know was where the cocaine was. As soon as I get that little piece of information, I think, "Thank you very much," and let the arresting officers move in.

We took this guy back to the police station, where we interrogated him. I said, "I'm curious. What were you going to do? Why did you want me to get in the car with you?" He broke down and confessed that he was trying to do a rip. Once I was inside with the money, he was going to drive away real fast, and the guy in the backseat was going to shoot me and toss me out of the car. He thought I was just another scumbag drug dealer, and his mentality was that murder didn't matter. He was thinking, "We'll get rid of this scumbag. We'll take the money and run."

A lot of rip-off artists have that mentality. As a cop, I have to be prepared to deal with that. If you don't keep control over the way the deal goes down, there's a good chance you'll end up dead.

*   *   *

JOHN FERNANDES [agent, DEA]: I had one case that ran for more than three months. Using an informant who was an ex-doper pilot, we managed to penetrate a cocaine ring in Miami. Our main target was a guy by the name of Julio, and he ran an organization that was smuggling cocaine into the United States.

Throughout the course of those three months, the informant and I met with these guys all the time, and all of our meetings took place in places that were controlled by Julio and his people. Most of the meetings were held in an apartment they had rented for their drug smuggling operation—they'd have navigational and air charts spread out and we'd use them to discuss smuggling routes into the U.S. DEA never could get any surveillance inside that apartment. I never wore a wire into any of those closed-door meetings because it was too dangerous. If we were meeting in a restaurant or some public place, then I'd wear a wire, but not when they had total control over the premises. They never displayed a bunch of heavy weapons like you see on TV, but we always knew they had weapons there under wraps.

Anyway, it took forever to get this operation going. It seemed like everything that could go wrong in an air smuggling operation did go wrong—we had engine trouble with an airplane and we had a boat capsize. All sorts of crazy bad luck. So I had to keep working the case, and week after week I was with these guys.

What made it weird was that Julio was a very likable guy. A real gentleman every step of the way. One time when we needed to have our informant delay his smuggling run to Colombia for internal DEA reasons, we told Julio that the informant's brother had died. Julio said, "Hey, family comes first. Don't worry about that flight. You take care of your family." Julio wanted to know how he could help, and he tried to pass along some money so the informant could get home for the funeral. You know, he was real sensitive, real understanding. He wasn't going to let business intrude on this family tragedy.

On a personal level, I couldn't help but like the guy. Outside of the fact that he was trying to move six hundred fifty kilograms of poison into the United States, he was a decent guy. I had to keep reminding myself of how he was making his money. The trouble is, once you've gained someone's confidence and become his partner in crime, you end up feeling that what you're doing as an undercover agent is not right. It's like you're betraying a friendship. There's that human side of you that feels guilty. The deception really got to me in this case because of the relationship Julio and I built up over those three months, and I had to deal with those deep-down emotions. I think it's important that you really believe what you're doing is morally right. If you don't have that moral certainty to hold on to, you'll end up crossing the line. That was the only thing that got me through to the end—when we made a successful smuggling run that resulted in numerous arrests.

LUIS FERNANDEZ: Through an informant I was told that a Mariel male [a Cuban who arrived in the Mariel boat lift], who was an established Miami businessman, was holding a large amount of cocaine and four million dollars in cash at his home. The informant couldn't get inside the organization, he just knew about it. I thought it would be difficult to get a search warrant on an unsubstantiated tip, and the only way I could pursue the lead would be to ask the owner of the house for his consent to search. This guy had a big quarter-million-dollar house, and he owned a really nice video store, so in addition to smuggling drugs he had a very lucrative legitimate business going. I was also told that he had a large amount of weapons inside his house, and that he was very violent.

We've had a lot of success with consent searches, and I figured I'd give it a try with this guy. What the hell? We had nothing to lose. All that could happen is the guy could tell us to go fuck off.

Whenever I ask someone for a consent to search, there's a technique I use. You can't just walk up and say, "Hey, I want to search your house. These are your rights. Now can I search?" First off, I'm very honest with them. I knock on the door and tell them that I'm a narcotics detective doing an investigation. When they ask, "What do you want?" I say, "I would like to talk with you. Do you have a couple minutes?" I'll be very polite, and everybody, whether they're in the drug business or not, will try to give the appearance of being good decent citizens. They'll tell you, "I'll help in any way that I can." It's just human nature to behave that way. Which is exactly what I want them to do. Once they open the door, I'll ask them a couple of innocuous questions that are designed to get them to agree with me. I'll mention how serious the drug problem is, and how important it is for the police to have citizen cooperation. Yes, yes, they'll agree with all that. The drug problem is very bad, and everyone should cooperate with the police. Then I'll ask, "Do you have any guns in the house?" They'll usually answer, "Oh, no. We don't have anything like that. This is a family home." Then I'll ask, "Do you have any large sums of money in the house?" "No, no. I might have four hundred or five hundred dollars, but no more than that. Just a little spending cash." "Do you have any narcotics here?" And they'll say, "No, no. Of course not. I don't have any narcotics." My strategy is to get them to tell me that they're willing to do anything to combat crime and drugs, and that they don't have anything illegal in the house. At that point, the situation is very nonconfrontational. We're agreeing with each other. That's when I'll say, "You don't mind if I look around the house, do you?" And I'll have a consent form that I'll ask them to read and sign so that they understand their rights. That puts them back on their heels a little. They're thinking, "If I don't let him look around he's going to think that I'm hiding something." Because of the way the conversation has evolved, people will almost always say, "No, I don't mind. Go ahead, take a look around." They'll almost always sign the consent form. If they've got narcotics on the premises, chances are it will be hidden, and they'll be hoping that you won't find it. After they've signed the consent form, I'll say, "Look, I don't want to tear anything up, or break anything, so I'll just bring the dog in." The dog will sniff, and no matter how well hidden the drugs are, we'll usually find them.

That's the strategy I was going to use with this Mariel guy my informant told me about. We got backup units in position around the house, and then I walked up to the front door. As I was walking up, I could smell ether, which is used for processing cocaine. I thought to myself, "Oh boy, this is going to be interesting!"

I knocked on the door, and heard a woman's voice shout, "Who is it?"

"Police officer. I'd like to talk with you."

All of a sudden, I can hear people running and scrambling all over the house. All hell is breaking loose inside. It's a crummy feeling to be standing all alone on the front porch listening to all that commotion. I'd been warned that this was a very violent guy, and for all I knew the people inside were grabbing guns. I was thinking, "A bullet is going to come flying through the door any second now." But what can you do? I was trying to keep cool and calm. I let a minute pass, then knocked on the door again. "Hello. Police."

I hear the woman's voice again. "Yeah, can we help you?"

"Yes," I say. "I'm doing a narcotics investigation, and I'd like to speak with you."

Then I hear the owner of the house, the Mariel, he's telling his wife, "Go ahead, honey. Open the door for the officer." You know, he's trying to sound very cool, very polite. Like nothing's wrong. She says, "I can't find the key." And they scramble around for a couple more minutes, looking for the key. Meanwhile, from upstairs their son is throwing kilos out the back window into the neighbor's yard. They don't know that we've got the house surrounded, and that officers are watching the whole time.

Finally, they get the front door open, and I go through the normal routine. I get them agreeing with me. Yes, yes, drugs are a terrible thing. No, no, we don't have any narcotics in the house. "You don't mind if I look around then?" After some hemming and hawing, the main guy finally says, "No, please, take a look around." And he signs the consent.

The K-nine officer brings the dog in, the dog alerts at a chest of drawers in one of the upstairs bedrooms, and sure enough, hidden in the clothes we find forty-four kilos of cocaine, and forty thousand dollars in cash. In addition, the officers outside retrieved eighteen kilos from the neighbor's yard. So the total seizure was sixty-two kilos of coke and forty thousand dollars.

We got all of that *without a search warrant!* All I had was a tip from an informant. A lot of people have a hard time believing that I can get a consent just by knocking on the door and asking for it. They'll say, "Man, you're forging signatures." But that's not true. I don't have to forge signatures. The trick is to use human nature as an investigative tool.

In this case, the guy would've been much better off if he'd told me to go fuck myself. If they'd wanted to, they could've barricaded themselves inside the house and little by little flushed their cocaine down the toilet. It would've taken a long time to flush sixty-two keys, but they had a long time. As police officers, we had no legal authority to enter the house until we obtained the consent. Even if we'd been able to go back and get a search warrant because of the smell of ether or whatever, they still would've had plenty of time to dispose of the coke. But they panicked. As soon as they started throwing kilos out the window into the neighbor's yard, we had them nailed.

When we went to court we seized all of that guy's assets, including his house, his business, and his car. He's in prison now, and that's where he's going to stay for the next twelve years or so.

*   *   *

JOYCE BALDASSARI [detective]: I'm from the Bronx. I grew up in
a pretty tough neighborhood, and was a streetwise kid. I thought I'd
already seen everything by the time I became a cop, but I was very,
very wrong. The violence, the dead bodies, the abused children—
those things are very shocking to the senses. It's not at all like what
you see on TV. It's a full sensory experience. You walk into an apartment where a body has been rotting for two weeks, and you see that
it's decomposed and all covered with maggots. It's awful. Worse than
anything you'll ever see in a horror movie.

I started to do undercover work in 1981. I was working with a
street crime unit in an area where gold chains were being snatched
off of people's necks. I was put out as a decoy. I had a big gold chain
around my neck, and acted like I'd passed out on Eighth Avenue—just laid out in a doorway with a bottle of booze. I ended up
getting molested rather than mugged. All the other cops were really
amused by that.

The majority of my work has been street-level work, just buying
all kinds of drugs—marijuana to heroin—all over the city. They say
you have to be a little bit crazy to do undercover work. It's true.
Undercover cops *are* a little crazy. You're out there all by yourself.
It's dangerous, and you're constantly being harassed and pushed
around by the dealers because they treat junkies and buyers like dirt.

There were a lot of heroin addicts in the neighborhood where I
grew up, and a lot of the kids I went to high school with did heroin,
but never openly. They always tried to hide it. It's not that way anymore, though. When I went to work on the Lower East Side, there
was nothing but junkies and dealers working these huge open-air
markets. People would actually line up to buy their drugs. You'd see
twenty or thirty people lined up waiting to get inside a building, and
enforcers who worked for the dealers would maintain order with guns
and baseball bats. They'd let five or six people into the building at a
time. I'd never seen anything like it. Completely blatant. The dealers
owned the streets.

Every operation I've ever worked, I've felt fear. I can't think of any
deal where I can honestly say I felt one hundred percent comfortable.
I had to look comfortable, but underneath the anxiety was always
coursing through my veins. I knew the rap, and there were times
when I'd mess my nose up and make my eyes all watery before trying
to make a buy. The dealer would look at me and say, "Oh, baby,
you're really hurtin'! You *need* some stuff!"

There were a lot of rough times, but the deal that caused me the most stress wasn't street-level. It was an investigation that we were doing uptown a block from Lincoln Center—very posh neighborhood, very posh building. We got a letter from a group living in a co-op saying that one of the tenants—a violinist for the Metropolitan Opera—was selling drugs and catering to prostitutes. So we decided to check it out. My job was to go up to the apartment, knock on the door, and try to make a buy.

I couldn't go up there looking like a street person, so I changed from my normal undercover appearance, and put on some nice clothes. The violinist answered the door. He was a short little guy, about five-four, and almost sixty years old. He invited me inside, where a lot of people were hanging out, drinking, getting high. He walked into a back room, and I followed him. When we got inside he locked the door with a dead bolt. This guy wasn't just into selling drugs, he was psycho. He had guns and knives mounted all over the walls, and he picked up this huge wrench and started to threaten me.

I told him that a friend had told me this was the place to come for a good time. He said: "No! No one ever comes to my place without calling first. Everyone knows the policy! You must be a cop!" He's waving this wrench around and getting very crazy. From the things I've seen out on the street, I know murders do happen. They happen every day. I'm thinking to myself, "I'm not going to let this crazy fool kill me. If I have to shoot him to get out of here alive, then I'm going to shoot him." I could all but see the headlines: PO-LICEWOMAN SHOOTS METROPOLITIAN OPERA VIOLINIST!

I was terrified, but I was also talking hard and fast. Telling him that I wasn't a cop, but that his friends were my friends, and they'd sent me over here. All I wanted was to buy some drugs. I managed to calm him down, and talked him into selling me some drugs. I felt a great relief getting out of there, but it wasn't over yet.

To firm up our case, we made a few more buys and then got a search warrant on the apartment. I went inside and made a buy to make sure there were drugs on the premises while the entry team waited outside in the stairwell. I came back out and told them, "Yeah, he's got drugs. Let's do it." The plan was to have me go back to the door, knock, and say that I forgot something. That would get the door open, then the entry team would come charging in from the stairwell.

I knocked, he let me in, and I took my gun out and told everybody to freeze. He grabbed for my gun, and we got into a wrestling match. Then the team came charging in. When he grabbed for my gun like that, we were lucky nobody was killed. Another officer grabbed him by the hair and lifted him off his feet.

We seized a few ounces of cocaine from his apartment and took all of his guns out. We had a solid case against him, but he never did any time for the conviction. He had tremendous social connections, and had all these people testify for him, saying that he was a musical genius. His attorney argued for a drug therapy program instead of prison, and that's what the judge gave him. That infuriated me. The guy was dangerous. I could've been killed when he resisted and grabbed my gun. He was a drug dealer and he should have been taken off the street and sent to prison. But because of his social connections he walked. He never spent a day in jail.

In the office, we always hang photos of seized material, and it's usually fun to look at. From this case, we had photos of all the guns he had in his apartment, and I couldn't look at those photos without getting depressed. It's really demoralizing to risk your life building a perfect case, and then watch the guy walk.

DARLA HUFFMAN [detective]: I started in narcotics and went to work undercover for the state narcotics bureau in Oklahoma because they needed a woman, and I was the only one trained for the work. One thing about the drug business is you have to be half-assed mean. But that's part of the allure. A lot of guys are narcs because they like to wear the badge and the gun. They like to kick ass.

In dope cases you've got to do whatever's necessary to make the case, and that usually means using an informant. Oklahoma has a lot of lakes, resort-type areas, that are well known for gambling and drug activity. I got a girl out of the Alabama penitentiary to be my snitch because I needed someone who wouldn't be known in these areas. I brought her in, got her a false driver's license, and sent her up there. She learned that one of the mayors in one of these small resort towns was into buying and distributing dope. She and I sat down and worked out a plan to try and make a case on him.

She was a cute thing, and she bleached her pubic hair blond and shaved it all into a nice heart shape. On Monday morning the mayor was in a meeting, so I put her in his office. When he came back, she was there waiting for him. She had on a short skirt, no underpants. He was a middle-aged man, and when she opened her legs there wasn't a thing he could do. For Chrissakes, he'd been waiting for something like this to walk up to him for forty-five years. She took him right there in the office.

After he got what he wanted, she told him she wanted some dope, which he was more than happy to supply. She was wired, and I was sitting in my car listening to every word. She made the buy from him, and that's how we got him. He took one look at that heart and couldn't say no.

That was a good case, and I didn't feel bad about using that girl that way. If we hadn't sent her in there, that guy would be still be mayor and he'd still be distributing dope.

LIEUTENANT JIMMY WHITE [detective]: Narcotics has always been a competitive position within the police department. What got me interested in it was my experience as a cadet—where they give you all the shit jobs in the world. The whole time I was working uniform, I knew I wanted a specialty job. Most cops want to work narcotics because it has the allure of glamour, intrigue, and fun. That's what draws you in.

Now that I'm in narcotics, I can say that it really *is* fun. You can be very creative—much more than in other types of police work.

There's a project area we work where a lot of dope dealing is going on—where people out on the street are selling crack cocaine. It's been a real tough area for us to work because of the way it's laid out. The layout makes it difficult for a bust team to do any surveillance without getting burned, and there are lots of escape routes and lots of places for the dealers to hide. Even if we make an undercover buy, it's tough to get the bust team in to make the arrest before the dealer disappears.

To work the area we had to come up with a good plan—something creative. We sent in a couple of undercover officers to make buys so that we knew exactly who we were going to arrest. But instead of sending a bust team racing in after them, we decided to rely on morbid curiosity. We got a hearse and dressed one of our officers up in a black suit, and we rented two Jeep Cherokees with the darkened windows—the kind the drug dealers drive. We put a couple of our big beefy guys in the Cherokees, and we formed a little funeral procession. Then we brought the funeral procession in, and drove up nice and slow. No excitement. No guns drawn. We backed the

hearse right up to where all the sellers were standing. It was beautiful. Nobody ran, and nobody threw down any drugs. They were all
standing there watching with their mouths open. The officer in the
black suit parked the hearse, got out, and walked around back to
open the door. The dealers are crowding around, just *dying* to see
who's dead. The officer opens the door, and two K-nine dogs come
flying out. The guys we'd targeted for arrest are standing right there,
and we took 'em all down. Easy as pie.

LUIS FERNANDEZ: I've been shot at a number of times. I've been
the target of sniper fire while doing undercover surveillances. I'll be
out watching a house and all of a sudden someone will pop a few
rounds at me from God knows where. That's because when we're
working undercover the drug dealers don't know we're cops. By looking at me, you'd think that I look more like a drug dealer than a
cop. What's worse is I look like the most dangerous kind of drug
dealer—the kind that does rip-offs. Most of the rippers are young and
muscle-bound. The drug dealers fear them a lot more than they fear
cops, because the rippers can be very violent. Every now and then,
we'll be doing a surveillance, and a drug dealer will realize his house
is being watched, but he won't think, "Oh no, cops!" Instead, he'll
think the house is being cased for a rip. So he'll have someone come
out and take a shot at us to try and scare us off. That happens to
narcotics detectives all the time. We have a sergeant who had the
rear window of his car blown out not too long ago.

RANDALL [detective]: As a cop, you hear about rip-offs all the time.
And it's not just stickup boys knocking off street sellers. There are
big-money rip-offs too. A rip-off artist will set up a deal saying he's
got ten kilos to sell, and the buyer will show up with three hundred
fifty thousand dollars in cash stuffed into a gym bag. The ripper will
show up, but he won't have any cocaine. Instead, he'll have ten or
twelve dudes jump out of the woodwork with automatic weapons and
machine guns. They'll pick up the gym bag and split. Or maybe a
dealer will show up with ten kilos, and it will be the buyer who has
the machine guns.

   My favorite rip-off took place about a year ago. Through an informant we learned that a transaction was going to take place at a motel,
and we had the room wired. On the day of the transaction a SWAT
team was ready to storm the motel.

When you've got an operation like this set up, you never know if it's really going to take place. A lot of informants aren't reliable. They'll feed you all kinds of bullshit, and you'll end up spending six hours staking out an empty hole. But on this particular day the relevant parties showed up right on time. The only thing was, the seller didn't bring any cocaine—he just brought guns because he was planning on ripping off the buyer. But the buyer didn't bring any money because he was going to rip off the seller.

I was at the command post listening on the wire laughing my ass off. All I could hear was these two dudes standing in the motel room shouting at each other, "You lying motherfucker!"

BARRY ANFANG [detective]: There are lots of abandoned buildings in New York. Frequently what happens is the drug dealers come in, take over a few apartments, and force the good people out. The good people get robbed and threatened. It isn't safe for them to walk in the front door, so they move. After a while even the landlord stops collecting rent. He leaves a situation like that alone. The place becomes a crack house or a shooting gallery, and it's these buildings where we do most of our work.

The dealers know sooner or later we'll be coming after them, so they set booby traps for us. They'll kick big holes in the upper floors and cover them with linoleum so that we fall through. They'll weaken the stairs so they collapse when we're about halfway up, and they'll drive a nail in the banister right where you're most likely to grab when you fall.

Recently, the dealers have started using pit bulls for protection. They use them not only against the police, but also to protect themselves from other dealers who are trying to rip them off. What they'll do is remove the dogs' vocal chords, and train them to go for the groin. You'll go into one of these dark buildings where you can't see a thing, and three or four dogs will come at you. They can't growl, so there's no warning. They just come leaping at your groin.

I used to be an animal lover, but not anymore. I shoot those dogs without hesitation. This year alone, we've shot hundreds of dogs.

LUIS FERNANDEZ: I've had to fire my weapon on numerous occasions. Mostly at attack dogs. The most gruesome case happened on my last day working SWAT. We were executing a normal narcotics warrant. I was part of the entry team. We had some trouble getting the door down, and were making a huge amount of noise banging on the damn thing. Whoever was inside obviously knew we were trying to get in. To keep them from setting up an ambush I went to a side window and tried to break it to create a diversion. I had a two-twenty-three-caliber machine gun, and was bashing the window with the butt of the gun, but the window wouldn't break. So I used my fist. I put my hand through the window, and as I withdrew it I could feel heat up my hand and arm from blood. I sliced the hell out of myself on a piece of jagged glass.

Right then, the entry team took the door down. Inside, we confronted two Latino male subjects, and we put them down in the hall. I wasn't working with my normal partner because he'd been shot in the eyes a couple days before, and another guy was assigned to me by the name of Doug. He was laying these subjects out, when I could see a door open at the end of the hall, and out comes a German shepherd attack dog. Doug was in front of me, and the dog was charging right at him. I was yelling, "Doug, look out! Dog! Dog coming! Look out!" He was messing with these subjects, so I swung the machine gun up, and with blood dripping all over the place from my hand and arm, I shot the dog three times. We were so close together that Doug could feel the muzzle flashes when I opened fire.

Outside, the supervisor heard gunfire, and didn't know what was going on. He thought we'd confronted fire. He saw me bleeding and figured that I'd been shot. He orders, "Back out! Back out!" I said, "No, no. I'm okay." I was the only Spanish-speaking officer in the house, and because the subjects were Spanish-speaking, he let me continue my search.

I got to the door at the end of the hall, and some guy was lying against it. I could feel his weight against the door. I pushed my way inside, and found the guy who'd released the dog lying in a pool of blood. One of my bullets had passed through the dog, and hit this guy in the center of the heart. He was a Santoria saint [religious group that believes in voodoo] who was heavily involved in drug dealing, and he was dressed entirely in white. It was a real mess. He was bleeding profusely because he'd been shot in the heart, and he was slumped over on the floor—already dead. He'd died instantly, so there was nothing I could do for him.

After it was all over, I had to go through an inquest. The judge listened to the testimony and ruled that I had committed an "excusable homicide." After that I went back to work, and didn't think too much about it. When you're young you don't feel a lot of fear. Even though you're involved in an occupation that is dangerous and violent, you don't think about potential consequences.

RANDALL: A lot of buyers driving in from the suburbs don't have any common sense. They come into these ghetto neighborhoods where white folks and money are scarce, but they don't even think about that. They just want to get high, and they think everything is cool.

They'll drive in wearing expensive clothes and jewelry, flashing wallets fat with money and credit cards. Now, imagine you're a street seller: Some guy comes up wanting to buy crack, and you see he's wearing a four-thousand-dollar Cartier watch. You'll say to yourself, "To hell with making three or four dollars selling this rock. I'm going to get that watch."

We had one incident where a seventeen-year-old girl was gang-raped after she bought her dope. We found her staggering out of an alley at about ten o'clock on a Friday night. Her dress was torn and bloody, and her underwear was gone. She was bleeding from the nose and the side of her mouth, and her eye was swollen shut. We tried to get her to talk to us, but she wouldn't do it. We kept on asking her questions, and she kept pleading with us to let her go. Over and over again she said, "My parents will kill me if they find out I'm in this part of town. My parents will kill me."

Most of the crimes committed against buyers tend to happen in areas where the dealers haven't established authority—neighborhoods where no one dealer or drug gang has consolidated control. In those operations that are tightly controlled, the honchos don't allow the local thugs to go robbing and violating their customers. It's bad for business. They want their customers to keep coming back. If some guy tries to get cute and starts ripping off customers, then the dealer at the top will use that guy to set an example. He'll send a couple of henchmen out to pump a few bullets into him.

As soon as that happens, the word hits the street: "No more rip-offs!"

SONIA CRESPO [detective]: Whenever I'm working the hooker detail, there are always guys that drive up and want to trade cocaine for sex. They say, "Hey, I don't have any money but I'll give you a rock."

The other day this guy came driving up in a Mercedes. He was a pretty good-looking guy—the kind of guy you'd think could go just about anywhere and pick up somebody decent. But here he was trying to pick up a hooker on Biscayne Boulevard. He knows all the girls are addicts, and he's trying to pay with crack. The girls on the boulevard jump for a little piece of rock. A five-dollar rock is worth more than a twenty-dollar bill.

I try to talk to some of the girls working the street, especially the pretty ones who are only sixteen or seventeen years old. After I arrest them, I'll say, "Don't you know how bad this is? Hooking is going to get you AIDS." That's because they give themselves to anybody in a crack house for a rock. A lot of the men they're having sex with are intravenous drug users that have contracted AIDS from using dirty needles. The girls will say, "Yeah, yeah. I know it's dangerous. I'm going to stop hooking." Then I'll go out the next day and see them back on the street.

Not too long ago I stopped a girl who's been working the boulevard for a couple of years. She was looking real bad. I said, "What's the matter with you? Are you sick?"

She said, "Yeah, I got pneumonia."

I said, "Pneumonia? Are you kidding?" One look and I knew she had AIDS.

LIEUTENANT JIMMY WHITE: There was a girl who'd been doing a lot of heroin, and she started prostituting to pay for her drugs. She had a baby, but it had been taken away from her. After arresting her, I got to know her a little, and every time I'd see her on the street all she'd talk about was getting her baby back. But her addiction was always screwing things up.

One morning we raided her apartment because she was storing dope for dealers. We had a warrant and searched her place, but we couldn't find anything. Still, I knew the dope was there. I kept asking her where it was, telling her I knew it was there, and that we weren't going to leave until we found it—even if it meant tearing the whole apartment apart. Finally, she told us where it was, and that was the only reason we found it. She'd taken her baby's little bronzed booties and stuffed all these bundles of heroin into the booties. There was something about pulling all that heroin out of those booties that made me sad. I was asking myself, "Is nothing sacred?"

T. J. WALKER: One night I got called to a domestic. Two sisters were living in a project where just about every third apartment was selling crack. They were having a mean, vicious argument. The woman that called the police was trying to kick her sister out, saying that her sister was a crack addict. That she had AIDS and wouldn't go to the hospital.

I looked around the apartment, and it was horrible. Piles of clothes thrown everywhere. A bare mattress on the floor that was the only bed, and at least one hundred empty little plastic bags—crack bags—scattered all over the floor. It was obvious to me that both of these women were hitting the pipe night and day.

Here in the middle of this are these two little children. They're skinny from malnutrition, and they have difficulty understanding what you say to them because they've never been to school. The little boy was walking around with nothing on but filthy Pampers—no shoes, no shirt. There's broken glass all over the apartment, and this kid is walking around with bare feet.

That gets you. These kids don't have a choice. They're the real victims. I see this kind of thing all the time, and I can't believe my eyes. I feel bad, but there's nothing I can do. Sure, it hurts to see people strung out like these two sisters who were fighting with each other. And it hurts to see people who have OD'd. But seeing a baby being brought up by a mother addicted to crack is a lot more painful. That's a sight that will tear your heart out. But as a police officer, there's very little I can do about it.

LIEUTENANT JIMMY WHITE: Working undercover, I had to go into a PCP house. I went in just to check things out, see if there was anybody in there who was either smoking or moving large quantities of PCP. When I got inside, there were a lot of people passing around joints of marijuana that had been dipped in PCP. They were white middle-class folk, and they thought it was a big laugh to inhale a big hit, then blow the smoke into the face of this little six-year-old boy who was there with his mother. They were shotgunning him to give him a contact high, and they thought it was the funniest thing.

I wanted to kill them, but I kept my focus on the job, kept thinking about making a case and locking people up. I put my energy there, rather than letting something like that get to me. I distinctly remember thinking, "This is terrible, and I'd love to kick your ass, but I've got a case to build."

TIM WELLS [investigative journalist]: The first time I walked into a shooting gallery, I couldn't believe my eyes. The gallery was located on the ground floor of a four-story apartment project in a notorious drug area. The entire project was filthy—bare concrete floors, with broken glass and needles lying in the halls and stairwells. I'm talking about grinding, urban poverty of a sort I didn't know existed in the United States until I saw it with my own eyes. It was like the sort of photo you see from some third world slum, where all these hungry children are staring at the camera with vacant eyes.

In the living room of this gallery, three junkies are sitting on a beat-up old sofa, and it's obvious they've just finished shooting up. Their eyes were wide and glassy, and they're nodding on from the high—you know, junkie heaven. I'm standing there trying to talk to one of them, when this three-year-old little boy runs up from behind me and starts pulling on my hip pockets.

I turn around to see what he wants, and he says, "Don't touch the needles! Don't touch the needles!" Then he points to all the discarded needles lying on the floor.

That damn near broke my heart. Instead of learning his ABCs, the first thing this kid's mother taught him was not to play with the needles because they'd give him AIDS.

I think it's difficult for most of us to imagine what we'd be like if we were brought up in that kind of an environment. It just boggles the mind. But one thing's for sure, that kid doesn't stand a prayer. And I'm ashamed to say, the thing I remember most vividly is the way I recoiled from that little boy. Normally, when you see a child in distress your instinct is to reach down and comfort him. But this little boy was so filthy I didn't want to touch him, and I didn't want him touching me. He had open sores on his chest, mossy teeth, and horrible, horrible BO. He'd probably never taken a bath in his life.

A cop saw me with the kid, and when we got back to the car the first thing he did was give me a Handi Wipe so I could clean myself off.

RANDALL: I have a partner who's still relatively new on the job. We work a beat that's a heavy drug section of the city. We get complaints all the time about crack joints, and when we go into these places it's not uncommon to find one or two grimy, starving babies that have been abandoned or swapped for drugs. We always take the baby to the nearest emergency room, and my partner carries the kid. He's a big, strapping guy—a weightlifter and a karate expert—and he looks mean as hell when you cross him. But every time we take a kid in, he's gets this mournful, wounded look on his face when he hands the baby over at the hospital.

SONIA CRESPO: I knew there was a drug problem in Miami, but I never knew how bad it was until I became a police officer. On my first day out, I saw seven- and eight-year-old kids out on the street selling drugs. I couldn't believe it. You hear that kind of stuff on the news, but it's a totally different thing when you actually encounter it face-to-face. Kids selling drugs, kids hooking.

Not too long ago I went into a crack house, and there was a nine-year-old boy in there holding on to a Coke can that had been used as a base pipe. That really got to me. You know that kid doesn't have a prayer. When I first came onto the force, I'd go home and fall into these really big depressions. My boyfriend was working street narcotics, and I could see it affected him too. He was going out to bars drinking every night. I'm talking seven, eight, nine drinks at a time. Some cops can cut themselves off from the tragedy they see day after day after day. They're totally cold. Immune. Those are the ones that last. Others can't do that. The problems get to them. They can't say to themselves, "I'm just going to do my job and not worry about the kids doing dope and the mothers selling their bodies." They can't cut themselves off from all of the tragedy they encounter. They start drinking and smoking three packs of cigarettes a day and inhaling coffee. They end up having a heart attack at the age of thirty-five.

Now that I've been on the force for a while, I'm learning how to control my emotions. I'm learning how to protect myself. I don't get depressed like I used to. When I come home I relax every chance I get, and I don't think about what I've seen during the day. I have a nice dinner, and think about other things.

T. J. WALKER: I've been a police officer for nine years, and I was married to a police officer—a black man who'd been brought up on the streets. He was using drugs, and I never knew it for a long, long time. Things seemed fine until one day he stopped giving me money to pay the bills. Then his car got repossessed, and he started disappearing for two or three days at a time. When he came home he'd always give me some lousy excuse, like he fell asleep somewhere.

That's when I started to suspect drugs. I was pretty naive, and I didn't know what signs to look for. I confronted him about it, and he denied ever using drugs. He said that I was crazy. We had some really bad fights, and he kept on denying it and denying it. Finally, I told him I wanted a divorce. He got really upset and said that he didn't want that. Please, not that.

I went out with a girlfriend that night, and he came after me. I was on the dance floor, and he walked up and started beating me. He was punching me, and slugged me in the jaw. I was thinking, "I'm a police officer. I handle these types of calls all the time. This can't be happening to me." My gun was in my purse, so I raced over to the table to get it. He had his gun too. I said, "Fine. What do you want to do? Shoot each other? You go ahead and shoot first." I was so humiliated at that point that I wouldn't have cared if he *had* shot me.

He finally left, and I went ahead with my plans for a divorce. We had a child to think about, and I didn't want our child to grow up in a house where the father was strung out on drugs. So we separated.

Eventually, he was fired from the police force and I didn't hear from him for a couple years. Then one day I was working an operation where we were targeting buyers. We had an undercover cop out on the street posing as a seller, and he'd radio us the description of each vehicle that came driving up to make a buy.

I responded to one of these calls, and we pulled a car over that had just made a buy. As I was getting out of my car, I realized, "Oh my God, that's my ex-husband!" He looked at me and said, "What's going on? Why are you stopping me?"

I said, "Don't even talk to me!" I couldn't believe that this was happening. Here I was, arresting my ex-husband. Some other officers arrived on the scene, and they all knew him because he was an ex-cop, and I could see that they had mixed emotions too. They were having as hard a time handling it as I was. I stood there and watched as he put his hands against the hood of his car and spread his legs to be searched.

That was the absolute worst experience of my life. When I hear people tell me that they have a son or a sister on drugs, I feel for them. I know what it's like. I know what hell it is for the family.

JOYCE BALDASSARI: One time I had a terrible experience with another undercover officer. Everyone thought he had a drinking problem, but it was worse than that.

I was working a street-level operation with him where we were busting dealers. To bolster our cases in court we needed to have at least two separate undercover cops purchase drugs from the same dealer before we arrested him. The guy I was working with went out with a hundred dollars to buy ten-dollar decks of heroin. Usually with a hundred dollars you can negotiate with a dealer and get him to throw in another deck or two to increase the quantity of the sale. Anyway, this guy went out and pretty soon radioed me, giving me the description of a person he'd bought from. The sergeant then told me to go find that person and make our second buy. Meanwhile, the other undercover cop was supposed to "ghost" me, which meant he'd follow me from a safe distance just to make sure there are no problems.

Instead, this guy raced up to the area ahead of me. I saw him standing on a corner talking to a group of people, including the dealer we had targeted. Suddenly all but a few of them take off in different directions. I'm still approaching, and I can see all of their eyes are on me. Obviously, something has gone seriously wrong. What had happened was the cop I was working with had given me up to the dealer for a free deck that he was going to keep for himself. He didn't have a drinking problem—he was a heroin addict.

The primary target walked right past me when I tried to make a buy from him. I had a hard time believing that another police officer—an *undercover* officer!—had given up his partner like that. I knew what he'd done, but I didn't have absolute proof. I met him back at the car and we exchanged words. I demanded to know what the hell had happened. He made a bunch of excuses, saying that they'd known for a long time that I was undercover. I told him he was full of shit, but he kept denying that he'd done anything wrong. Without any solid proof, there wasn't much I could do.

The only way the police department was finally able to nail this guy was because he played softball on a DEA team in a recreational league. They were playing up on Governor's Island one day, and he left his gym bag on the playing field after the game. Park security came by, picked up the bag, and found his credentials, his gun, and some heroin inside. They turned it over to Internal Affairs, and that was the beginning of the end for that guy. But he'd been out there working undercover for a long, long time.

JUDD [detective]: If a street dealer runs when we try to arrest him, I chase the guy down in my car, not on foot. I want the protection of the car so I don't have to worry about being shot. If need be I'll run the son of a bitch down.

Working buy-busts in Liberty City one time, our undercover buyer gave the signal that a buy had been made, and we moved in. I was getting out of my car to help with the arrest when the guy ran. I jumped back in the car and started chasing this kid down the street. Other backup cars were coming up the street. The kid turned around and started running back in my direction. He was on the sidewalk, so I pulled onto the sidewalk and drove right at him. The kid jumped back into the street, right into the flow of traffic, and a passing car hit him—and hit him hard. The kid went spinning cartwheels flying through the air. He hit the ground and was dead still. I remember thinking, "There's no way he survived." Then all of a sudden the kid shoots straight up and is running again. He ran for about ten seconds, then collapsed in a heap because he'd broken just about every bone in his body. I'm sure it was a burst of pure adrenaline that had picked him back up. We called an ambulance, and they scooped the guy up and took him to the hospital. I was amazed that the guy was still alive.

CHARLES BROWN [agent, U.S. Border Patrol]: I'm scared every time I hit a house. Anybody that says they're not scared when they kick in a door is a liar. The adrenaline goes up, the heart's pounding. A couple of times I've been ready to drop the hammer on anything that moves. You never know what's going to happen on a raid.

One time we had a task force working with DEA, and they were going to do a buy-bust for two hundred pounds of weed. That's the kind of minor deal that normally goes down real easy. And that's the way this one started. The buy team goes in and makes the deal, and the bandit is sitting in a chair. The bust signal is given, and everybody goes charging in—screaming, yelling, "DEA! Police!" We're all wearing body armor—raid shirts, raid vests—and the guy's just sitting there. Then he reaches down and pulls a nine-millimeter out from under his seat and—wham!—pops off a round. The bullet goes flying over our heads.

Right then, all hell broke loose. That guy was shot about seventeen times.

RANDALL: Four years ago I had to shoot someone. I was working street narcotics when we got a call over the radio. A juvenile had shot some other kid in a dispute over drugs.

My partner and I were working nearby, and we arrived on the scene almost immediately. When I jumped out of the car, I spotted the assailant and shouted, "Police! Drop your gun!" He turned on me with the apparent intent to open fire. I shot first. I unloaded three consecutive rounds, and struck him in the head and chest. After he went down, we secured the crime scene and called in emergency medical, but there wasn't much they could do.

It doesn't bother me that I had to shoot him. When I became a police officer, I knew that I'd be involved in situations where I might have to kill someone. It's not something I'm ashamed of, and it's not something I brag about. I consider it a normal police function.

After going through a situation where you have to blow someone away, my major concern was not my conscience but whether the department would justify the shooting. Every time a police weapon is discharged, we have an internal investigation and the officer involved is required to appear before a review board. That was my biggest concern.

RICHARD [detective]: I've had two partners get shot. One was shot in the head and killed. The other was shot in the chest three times. He was lucky, he lived, and we nailed the guy that shot him.

Five years ago you didn't see the kind of gang violence that you see today. Crack has revolutionized drug markets and drug-related violence. A heroin dealer would never shoot a cop. Even though what they were doing was pretty hard-core, they were basically nonviolent people. But drug gangs dealing in crack carry automatic weapons, and they use them.

What's frightening is you never know when the violence is going to erupt. The guy that shot my partner in the chest was just some guy we were trying to pull over for a traffic violation. As my partner pulled our car up behind him, this guy opened fire, blew out our windshield, and tried to get away. My partner took three slugs in the chest. Fortunately, the guy that shot him turned down a dead-end street, and we had two other cars in the area. He was surrounded right away, and he opened fire on a squad car. One of our officers returned fire, and got him right in the forehead. He was killed instantly.

I'll tell you, being on the receiving end of that kind of violence works on your head. You know the people who are getting shot, and that makes it too real. There isn't any romance in being an under-cover cop—even when you get the bad guy. It's too ugly to feel any joy or satisfaction.

EMMET [detective]: On the day that he becomes a policeman, every cop thinks he's going to change the world. He's going to be the cop that puts all the bad guys in jail and makes the streets safe. He's thinking the world is going to be a better place because he's got a badge and a gun.

But pretty soon you find out that's not the case. You learn that the system isn't set up to keep people in jail. A lot of the bad guys you arrest, who really do belong in prison, end up copping pleas and don't do any serious time. No matter how many arrests you make, there are still thousands of dealers standing on street corners selling drugs. The murders and robberies and ODs keep on coming. The city is like a giant cesspool, and no matter how hard you work you can't clean it up. The judicial system stinks, and that hardens your attitude. Makes you a little cynical.

Pretty soon, you slow down. You don't try as hard. After you've been shot at once or twice, you shy away from potentially dangerous situations. Instead of telling yourself, "I'm the cop who's going to make the world a better place," you're asking yourself, "What the fuck am I risking my life for?"

CHAPTER 5

ADDICTION

"We who do not use drugs cannot understand why people can't just stop," says a doctor who treats recovering addicts. "After you've lost your job, your home, your family, why can't you just stop?"

Unfortunately, drug addiction is a progressive disease that frequently evolves in an insidious manner. "I was addicted to cocaine for five years before I even realized it," says a recent law school graduate. "I was going to see a psychiatrist because I had all these problems. I wasn't getting along with my parents, I was irritable and prone to outbursts of anger, I was drinking too much and doing irrational things. My psychiatrist and I would talk about all sorts of things, but I never once mentioned cocaine to her. That's because it didn't seem significant. Cocaine was one of the few things in life that would actually make me feel better. So how could that be part of the problem?"

In making the transition from recreational use to drug abuse, most addicts go through prolonged periods of denial, where they struggle to maintain the appearance of a normal life. "I would go to work completely stoned," explains one such addict, "and I would work hard. I was always a high-level performer. In fact, I realize now that part of my being able to function like that helped me in denial. My feeling was, how can I be an addict when I can keep my job and keep on functioning?"

The truth is, most addicts would like to quit, but can't. "On one level," says a drug treatment counselor, "the addict knows that his life is falling apart, but he refuses to admit it. Cocaine or crack or heroin has become an obsession, and the addict just cannot see—or refuses to see—that his behavior has become distorted and bizarre."

———

ALLAN: Alcohol used to be my demon drug. Then when I started doing cocaine, alcohol became a tool I'd use for modulating my intake of coke. I'd monitor my heart rate, and when I felt my heart was getting ready to burst, I would slow it down with a massive dose of alcohol. This may sound crazy, but if you're going to become involved with cocaine, my advice is that you should take the time to become an alcoholic first. Alcohol provides a wonderful way of maintaining your equilibrium between periods of snorting up.

ALEXA: Most people think of drug addicts as being down-and-out—people who are living on hard times and look like skid row derelicts. At least that's the way I used to think until I became a cocaine addict.

Now I realize we have a lot in common with alcoholics. A lot of addicts are "functional addicts." We get up in the morning and go to work every day, just like a lot of alcoholics who drink seven nights a week but hold on to their jobs no matter how rotten they feel.

SANDRA: After my first year of heavy cocaine use, I found that most of the changes in my life were rather subtle. They involved the sorts of things that were easy to hide, or easy to explain away. For example, I started hanging around with people that I normally wouldn't hang around with, and I started dating men who were heavy into drug abuse—men that I normally wouldn't have given the time of day to. But here I was, going to bed with them. A lot of times I'd do it just because I knew they had cocaine in their apartments, and it was an easy way to get some free coke. Then I'd pop up in the morning, rush over to my own home, dress real nice, and go to work.

*   *   *

STEPHANIE: When I got out of high school I went to secretarial school, and got a job working for the power company. It was a good job, and for someone fresh out of high school I was making a lot of money.

I was dating this guy, and the two of us were doing a lot of cocaine together. I had a card key so I could get into the building, and late one night we went up to the top floor and did some coke. The next day I told one of the girls I worked with about it, like it was real funny, and she told security. I ended up having to quit my job so I wouldn't be fired.

I suppose that was a warning sign. But I didn't think I had a problem. I just thought it was a bummer that I got caught.

I was continually abusing cocaine and alcohol, and I started screwing around a lot. I'd hang out with this girl who was really loose. The two of us would go to bars together, get drunk, and pick up guys. I really loved my boyfriend, but because I was drinking and drugging I'd do things I normally wouldn't do. One night I met this guy at a bar and he asked me if I wanted to do some coke with him. I said, "Yeah!" We went over to his place and I ended up screwing both him and his roommate. My boyfriend heard about it later, and that was really horrible. I felt awful. Another time I went to bed with my boyfriend's brother, and he found out about that too.

Eventually, the two of us broke up. Of course, that didn't slow me down. I kept right on drinking, and I'd do cocaine whenever I could get it. During that time, I was very promiscuous. I was always going to bars and picking up guys. I could never go to bed with a guy unless I was drunk or doing coke, and sometimes I'd sleep with three or four different guys a week. One time I slept with this black guy who worked in a parking garage. I used to buy cocaine from the guys in the garage, and I brought this black guy over to my apartment. We did our thing, then he got me some coke. It makes me sick to think about it. He was a heavy drug user, and I worry about AIDS. Sometimes I lie in bed wondering if I've got AIDS because of what I've done.

Every time I'd go out and sleep around, I'd feel real bad the next day. I'd feel like I had this terrible secret, and that nobody understood what a bad person I am. I have these deep depressions, this horrible guilt.

JOE: There were several years there when I was buying marijuana by the pound, and one day the guy that I regularly did business with was unavailable. Because I'd been such a good customer over the years, he sent his cousin out to see me. This young black kid shows up at my office, and supposedly he's going to get me an ounce of this extra-special super-quality marijuana. So I give him two hundred dollars, and he strolls out the door saying he'll be back with my stuff at three o'clock.

Well, four o'clock rolls around and I haven't seen hide nor hair of him. I get on the phone, and I ask, "What the fuck's going on?"

He says, "Man, I'm having a little trouble, but don't worry. I'm getting your stuff. I'll be there."

"When?"

"I'll be there by five."

I wait around till six, but he never shows up at all that day. So the next morning as I'm getting ready to go to work, I load my gun and toss it into my briefcase. An Iver-Johnson cowboy-style forty-five—which is a big fucking gun. You shoot somebody with that and it'll put a mammoth hole in the poor bastard.

I go to work and get this kid on the phone and tell him, "Either you bring me my dope or I'm coming to get it!"

He says, "Don't worry. Don't worry. I'll be there."

I sit there the entire day, and I'm getting plenty pissed off, because it's becoming obvious that this kid is ripping me off. Right as I'm leaving work he shows up and the two of us are standing on the sidewalk in the middle of the downtown business district having a little discussion right at rush hour. Tons of people are walking by. This is the heart of the business district so they've all got coats and ties and nice dresses on, and they're hurrying to catch the bus home or they're jumping into their cars. This kid is giving me all these wonderful excuses as to why he doesn't have either my money or my dope. It's obvious to me that he figures he can bullshit the pants off a honkey motherfucker like me. To him I'm just another dumb white guy in a suit.

As he's giving me these excuses I say, "Motherfucker, you ripped me off! That's what happened to my money! Don't give me that shit about getting it tomorrow!" Then I pulled that Iver-Johnson forty-five out and I put the barrel right on the end of his nose. All day long I'd been sitting there getting more and more pissed off, and listening to his bullshit just got me that much hotter. I mean to tell you I was steaming. I said, "Motherfucker, I'm going to blow your head clean off your shoulders!"

His eyes got real wide, and I could see the sweat rolling down his face. He was saying, "Don't kill me, man. Don't kill me."

Meanwhile, all these people are walking by looking at the two of us. That gun had 'em doing some double takes. It was like, "Jesus Christ! That guy's got a gun!"

I'm screaming at this kid because he's ripped me off, and the kid was doing some serious sweating. He was trembling with fear. I looked at him and said, "I'll tell you what I'm going to do. I'm going to let you run, and if you can outrun this bullet you'll live, but if you can't you die."

He took off running, and I leveled my gun dead at his head. But for some reason I never squeezed off a round, and I'll never know why. To this day I don't know why. I was so pissed off that I could've killed the motherfucker in a heartbeat. My instinct was to do it. For a moment I was standing on the street coming within a hair trigger of killing this kid in front of hundreds of witnesses.

I had a good job, a college education, and a good woman waiting for me at home—and I was going to put all that in jeopardy over a two-hundred-dollar bag of dope.

JEROME: When I was on drugs most people couldn't tell, because I was doing everything I could to hide it. I always had access to dope, so I never got that desperate look that junkies get, and I always took care of my hygiene. I'd comb my hair, brush my teeth, shower and bathe, and wear nice clothes. You know, I kept my appearance up.

It's the same thing with a lot of rock stars and movie stars. Every now and then you'll read in the newspaper how one of 'em checked into a treatment center. They might be addicted to heroin or cocaine, but when they're on stage they look good. A rock star will put on his show, and you can't never tell. Or an actress, man. You might see this actress who's got a habit, but on screen all you can see is that she looks really beautiful. Really glamorous. Inside she might be sick and spiritually disrupted, but all you see on the outside is this beautiful woman who is very successful at what she does. People like that can keep their habit up for a long, long time, because they got lots of money.

I know you can hide it, because I was addicted to heroin for ten

years and even my wife never knew. When she was around I'd drink
Grand Marnier on the rocks to cover my addiction. I'd come in the
house high on dope, I mean *twisted*, and the first thing I'd do was
pour me a drink. I'd jive and fool around, and my wife would be
thinking that I'm drunk. She'd tell me, "You got to slow down this
drinking. You don't make no sense." A couple of times she got mad
and threw all my liquor bottles out. Which was no big deal, because
I could always buy more. The important thing was that she didn't
know I was messing with heroin. I was snorting every day, but I
always kept it hid. I never brought it in the house. My wife's a decent
person, and if she knew I was into heroin she *never* would've stayed
with me.

It's only when an addict runs out of money that you can *see* he's
an addict. That's when they get desperate. A dude like that will be
runnin' around like a wild horse trying to get him some stuff. He
don't care where the money comes from. He'll be robbing and stealing, and eating out of garbage cans. He ain't got time to brush his
teeth or put on clean clothes. He's desperate, man.

But as long as you got money, man, you'll never slip to that state,
because when you got money you can get all the drugs you need.

DARYL: I was selling Boat [marijuana laced with PCP] when crack
'caine first came out, and right away everybody started putting their
money behind crack. So I switched over and was selling crack. I seen
how crazy people was acting. I seen how dudes was getting shot and
beat over the head for smoking up product. I seen how women would
sell their bodies just to get a little hit. I seen how mothers would
leave little babies in the crib, and not feed them or nothing. I been
in houses where there'd be a little three-, four-month-old baby crying
upstairs while the mother was next door selling her body. I'd look in
the icebox, and there was no food in there. The only thing I'd see
in the icebox was some baking soda and some water. I said to myself,
"That ain't right. The baby ain't got no food. No matter what happens, I'll never let myself get this desperate."

Even though I was selling, I didn't smoke crack 'caine because I
seen how crazy people was acting behind it. But it made me curious.
I figured, "This has got to be some righteous shit for people to be
going this crazy." I'd experienced everything else—powder cocaine,
PCP, acid, heroin. I'd done it all, and I just didn't believe that anything on this earth could control me. In the back of my head this

voice was sayin', "You can handle that shit. I know you can handle it. You've handled everything else. Just try it. Try it one time. See what this shit is all about."

I entertained that thought for a whole month. Then one day my old lady took her mother to the grocery store in my car. While they were gone, I cooked up a rock and said, "I'm gonna try this stuff. I'm only gonna do it this one time. I'm gonna see what all the fuss is about. And after that—no more." I cooked up a fifty, put the rock in the pipe, lit it, and took a hit—a long, deep hit. I held the smoke in my lungs for thirty seconds.

Then I said, "Lord have mercy! This shit ain't to be fucked with!" I felt so free. The feeling is undescribable. I was standing there in front of the window saying, "Man, this son of a bitch ain't to be fucked with!"

The rest is all history, man. That first hit there, that was my downfall. Crack is the worst addiction there is. It's worse than heroin, and it's worse than PCP. The craving is so powerful it makes you lose all your morals and principles. It robs you of your dignity.

I've seen grown men and grown women sitting down crying, saying, "I've got to stop living like this. I've got to stop hittin' the pipe. I've got to get some help."

But five minutes later, when somebody is knocking on the door with a rock, all the cryin' and shit is history, man. All they thinking about is gettin' a hit on the pipe.

JACK: I make pretty good money. I work in real estate development and bring in better than seventy thousand dollars a year. When I was growing up I experimented with all kinds of drugs. I had this buddy that I went to school with and the two of us had a reputation for being real wild and crazy. We used to party and over the years we did a lot of powder cocaine together. We also freebased—which I thought was great. Back then, cocaine had the reputation of being a glamour drug, and we had a lot of good times. About five or six years ago he moved out of state, and I lost touch with him. I got married, settled down, and didn't hear from him again until February of 'eighty-nine, when he called me for the first time in three years. He was back in town and wanted to get together for lunch. I said, "Great." So we hooked up and decided to catch a buzz for old times' sake.

That's when I was introduced to crack cocaine. I'd loved the high

I got from freebasing, so crack was too good to be true. It was so easy, so cheap. My friend knew these open-air markets in the projects where we could go to get it. I didn't feel comfortable driving into those neighborhoods, but my buddy knew what he was doing and we didn't have any problems. The dealers were standing on the curb saying, "We got rocks. We got rocks."

Crack took me back to the feeling I'd gotten from free base. An instant high. A great high. I was sitting there thinking, "This is so damn easy. All we've got to do is buy a twenty-dollar rock and light the pipe!" We didn't have to mess with buying powder and cooking it up ourselves, which was always a hassle.

Unfortunately, crack is just like they say it is. Once you get started you can't stop. You have a desire to do more and more and more. It's unreal how powerful the high is. It grabs you and won't let go. When I first started, I tried controlling it. I'd only smoke one or two rocks at a time, and I'd only smoke two or three times a week. But that only lasted a few weeks. I found myself smoking more and more often, and trying to hide what I was doing from my wife.

My job performance really suffered, because I was always high. At six o'clock in the morning I'd stop by the projects on my way to work and buy some crack. I'd smoke as I drove in. Then when I got to the office I'd slip my pipe in my socks and shove the crack in my pockets. I always had to have some crack on me. I'd do my paperwork, make a few phone calls, then go into the bathroom and take a few hits. Or I'd go into the storage room, lock the door, and smoke in there. Sometimes I'd tell my secretary, "I have a lot of work to do and I don't want to be bothered. If I get any calls, just take a message." Then I'd close the door and smoke crack at my desk for hours at a time.

Without even realizing it, I'd become a crack addict, and I was sneaking around the house, lying to my wife. She'd be watching TV, and I'd sneak out to the garage, do a few hits, then come back into the house. At night I'd keep getting out of bed to go to the bathroom. I'd sit in there for ten, fifteen minutes at a time with a towel shoved under the door so my wife couldn't smell the smoke, then after smoking a couple rocks I'd sneak back to bed.

I wanted to quit, but I didn't know how. I kept trying, and sometimes I'd have a little success. I'd stay straight for three or four days in a row, and that would be great. One time I even went a full week. But then I'd go right back to it. I can remember many, many times driving down to the projects telling myself, "You don't want to do this! You don't want to do this!" But I'd do it anyway. It was like my car was on automatic pilot. I had no control.

I'd drive into this nasty crime-infested project area, and as soon as I pulled up to the curb five or six dealers would come running to me hollering my name. "Jack! Jack! Here I am. I've got it for you, Jack!" They'd fight among themselves over who was going to serve me. I bought large quantities, and was guaranteed money. I always had several hundred dollars on me at any one time. And I always carried a baseball bat and a knife, which I'd have lying on the front seat where everybody could see them. The dealers thought I was crazy—this white dude in the ghetto with a baseball bat and a knife.

Some people selling on the street were lowlifes. They'd play con games and try to rip me off. They'd sell little balls of wax wrapped in a plastic bag so that it looked like crack, or they'd sell Ivory soap. One guy even tried to sell me a peanut one time. I had my money in my hand and he passed me this peanut wrapped up in a baggie. I guess he thought I'd take it and drive off, but I'd been ripped off before so I always checked. Coke has a bitter taste, and whenever somebody passed me something through the window I'd bite through the baggie to taste it and make sure it was crack. I just threw that peanut back at the guy and said, "Man, you're full of shit! Get out of my face!"

After a while I got to know which dealers had the best stuff. They knew I was spending money, and they wanted to keep me coming back. So they'd look out for me. Sometimes, when I drove up they'd sit in the car and we'd bullshit for a while. They'd turn me on or I'd turn them on. They were decent guys and we'd have these friendly conversations. You know, they were businessmen. They'd treat me like a customer, someone whose business they valued. They'd give me special deals, or they'd throw in a free rock every now and then. They let me know that they were looking out for me, taking care of me.

It got to the point where I was spending four, five hundred dollars a night on crack. I couldn't go home because I didn't want my wife to see me in that condition, so I'd stay out all night. I'd get in my car and drive all over the state. I'd smoke and drive, smoke and drive. I made this little pipe that had a long tube, so that I could hold it below windshield level when I hit on it. That way if there was a cop around he couldn't see me lighting the pipe.

In the morning I'd call my wife and lie to her—tell her I'd been out drinking with a friend and that I'd spent the night at his place because I'd gotten drunk. Of course, that's not the kind of situation you can live with for very long. I mean, it wasn't that hard for her to figure out what was going on. At first, she was lenient. She'd done cocaine before so she understood the attraction of getting high, but she didn't understand addiction. She kept hoping that it was a phase I'd pass through. Something I'd get tired of, and that I'd get better. But I continued to deteriorate. My boss would call her because I wouldn't show up at work and she'd have to lie for me and make up excuses. Finally, she'd had enough, and she put her foot down. She told me that she was going to leave unless I entered a treatment program.

By this time I was really obsessed. My attitude was "Fine. Leave." I was thinking, "If she leaves then I can sit at home and smoke crack all night. I won't have to sneak around anymore." When she moved out, I thought having her gone was a big luxury.

She left on a Sunday, and for the next five days all I did was smoke crack. I didn't eat; I didn't sleep. I just sat there in front of the television hitting the pipe, hitting the pipe. Then I'd get into the car and drive down to the projects to buy more crack. After a couple days I was really miserable. But I had this intense physical craving to keep going, keep hitting the pipe. I was dehydrated and sweating, my muscles were cramping, and every time I'd start to come down I'd tell myself, "C'mon, hurry up! Do another hit!" The only way I could get rid of the physical symptoms of withdrawal was to stay high.

The drug had taken control of my mind. The drug was doing all the talking. I felt like I was in the ring with a fighter, and I had my hands tied. I wanted to quit, but I couldn't fight back. The addiction was just too overwhelming. I *had* to have more crack.

SLICK: After I lost my job I went back to workin' the street. I hooked up with this guy who was a professional car thief. He'd steal cars, chop them, and sell the parts. I went into business with him. We'd grab cars, take them out to this place we called the Weeds, dismantle them, load everything onto a truck, and drive the truck into Brooklyn. Every morning we'd get paid for what we brought in.

Me and my partner would spend our days sitting in my backyard getting high. All we'd do all day long is smoke crack. Then at night we'd go out and steal cars. After getting paid in the morning, we'd buy more crack and smoke all day.

At this time I was planning on getting married to this woman that I really loved. She didn't know that I was strung out on crack, because I kept my appearance up and never smoked when she was around.

Then one day me and my partner were in the backyard smoking and she walked up and saw me with the pipe. She saw what I was doing. She was really hurt bad. She turned and ran out of there. I went running after her, trying to make her stop, but she just kept on going. Then this voice in my head said, "Let her go! Forget about her!"

That's what crack does. It makes you forget about the people you love.

I was smoking crack all the time. I mean *all the time*! I got so fucked up that I couldn't even steal cars anymore. So I'd go out and panhandle. The only thing that made me different from a homeless person was I had a car to sleep in. But outside of that I was just like the rest of 'em. I was out there bumming money and stealing whatever I could. I lost forty pounds. I had the belt loops on my pants tied together, and I had grease and dirt all over me. Then one day I was walking down the street and I heard this lady call out my name. I recognized the voice, and thought, "Oh no, it can't be!" I turned around and there was my mother looking straight at me. She was shocked. Absolutely shocked. There was nothing but hurt in her eyes.

JOE: Even though I didn't know it, I never stood a snowball's chance in hell. I was doomed from the very beginning. My mother and father were alcoholics, both of my grandfathers were alcoholics, and all of my father's brothers were alcoholics, as were my mother's brothers. We're talking about a family where heavy drinking was the thing to do. Back in the fifties and early sixties, when I was growing up, no one knew that there is a strong link between heredity and alcoholism. So come hell or high water, I was going to drink.

My father was a used car dealer. They're infamous for drinking, as are the people associated with them—automobile painters, mechanics, and the like. Early on, when I was seven, eight years old, they'd all come over to the house with my father and pass the jug after work. The drunker they got, the more frequently I got hold of the jug. To be like the big guys, I'd sip on it. I'd do my best to hang in there with them. My father and his friends all thought that was really funny. They got a big kick out of seeing this seven-year-old kid get totally blitzed. Which I guess is kind of sad, but I can't hold it against them. They didn't know any better.

Unfortunately, alcoholism is an extraordinarily insidious disease. All through high school and my time in the Air Force, I had this incredible tolerance, and I was into the whole macho thing of being able to drink and hold my whiskey. The thought that I had a problem never crossed my mind. To the contrary, I thought I could handle alcohol *better* than anyone else because I was drinking so much of it.

In 1970, after I got out of the military I went to work for this corporation in my hometown. It was a PR job and my responsibilities included wining and dining clients and corporate executives when they came to visit the national headquarters. That was right up my alley because it meant a lot of drinking. A couple nights a week I'd take these guys out, show them a good time, drink them under the table, then take them back to their hotel and put them to bed. As soon as I'd get them tucked in I'd go straight to a bar, and start my *serious* drinking.

Right about this time the Vietnam War was just beginning to wind down. For people of my generation that was a strange, eerie time. I had a lot of friends go over to 'Nam—a lot of 'em came back and a lot of 'em didn't. Every time the phone rang you'd have this nagging fear, you'd almost be afraid to answer, because you'd be wondering, "Who got blown away this time?"

I think that's one of the reasons drug abuse was so prevalent back then—so open and accepted. It was a way to numb our anger and pain, and we had a lot to be angry about.

My drug of choice was alcohol, but I was something of a garbage can. I'd take anything I could. I smoked a lot of pot, ate a lot of speed, fooled around with LSD, uppers, downers, mushrooms, cocaine. You name it, I did it. And I was hanging out with people who were doing the same thing. We thought we were a bunch of hippies in search of peace, love, and understanding. Drugs elevated us—took us to a higher plane of consciousness. You know, that mellow euphoric feeling that comes from getting high was a regular part of our lives, and we attached great intellectual significance to it.

I must've been about twenty-five, twenty-six years old when I began to realize that my job was interfering with my drinking. Having a job meant having to get up in the morning, and it meant trying to stay sober most of the day. I wasn't into that. So I did the logical thing: I quit my job and started collecting unemployment. That way I could sleep till noon, hang out with my friends drinking and getting high, and then party all night. Working just wasn't the thing to do.

JOHN: I'd first started using drugs on a regular basis in Vietnam, and after I got back to the States I continued to use. I was getting drunk and stoned almost every day, but I never thought I had a problem. I figured if I could survive in a war zone while drinking and drugging I could certainly function in a normal, sane environment, where all I had to do was get up and go to work in the morning. That was a thought I held on to for many, many years.

I was out of control. Just totally whacked out on cocaine and booze. Sure, I felt a fall-off in my abilities at work, but not to the point where I was concerned about it. I could still function. A lot of my business associates weren't returning my calls, but I didn't pay much attention. Then one Monday morning I went to my bank machine to get some money and my account was empty. I thought, "Hell, this can't be right. I just put two thousand dollars in here the other day. What's going on?" Of course, I'd spent it all on cocaine.

Everybody was telling me how bad I looked, but the people I was closest to looked just as bad as me. I couldn't understand what those other people were talking about. Everybody I drank and drugged with partied their brains out. Drinking and drugging was normal. There wasn't anything wrong with it. They all had jobs, they all had families. Nobody I knew had ever been fired or gone to jail. And as far as the law went, I didn't think of it as being any big crime. Hell no. I'd been to Vietnam. I was thinking, "Hey, I went to 'Nam. If a cop tries to stop me, he probably didn't go to 'Nam. So fuck him. I've paid my dues. This country owes me."

WALLACE: Drugs and alcohol saved me from the military. I was in the Army for a few months, and although I didn't know it, I was an alcoholic. One afternoon I'd been drinking and had swallowed some mescaline, so I was definitely under the influence. This sergeant walked in and gave me an order. I was drunk and high and didn't feel like doing it. So I said, "Sir, would you kiss my ass?"

A bunch of other men were there, and that sergeant got hot. The veins were popping in his neck. He said, "Would you repeat that?"

In a louder voice, and with greater pride, I shouted, "Would you kiss my ass, sir!"

That was my last day in the Army. They made me sign a piece of paper and gave me a discharge. They said that I didn't have the right attitude to be a soldier.

SNAKE: I was working at the stock exchange, and I started stealing checks and bonds, and embezzling money from the firm. I knew people who could cash the checks, and we'd split the money. I even stole entire payrolls. I was getting real well known on Wall Street—but by the wrong people. I had to get out of there before something happened.

I was twenty then, and living with my parents. I started stealing cars, dealing with the chop shops, the whole bit. I got in on some robberies, although I never went inside and did the stealing. I sat in the car and was the driver. I needed money to live, but mostly I needed it for dope. My number one priority in life was to get high. I did any drug I could get ahold of. You know, the garbage can syndrome—cocaine, heroin, you name it. My father knew, and he tried to keep me straight. He'd beat me, he'd take my car, he'd even flatten the tires so I couldn't drive around at night. But I'd still get out.

I was locked up three times for assault. I wasn't really picking fights but I was putting myself in situations where it would happen. Why? I don't know. I didn't care. I got stabbed twice—once in the ass. It took nineteen stitches to sew me back together. But at least I'd gotten one in on the guy before he stabbed me. I hit him with this belt that had big metal spikes on it and busted his jaw. I got arrested for that and ended up sitting in jail with a bleeding stab wound.

None of it mattered, though, except for dope, getting high. I was smoking a lot of Angel Dust, which was affecting my speech and my sense of balance. I was slurring my words and having trouble walking. I'd wake up with blood on me and not know whose it was or how it got there. My father was threatening to throw me out of the house.

But I never thought what I was doing was wrong or abnormal, because all the people I hung out with were just like me. I was "normal." Anytime somebody would say something, I'd say, "Aw, you're just jealous because I've got drugs and money."

DONNELL: One of the stereotypes you always hear is that an addict will do anything to get a fix. But that's not true. I know a lot of people who are addicted to heroin but still have principles. They won't break into somebody's home and steal things. They won't use a gun to commit robbery. They won't do anything that would hurt their friends. Those are principles they won't violate. Most people supporting heroin habits through crime are professionals at what they do. Some specialize in shoplifting, others in writing bad checks. The shoplifters know how to clean out a department store in the suburbs, or how to case a warehouse by posing as a deliveryman. Even though they're out there stealing, their victims are not individuals who get hurt. They're going after large corporations that are well insured. They're not into violence, and they never hurt anyone.

ANNE: My cocaine habit got so bad, I started stealing off my job. At night, after everybody'd gone home, I'd run through the office building and go through all the desks, stealing whatever I could. If somebody left an overcoat or a Christmas present behind, I'd take it. I'd steal anything I could get my hands on. I wanted to slow down and stop stealing, because I was taking from innocent people. I was taking from the people I worked with every day, and I was afraid I was gonna get found out. But I didn't stop.

No matter how much I stole at work, I needed more money. It got to the point where I was going outside of work to rob people. I'd run to the downtown hotels, and I'd rob the guests in the hotel. I'd have a gun sometimes, or I'd use a knife or a club. It didn't make any difference—anything that would do harm I'd use to take money off people.

As much bad stuff as I was doing, I never really hurt anyone. At least not physically. I was hurting myself, though. I was hurting inside for all the bad things I was doing.

ESTELLE: I have a brother, and he's on drugs too. He shoots heroin. I don't do that. I ain't sticking a spike in my arm. If I can't smoke it, I don't do it. Mainly, I smoke PCP and crack cocaine. To get the money to support our drug habits, me and my brother used to embezzle money out of banks. People that use heroin, they have a talent where they can just sit back and observe things. Where there's a way to make money, they know about it. My brother used to stay up all night long. I'd be at home, and I wouldn't know where in the hell he was going or what he was doing, but when he'd come back in the morning he'd have all these bank statements. I guess he got 'em by going through the trash. He'd go to the dumpster behind the bank and get the trash. Or he'd steal mail. Every day we'd have the names of fifty different people, and the balance of their bank accounts. I'd get up in the morning, get dressed nice, and go out and help my brother embezzle. I'd go to the bank, write out a with-drawal slip using one of the names and account numbers from the bank statements he'd get, and then I'd approach the teller and make a withdrawal. I'd do that for all the women's names, and my brother would do it for the men. Mostly, we'd withdraw small amounts, so the teller would never ask for any identification. When you do that several times every morning, the money starts to add up. We could embezzle two thousand or three thousand dollars in a couple of hours just by going around to different banks.

We'd do this three or four days a week, and we'd wear different disguises. I'd never wear the same outfit, and sometimes I'd wear a wig, or I'd put on some glasses. I'd always wear nice clothes, so I looked like a businessperson. Once we went to a bank, we wouldn't go back there for a while, or we'd go to a different teller. We did that for several months and never got caught. We had a couple of close calls, but we never got arrested or nothing like that.

DOUGLAS: I've been an addict for seventeen years, and the way I supported my habit was to go out robbing people. My partner and I would get in a car and cruise around and rob people on the streets. I had a pistol, and I was always the one who would do the robbing. My partner would drive the car and stand lookout. We'd do ten, fifteen robberies a day. A lot of times it wasn't because I needed the money. I might have had money, but going out and robbing was something to do. Or maybe my partner needed money, so I'd help him get some.

Robbing is an easy thing to do. It's easy to avoid the police, be-cause it happens so quickly. I've robbed hundreds of people on the street, and never once got caught. You come up fast, and never take more than fifteen or twenty seconds. When you put a gun in some old lady's face she has a tendency to get very quiet and do exactly as she's told. By the time she calls the police and they show up, we'll be on the other side of town.

One time I was robbing this woman, and when I snatched her purse she wouldn't let go. She started tussling with me and screaming, "Help! Help! I'm being robbed!"

This man who was walking down the street heard all the commotion, and came over. My partner was standing lookout and he had a little twenty-two caliber pistol—a little Saturday night special. He saw this guy approaching to assist her, and he fired a warning shot past the guy. He didn't try to hit him. He just blasted a bullet by his head to give him something to think about. Well, that bullet changed the guy's mind about trying to assist this woman. He stopped dead in his tracks.

But this woman still didn't want to let go of her purse. She was fightin' and screamin' and holdin' on to that purse. Finally, I had to hurt her to make her let go. I had to get rough and smack her face. I felt bad about having to do that. I didn't want to hurt that old woman. I just needed to get me a bag of dope.

GOOD FEELIN' FRED: Getting near Christmas one time, I was in a supermarket in New Jersey. I had a long coat on, and there was this lady there who was living on welfare. She had six children with her, and they were running around the store in six different directions. Her pocketbook was in the shopping cart, and she was running all over the place trying to get ahold of her kids. So I threw my coat over my shoulder, winged it over the cart, and grabbed her pocketbook.

When I was on my way back to New York, I looked inside the pocketbook, and it was full of all these brand-new hundred-dollar bills. She'd obviously just cashed her monthly welfare check. I remember saying, "Thank you, Jesus!" There was about seven, eight hundred dollars in there. I was thinking my belief in God had taken care of me.

I never even gave a second thought as to how that lady and her children must've suffered because of me. You see, when you're an addict you don't think about whether what you're doing is right or wrong. The only morality you know is that if you don't take drugs you'll get sick. Taking drugs isn't bad, it's not taking them that's bad.

DOUGLAS: One time my buddy and me were going out to buy some dope. We were getting into my car when this dude walks up and asks us if we had any heroin. I didn't know this dude's name, but I'd seen him around and knew he was an addict. We say no, we don't have any, but we're going to get some. So he gets in the car.

As we're driving over to make our connection, my buddy reaches down under the front seat and brings up my pistol. He puts it in this dude's face and says, "Give me your money." You know, he's robbing the dude of the money he was going to use to buy his heroin with. I pull the car over, and we let the dude out minus his money and his watch. Then we go on about our business.

Eight hours later we're driving around the red-light district looking for action, and a police car pulls me over. These cops jump out of their car with their guns drawn—just like you see on TV. They're telling us, "Put your hands on your head and get out of the car!"

I get out of the car and say, "What's going on?"

The cop says, "You're under arrest for armed robbery."

Well, I heard that and breathed a sigh of relief. The only dude I'd robbed all day was that junkie. I figured someone had hit a store or something, and the cops had pulled me over by mistake. It never occurred to me that a drug addict who was on his way to commit a crime would go to the police and report that his money and watch had been stolen. But that's exactly what this dude did. After we kicked him out, he took down the tag number on my car and called the police.

The cops put me and my buddy in a lineup, and that junkie picked us out. Then he went to court and he testified. We were charged with armed robbery and kidnapping, and there's no question we fucked up on that one. When the cops pulled us over we still had the dude's watch, and we had some drug paraphernalia in the car. I was convicted at the trial and the judge sentenced me to fifteen to forty-five years. But the sentence was suspended on the condition that I enroll in a drug treatment program. I enrolled in this program, and held on to my life-style. I'd hang out with all the dudes in the treatment program, and after our rap sessions we'd do drugs together.

STEPHEN: I'd gotten my own apartment and a job with the sanitation department. I was driving a truck for them. I was always a friendly worker, a friendly junkie. I figured I could do my job and get high, no problem. I was leading a double life—at work I was fine, but at night it was like Jekyll and Hyde.

One night I was smoking crack with a friend. We ran out, and went to get some more. He had sixty dollars, and pulled up to this place in the projects where they sell. The guy came running up to the car, my friend gave him the sixty dollars, the guy put the shit in his hands, and we drove off. We only got maybe fifty feet away when we saw that the guy had sold us soap. Fucking soap rocks. We went crazy.

My friend threw the car in reverse, stomped on the gas, and yelled for me to reach under the seat. I reached down and found a twenty-five automatic. We were flying back in reverse, and I seen the guy running into an apartment building. I jumped out, aimed the gun at the door he'd just run into, and emptied the gun. A complete maniac! I don't know what happened inside that apartment, if I hit him or anyone else, but there was busted glass and splinters flying everywhere. I unloaded the clip, jumped back into the car, and we drove off. I figured I'd taught that fucker a lesson.

Another time, I went traveling with a buddy of mine one after-noon, and the two of us ended up on the east side of New York. My friend was driving. He owned this van, and the two of us were hitting the crack pipe. As we were driving along, I seen this guy on a bicy-cle—he was riding right in front of us. My friend was coming up from behind, getting real close to him. So I said, "Watch out, man!" Instead of jamming his foot down on the brake, he smashes the ac-celerator and plows right into the guy on the bike. That guy went flying—hit our windshield and went right over top of us. I think it was an accident. I think my friend meant to hit the brake. But I don't know. We just kept on going. I have no idea what happened to the guy we hit.

ROGER: I was up in the West Virginia mountains with a couple of my buddies, and we got caught in a flood. We were stuck in this little redneck town, and couldn't leave because the roads below were washed out. Between the three of us we had an ounce of pot, a few hits of speed, and a case of beer. There was a little country store nearby, and we went in there to buy some bean soup and some more beer. That's what we lived on for the next few days—pot, speed, soup, and beer.

There was a bar in town, so of course, we had to go out drinking whiskey while we waited for the rains to stop so the roads could be repaired. There were some rednecks in this joint, and words were exchanged. I don't know how it started, but there was some antago-nism between us. Nothing much happened that night, but the next day, right when this bar was opening back up, we ran into the same group again. We'd been speeding and drinking day and night, and were not to be messed with.

This time, major fisticuffs broke out. One of my buddies is a great boxer. He's very quick with his hands, and he throws a vicious punch. He took on this one redneck who'd been eager to mix things up, and after knocking him silly, he mashed this guy's face down on top of a chain-link fence. The fence coil caught the guy in the eye, and poked his eye clean out. My buddy blinded the bastard, and left him whimpering.

I remember standing there watching, and laughing at the guy when he lost his eye. I thought it was real funny. You know, a big macho event.

LURISA: When I was using PCP I did a lot of crazy stuff. Don't ask me why. PCP just sent me crazy. It put my mind to a state where it's a black-white thing. Here I am a black person, and smoking PCP would click something in my mind that made me very violent, very angry toward Caucasian people. Automatically, I would go out of my neighborhood, around in the suburbs, where I know white people be at. I'd be on a mission. My mission was to hurt Caucasian people. I'd rob 'em, beat 'em, steal from stores. All that kind of shit.

I've never killed anybody, but I've bodily harmed people. I've sprayed Mace in the eyes of white people just to get my rocks off. I've beat 'em over the back of the head with a pistol, and I've used knives on 'em. I know of two incidents where people have been hospitalized on account of what I done.

PCP put me in a state where my rage was my strength. When I'd be on a mission, bringing harm to a white person would make me feel better. After I robbed or beat someone, I'd be thinking, "I got that motherfucker! I ripped that motherfucker off and made him bleed! Now I'm going to get another one!"

NAP: I'd learned all the angles and con games, and I was stealing a lot. I was stealing so good that I was spending anywhere between one hundred to one hundred fifty dollars a day on dope. But I was getting busted a lot too. I never did much time, though. I'd always plea-bargain—you know, promise not to do it again and get off on a lesser charge. But that kind of shit can't go on forever, man. Eventually, a judge decided he'd had enough, and he threw me in the penitentiary for four years.

I got a real backwards kind of education in the joint. I learned a lot about gambling and dice and hustling and pimping from the older guys. They even told me what to say to the whores, when to say it—the dos and don'ts of pimpology. But I also read some classics and a lot of stuff like that, because I was at the end of the cell block. By the time the books got passed down to me, all the fuck books and cowboy books was gone. I didn't have nothing to read but *Bartlett's Quotations*, and *Abnormal Psychology*, and Plato's *Republic*, shit like that. When you're in a cell by yourself, you read that shit. And consequently, it makes you think.

When I got out of the joint I thought I was slick as eel-oil, boy. I was ready to turn my world around. I was going to stop this dope shit. But then I met this bitch—a fast-walking, big-hat, boosting lady—and she took dead advantage of me, Jack. She was a top-flight thief, man, pulling in designer clothes and selling them for *big* money. She was stealing shit for me too—Walter Morton suits, Hickey Freemans, silk drawers, shit like that.

She was doing all the big work, and I got a real job as a short-order cook. I wanted to become part of the regular world. I wanted to be like other people, and I thought this job would help me do that. But the bitch say to me, "Shit, man, the little bit of money you make slaving away like that, I'll pay you that much just to be with me all the time!" So I quit the job. She was giving me all the dope in the world, and I was back on it.

I was hanging out with her until one day I sold some dope to a guy I'd been knowing a long time. He snitched on me. The police came and kicked my door down. I must've flushed an ounce of dope and a half ounce of coke down the toilet before they got through the door. The police come busting in, and they're searching all over the place, and I'm saying loud as I can, "Everything in this place is mine!" I'm saying that because one of us had to raise bond, and if they lock both of us up it ain't gonna happen. I need her on the street where she can make some money. The Man is searching the room, and we had one of them big bookcase headboards on the bed, and when the Man goes to search the headboard, my woman grabbed a pill bottle full of dope.

The Man says, "Everything in here might be yours, but your woman's got dope in her hands. We got her on possession!" The larceny-hearted bitch was afraid of losing her fucking dope, but didn't give a damn when I was flushing all mine down the toilet.

I ended up with a seventy-two-count indictment against me. Possession, distribution, conspiracy, carrying a dangerous weapon, all sorts of shit. I had this big old knife that I used to carry, and the day before my court appearance I feigned a suicide and ended up in the hospital. Some little district attorney came over to see me, and I told him I was trying to kill myself because I'm a dope addict and I can't stop thieving. Going on and on about how I don't know how to stop except by killing myself. You know, laying this big sob story on the dude. He said if I'd agree to go to Saint Elizabeth's [mental hospital] they'd agree to drop the possession charge. I thought, "Well, if they drop the possession charge, maybe they'll drop the rest." I said okay, and I ended up getting off all the charges by being declared not guilty by reason of insanity.

They sent me to Saint Elizabeth's and subjected me to all kinds of therapy and shit. Strange to say, it worked—they got me off the dope, at least for a little while. I met a nurse while I was there, a white woman, and I married her when I got out. I was doing okay, trying to get my American Dream together. I was working and all—but I couldn't stop fucking around. I don't know why, I just couldn't stop. Pretty soon, I slipped and went through the same damn progression all over again—alcohol, marijuana, heroin. I was back into the junkie thing one more motherfucking time.

By now, though, I was absolutely convinced that it was not my fault. In my mind, it was the system's fault. And being married to a white woman was a great way to get back at the system. "Okay, motherfuckers," I said, "so this is your most prized possession? Well, I got me one now, and she's mine. So fuck you. I'm a dope fiend because you motherfuckers are locking me up all the time! If this is how your system works, then I'm gonna be just as mean and nasty and cruel to any one of you motherfuckers as you are to me!"

I went back to being a crook. If you had something nice, I was taking it—simple as that. I was not trying to be like other people anymore. I was trying to be the worst motherfucker I could be. Morality, ethics, all that shit went out the window. It had to, because if you accept responsibility for all the negative shit you're doing you couldn't stand it, man. You've got to believe that even the mean, hurtful stuff is justified. You've got to believe that you are right.

My attitude was, it's everybody's fault but mine. I figured, "This is it, man. I'm a dope fiend and it's never going to change."

*   *   *

ERNIE: A lot of the people I partied with in high school don't party as hard as they used to. They don't drug to excess because they know better. For them, drug and alcohol abuse was a phase they passed through. A lot of that was due to peer pressure. They wanted to belong to their cliques, and in order to belong you had to get fucked up and tell people about it. But as they grew older, they got on with their lives—they went to law school or med school, and they got married and had children. They found other things in life that were more important than getting high. A lot of them probably use cocaine, marijuana, and alcohol recreationally, but they've never let it dominate their lives.

For some reason, that never happened to me. Getting high was always the most important thing in my life. I'd started messing with needles when I was still in high school. I was shooting a lot of crystal meth and a lot of cocaine. Five or six of us would get together and we'd shoot speed all night long. There was also a lot of real good cocaine around, and I much preferred shooting it to snorting it, because the gratification was so much more immediate. Once I learned how much better the high was from the needle, I was hooked. I never did heroin, because I was afraid of it, but I'd shoot anything else I could get in the syringe. I knew a guy that worked at a veterinary clinic, and he had access to the Demerol they used to put the dogs to sleep. He'd bring that home, so I was shoooting a lot of Demerol. The great thing about the needle was I liked the rush. I liked the instant high. I used to boot four or five times, because I liked to watch my blood rush back and forth in the syringe. I liked the way the blood felt when it reentered my veins.

There was no way I could've held down a job even if I'd wanted to. My hygiene was bad, and I smelled bad. That didn't bother me, though. I wasn't thinking about the fact that I was walking around in urine-stained pants, because my mind was on getting high. I was always trying to figure out how I could score my next fix. Believe me, a little physical degradation doesn't bother a drug addict. I remember one time after getting arrested on a drunk in public charge, I woke up in my jail cell and the little silver faucet beside my bunk didn't work. I was dehydrated and *needed* a drink of water. So I got down on my knees and started drinking out of the toilet. Most anybody else would've waited. The last thing they'd do would be drink out of a smelly jailhouse toilet. But in my addiction I didn't see anything wrong with it. Hell, self-respect and hygiene had gone out the window a long time ago. As far as I was concerned, I needed a drink, and if the toilet was where the water was, then that's where I was putting my face.

JOE: Eventually, I got to the point where my addiction was so bad my motorcycle was repossessed and I was evicted from my apartment. I had no place to live, so I lived on the streets. I was sleeping under bushes and in old abandoned cars. I'd go for weeks without changing my clothes. Occasionally, I'd find somebody who'd let me take a shower, and I kept my toothbrush in the pocket of this field jacket that I always wore. I never had any toothpaste, but that didn't matter, I'd brush my teeth with beer, wine, or whiskey—whatever I had.

Even though I didn't have a place to live, I could always find a way to get my hands on some booze. Sometimes I'd steal it, and sometimes I'd do odd jobs. Other times I'd panhandle until I had enough to buy a bottle of wine. Drinking was more important than living.

I was homeless for several months, and finally checked myself into a halfway house. This place had strict rules, and I managed to straighten myself out. I was going to AA meetings and staying sober. I stayed sober for three months, and was doing really well.

Unfortunately, this was a coed halfway house, and one day they brought in this young lady. She was in her early to mid-twenties, had red hair, and was very attractive. Needless to say, she turned the head of every man in the place.

The house was laid out so that the women slept downstairs in small rooms, and the men slept upstairs. Everybody had little jobs to do, and one night after I finished my duties I went upstairs to bed. I was lying in bed reading a book, when I heard someone moving in the hall. I assumed that one of the guys had gotten up to use the toilet, so I didn't think anything of it.

The next thing I know, that young lady is standing beside my bed. I look up, and she's smiling down at me in her bathrobe. My eyes got big, she opens up her robe, and there she is, buck naked. I've never had any power over women, but that redheaded gal was on me in a heartbeat. I was a street drunk, so it had been months and months and months since I'd any sex with anybody. Good-looking young ladies just didn't want to have anything to do with guys like me that slept in the park and didn't bathe. There were a couple of homeless women that were as smelly and dirty as I was that I fumbled around with, but on the street I was injesting so much alcohol that I really couldn't perform sexually. All we'd do was sort of paw at each other. But on this night, I'd been sober for three months, and everything was working. That was a lovely evening to say the least. She was good. She was absolutely phenomenal.

In the halfway house sex was strictly taboo. If they found you screwing around, you were immediately ejected. That young redhead was the temptation I couldn't resist. Here I was with no money, and no place to live, lusting after this hot little babe. All I could think about was getting her back in the sack. Well, to make a long story short, she and I ended up in a motel room together. I'm a good mechanic, and I stole some expensive parts off of some cars to get us a stake, and we went off to shack up in this motel. We're both drunks, and we proceeded to get absolutely blasted. We went on a four-day binge the likes of which you've never seen. The maid would come in to clean the room in the morning, and the floor would be absolutely covered with beer and wine bottles.

By the fourth day, I was out of money, and we were down to the last fifth of wine. She wanted a drink, and I wanted a drink. I opened the bottle and gave it to her, and she took a bigger drink than I thought was fair. That pissed me off. It was *my* bottle. I grabbed it from her, opened the door, and kicked her ass out in the street. Told the greedy bitch I never wanted to see her again. Then I sat down on the edge of the bed and finished my bottle of wine. Here I'd given up my sobriety so I could be with this girl, and then I turned right around and kicked her out over a few slobbery ounces of wine. I was right back to where I'd been before, drinking with the desperation of a man to whom alcohol means more than sex or friendship.

After that, the next fourteen months were spent on the street. There were a couple of times when I damn near killed myself. For a while, I was sleeping in this old abandoned car, and one cold winter night I built a small fire on the floorboards so I could stay warm, but the upholstery caught fire, and I almost died from asphyxiation. I woke up just in time to save myself from suffocating to death.

Another night, I almost froze to death. It was twenty-two below zero, and I spent the night in a ditch because I had no place else to go. I stopped by my aunt and uncle's house, and asked my uncle if I could sleep on the sofa since it was so cold outside. He could see that I'd been drinking, and said, "Well, having you here makes your aunt very nervous." That was all I needed to hear. I took off, because I knew no one likes to have a street drunk in their house. I crawled into this ditch so that I'd be out of the wind, then I covered myself up with leaves to get whatever insulation they'd provide, and I laid there very still, trying not to move, hoping I'd live to see the morning.

ROGER: I wasn't working because it was easier to collect unemployment, hang out, and spend all my time drinking and drugging.

I was taking in so much alcohol that I developed pancreatitis, which is an inflammation of the pancreas brought on by alcohol abuse. If you've ever known anyone who's had pancreatitis, you know how painful it is. It feels like someone took a piece of hot iron, shoved it in your back, and ran it up your shoulder. It's the most piercing pain I've ever experienced. The pain is so severe it brings you to your knees and completely immobilizes you. Nothing can stop it. I've been given morphine, and even that wasn't enough to stop the pain.

Of course, I wasn't going to let pancreatitis stop me from drinking. Every day, every night, I was out partying, scoring drugs, and drinking booze. Finally, my pancreatitis got so bad I had to be hospitalized for three weeks. While I was in the hospital a couple of my unemployment checks came in. So when I was released from the hospital, the first thing I did was walk down the hill to the first liquor store I came to. I walked inside, cashed one of my checks, and bought a gallon of wine. Then I walked outside, sat down on the curb in front of the store, and drank the entire gallon of wine.

That gives you an idea of how insane I was. I knew I'd just been released from the hospital because of a serious medical problem brought on by alcohol abuse, and I knew it was absurd to be sitting there on the curb drinking wine. But I didn't care. My life didn't mean anything to me. The only thing that mattered was feeding my addiction.

Now I can tell you that story, but no one other than a fellow addict can understand what it is that I'm talking about. I'm talking about a force that is so incredibly strong that it overrides intellect, emotion, and basic common sense. Drug and alcohol addiction are outrageously powerful. A sane person will say, "Just don't drink, and you'll be okay." But an addict doesn't even perceive the option. An addict drinks because he *must*.

Of course, I ended up right back in the hospital, where I stayed for another couple weeks. This time, I was released on a Wednesday, and that Saturday I went out and got drunk again. There was nothing, absolutely nothing, that was going to get me to voluntariliy stop.

DONNELL: A shooting gallery is a place where people come to shoot up. Everything you need is already there. The needles and the hypodermics are available. It may cost you two dollars to get in the door, and two more dollars for the needle and the hypodermic. If you can't inject the drug yourself, then there's somebody there that will inject the drug in you for five dollars.

Some shooting galleries are nice places where they don't let nobody in but the people they know. Others are run-down and trashy, and they'll let anybody in. When you walk into a shooting gallery, you'll see people getting high and talking shit. Some people will hang out, others will come in, get injected with drugs, and walk right back out the door. You'll see a lot of people who've got jobs, they'll come in on their lunch break, get their hit, and go right back to work. People are constantly coming in and out twenty-four hours a day.

It was only after I started selling heroin and working in galleries that I became aware of things I hadn't been aware of before. I started seeing dirty junkies with physical deformities—swollen hands, swollen feet, missing teeth. I saw women selling their bodies to get the drug, and kids abandoned because the mother was a junkie. I saw violence, disease, and death.

I felt like I was contributing to that, and I felt bad about it. But there was nothing I could do to change. I was addicted myself, and selling heroin was the way I supported my own habit.

GOOD FEELIN' FRED: In the galleries a lot of the women wear those little black Chinese slippers because their feet have swollen up so bad, and the men wear sneakers without shoelaces because they can't tie their shoes. I've seen people with hands so swollen they look like they're wearing boxing gloves. Then there are the people with running abscesses.

Whenever I saw that, it had an effect on me, but not the kind that would make me say, "This is crazy! I got to stop this!" Anytime I saw something like that, it only impressed on me the need to get new works [needles, syringes, etc.], or to get some alcohol and clean my works. If I did that, I thought, I wouldn't have no problems.

But then I ran into a bigger problem. I shot some dope, and, man, I knew it was an OD. As soon as I shot it, it tasted bitter in my throat. I started sinking—not falling down, but it felt like my legs was moving away from me. I had this feeling like I was moving toward this bright light. And I started talking. I told this brilliant light that I was too young to die. That I was not ready to die. And I knew that God was that light. That it was God that I was talking to.

The next morning I came to. Apparently, I'd convinced the light, because I was still alive. But I didn't quit shooting drugs. I had this feeling: "Yeah, man, I can go on and keep shooting drugs. I won't die. If what I was doing was wrong, I'd already be dead. If I was gonna die, I would've died last night."

DONNELL: I've seen a lot of violence working in shooting galleries. I've seen people come up to rob dealers and get their asses blown away in the process. And I've seen people overdose and die on drugs. They'll come into the shooting gallery, get their injection, sit back in a chair and tell me how good it is. Then I don't hear from them for a while. They get real quiet. So I'll go over to check them out. I'll touch the dude and say, "Hey man, you okay?" But I'll be too late. The dude will already have died, or be in it so deep I can't wake him up. That's happened to me lots of times.

I've also saved a lot of lives. Heroin isn't like cocaine. It doesn't kill you by blowing out your heart. It kills you slowly. It gives you enough time to get help. If some guy nods out, I'll run over and slap him around. I'll wake him up. If a guy has OD'd, and I can get him to respond, get him on his feet and moving around, I know he'll be okay. The trick is to get to them early and keep them from going in too deep.

DOUGLAS: When you overdose you don't feel a thing. I've over-dosed three times. The first time was in 1969. Three of us were running together, and we got some really potent heroin. The quality of it was much better than what we'd been buying in our own neigh-borhood.

I loaded the needle up, injected it, and within a minute or two I felt drowsy. Then I didn't feel a thing. I just nodded off. My buddies had to smack me around to wake me up. And they kept on smacking me around to keep me alive. One of them was saying, "Let's take him to the hospital." And I was saying, "No, man, don't take me to no hospital." Even in the middle of all that crazy madness, I had a sense of well-being. I didn't fear a thing.

TYRONE: Even though I'm a junkie, I've still got my pride. I never let anyone *see* me shoot up. That's because I don't want anyone to know what I'm doing. Whenever I inject heroin or cocaine I'm alone. I'm sitting behind a closed door. My friends, my wife, my daughter—they might know what I'm doing, but none of 'em can say they actually seen me stick the needle in.

I figure, if I OD I'm going to die. I won't have nobody slapping me around and there won't be nobody calling no ambulance. I'll die with my privacy and my dignity intact.

TRAVIS: What's happening on the streets is tragic. So many young people dying. Sometimes it gets me depressed. I seen a lot of violence. I seen bodies lying dead in the gutter. I seen pools of blood. One time, I helped a couple of my friends die.

What happened was I gave them drugs that was too powerful. We were mixing cocaine and heroin together. That's called a speedball. A lot of my friends make a speedball by cooking the heroin and the cocaine up together. First they'll cook the heroin, then put the cocaine in the spoon and squirt the warm heroin on the cocaine. The mixture will dissolve, and they'll draw it up into the hypodermic and inject it. But what we was doing was using two hypodermic needles in the arm at the same time. I drew seventy-five cc's of heroin into one hypodermic and thirty-five cc's of cocaine into another, and they'd stick both needles in their arms. First you push a little heroin in, then a little cocaine, and when you feel the rush, you kick 'em both in all the way. That's what my two friends were doing with the drugs I gave 'em, and they both OD'd from the mixture. I tried to revive them, but I couldn't. There ain't no coming back off a cocaine overdose. So I left town for a couple of days to try and get my head together.

After that I never gave anybody any dope without trying it out on myself first. I used myself as a guinea pig. I have a strong suicidal instinct. Sometimes I feel like life ain't worth living no more. It's nothing but dope, crime, and disease. It makes me feel bad. If I OD, I ain't scared of death. Sometimes I feel like death would be a relief.

*   *   *

JENNIFER: I was in junior high when I started using cocaine. My parents knew something was wrong, but whenever they confronted me with it I'd sit there and lie to them. I'd tell them that I couldn't have a drug problem because I didn't do drugs. Then I'd steal money out of my dad's wallet to buy cocaine with.

I've always thought of myself as a really beautiful person, and I always knew my parents loved and cared about me. I never had any trouble getting dates, and I always had a lot of good friends. I didn't even know I was addicted to cocaine. But when I was sixteen I started doing things that made me lose respect for myself. I got into prostitution so that I could have enough money to buy drugs. I was working for escort services, and making a lot of money doing that.

One afternoon when I was at school my mother found out that I was into prostitution. She found a list of phone numbers in my bedroom. They were the phone numbers to the escort services I was working for and she called them up. Right away, she knew what I was doing. That was the last straw as far as my parents were concerned. They couldn't live with me anymore. They told me I had to go into treatment and quit using cocaine or leave the house. Basically, I had to choose between drugs and my family.

I chose cocaine. I dropped out of school, hooked up with these two guys who were dealers, and moved in with them. At first, they were really nice. They bought me beautiful jewelry and clothes, and took me to nice restaurants. They even bought me a car. I was still working for the escort service, so I always had lots of money. My attitude toward my parents was "Screw you. I don't need you."

Because these guys were dealers, I always got all of the drugs I wanted for free. I didn't have to pay for my cocaine anymore. One of the dealers sort of became my boyfriend, even though he was thirty-three years old and I was only sixteen. He had an overseas connection, and he'd buy cocaine by the kilo and cook it into crack right there in the house. Then he'd go out and deliver it to his customers. I thought only the lowlife black population smoked crack, because it has the reputation of being a ghetto drug. But hanging around with these dealers, I learned that crack is everywhere. A lot of professional people living out in the suburbs do it. My boyfriend wasn't selling on the street in the ghetto, he was selling to white people who had good jobs, plenty of money, and beautiful homes.

We never worried about the police. Out in the white neighborhoods the cops are blind, because there isn't the violence and murder associated with crack that you hear about in the inner cities. My boyfriend was making thousands of dollars a week selling crack, and the police never had any idea what was going on. It was like they didn't even exist. Out in the suburbs crack is an invisible epidemic.

My boyfriend didn't care if I used powder, but he didn't want me to use crack. He would always tell me, "Crack destroys you. Never mess with it, because it's the worst drug there is." That was fine with me. I always thought crack was the last thing in the world I'd ever do. But some of the men I went out with from the escort service liked crack. We'd have sex, and they'd light up the pipe. It was one of those drugs that was always around. So one night I tried it. I wanted to know why it was such a big deal. When my boyfriend found out he got very angry. We had a big fight. He beat me up and told me never to do it again. I was already addicted to powder, and once I smoked crack it was like I was ten times more addicted.

For the next six months I was smoking crack *all* the time. I'd do hit after hit after hit, and would go three, four, and five nights in a row without sleep. It would get to the point where I couldn't hold my body up anymore, and I'd sleep for two or three consecutive days. When I'd wake up the first thing I'd do would be put the pipe in my face.

Within four or five months of heavy crack use, I didn't even look like a human being. I lost a lot of weight, and my eyes looked terrible—all bloodshot and wired out. I looked like a person of the streets. My boyfriend let me have all the crack I wanted, but he wasn't nice to me anymore. Him and his friends would beat me and rape me. At parties they'd get real rough and throw me around the room. They'd tear off my clothes and screw me with a bunch of people in the room. Here I was sixteen years old getting raped by these men who were thirty and thirty-five years old. But I didn't try to leave. I continued to live in that environment. I continued to let them beat me and rape me, because I wanted crack.

A lot of the time, I'd hide in the closet and sit in there with my pipe. My body was bruised and scarred, but I couldn't feel any pain. I was afraid of the men I was living with, but all of my emotions were gone. Physically, I was still alive, but emotionally I'd committed suicide.

*   *   *

JAY: Shit, man, I'd been doing acid for about ten, twelve years. I never got too heavy into cocaine, though, because it screwed my sinuses up. I had problems with my nose every time I snorted. But when crack came out, I really liked that. I thought crack was a great high.

Because of all the drugs I was doing—acid, speed, PCP, crack, pot, alcohol—my thinking was really fucked up. I couldn't control my anger. I was having anxiety attacks, and I couldn't sleep. I was getting real paranoid. My temper was so bad that I beat my wife, and I was having all these weird, irrational fears. But the strange thing is, I never thought my problems were drug- or alcohol-related. I was telling myself, "I'm not an addict, and I'm not an alcoholic. What's happening here is I'm losing my fucking mind. I'm going crazy, and I'm going to end in a fucking mental institution."

Then I thought, "Well, shit, man. I'll end it before I let that happen. I'm not going to sit drooling in some corner. I'm not going to be like Chief Murphy in *Cuckoo's Nest* [reference to *One Flew Over the Cuckoo's Nest*]. They ain't doing lobotomies on me. I'll just end it."

I'd especially think like that when I was smoking crack. I'd remember the way Len Bias died, and I'd tell myself, "Maybe Lenny knew something. Maybe this is the way to end it."

I'd be hitting the pipe, and I'd feel my heart beating faster and faster. And I'd be thinking, "Yeah, this is going to work. I'll load up on more rock, and keep smoking until it blows my heart clean out of my chest."

LEE: I'm fifty-one years old. For seventeen years I worked as a truck driver. I've got a wife, five children, and seven grandchildren. After I got addicted to crack, I lost my job and my wife left me. I was no good to her.

I feel bad about that. Of course I do. I feel bad about the way I look. Do you think I like dressing in these filthy clothes? Do you think I'm proud of spending time in jail? I feel bad that my life got ripped up, and that my children are so ashamed of me they won't let me see my own grandchildren.

But I'm not going to quit smoking crack.

This is something you've got to understand. No addiction can get ahold of somebody so bad that they can't quit. And no drug treatment program in the world can save you. To quit, you've got to want to quit. You've got to want it more than you want the drug. And I don't want to quit. After losing my job and my wife, crack is all I got left. It's the only thing in the world that can still make me feel good.

CHAPTER 6

MEAN STREETS

Armed robbery, theft, and murder have soared as a consequence of the nation's drug epidemic. Police estimate that drug-related homicides have more than quadrupled in the past four years. When shootings that do not end in death are factored in, the statistics become even more staggering. Of course, the body count does not begin to measure the real costs of the drug war—the young careers ruined by the allure of easy money, the broken homes, the crime, the years lost to prison, and the tax dollars spent trying to control the epidemic are all part of the toll.

Spiraling murder rates are largely attributable to the internal warfare that is taking place among drug dealers in America's inner cities. "What most people don't understand is that drug violence has a logic behind it," says a young dealer currently serving a lengthy prison term. "It's like the Mafia, man. For the Mafia violence is a way of doin' business. It's the same thing in the dope trade. You don't go out killing 'cause you on a joyride. You got reasons, man. You doin' it to keep control of your business. If you want to rise in the drug game, man, you got to control your people. You got to control your turf. That's why you see so many Uzis on the street. Dudes is laying down the law, takin' control."

Street Justice

MICHAEL: The rule on the street is, you don't pay for nothing 'less the man can make you pay. If I can't make you pay me—why pay me? See, you got to be ready to do something to somebody, and you got to *be* doing things to people sometimes just to make sure everybody knows you got to be paid.

Sooner or later I got to shoot somebody or my worth on the street is gonna dwindle. A guy shot me two months ago, and I ain't retaliated yet. People gonna start to think I'm a punk. So it's got to happen. And it's gonna happen. It's part of the occupation, man. Just like you got to do certain things every now and then in your job, I got to do this myself—I can't have it done for me, and I got to do it where people gonna see it. I got a reputation to protect. I worked too long to get this reputation to see it go down the drain.

MARSHA: My sister and I and her boyfriend were in the car one night coming back from a movie. We stopped at the twenty-four-hour store on Indian Head Highway to get a few things, and as we were coming out we ran into this guy my other sister used to date. He was saying he had to go down to Condon Terrace to pick up money for the drugs he'd left there and had never got paid for. He was going on and on about how he had this "Uzi" and how he was going to force these people to pay him the money they owed him. I was wondering, "What's a Uzi? What's this crazy boy talking about?"

Well, we got back in the car and pulled out to the light. He pulled up next to us in his car, held up this thing that looked like a miniature machine gun and started waving "bye-bye" to us with it. I was saying, "Is that a Uzi? Is that what he's talking about?"

JEREMY: I've been all over this city, and I ain't never experienced nothing that caused so much misery as cocaine. Murders happen all the time. Killings is nothing, man. I've seen dudes get blown away, and I've seen dudes get beat to death with baseball bats. I've just barely escaped death myself.

Shit, I came out of my house one day and was just standing on the street. This was near where the hustlers was selling hand-to-hand. I was standing there, and this guy pulled up with a shotgun, jumped out of his car, and pointed the gun dead at me. He said, "Where's

my goddamn money?" Some dude on the street had just beat this
guy, and he thought it was me. The dude had sold him a bag full
of soap flakes, or stones, or something.

I said, "Man, it wasn't me. I just came out the door. I swear to
God it wasn't me."

This guy was real pissed off. I mean, he looked crazy. He kept his
gun on me, and was screaming, "It looked like you! You look like
that motherfucker!" I was sure he was going to shoot me. I was so
scared I shit my pants. I'm not joking, man. I crapped my britches.

One of the guys who was hustling on the street saw what was happening, and he came over. He told the dude that I didn't do it. He
said, "C'mon now, put that shotgun down. I'll take care of you." He
gave the dude a couple rocks, and got him all calmed down.

If that hustler hadn't come over and given him some cocaine, the
dude would've blown me away. That's the way it is on the street.
You can get killed for no good reason. Shit like that happens all the
time.

ELEANOR: There will be times when I'll be the only female out on
the strip selling drugs. I'll be out there with nothing but guys. My
product is always good, because if it isn't, I'm not going to be working. But some of these hustlers, they don't think like that. They
might be having trouble with their money, and they'll be trying to
rip the customers off. They'll sell demos. They'll wrap up soap or
candle wax or plaster so that it looks like crack cocaine, and they'll
sell it to the buyers driving up in their cars. You might be trying to
buy four fifties [fifty-dollar rocks], and this hustler will say, "Yeah,
yeah, man. I got fifties. Look at these here." And he'll show you
four rocks. You'll give the guy two hundred dollars, and he'll pass
you the four rocks. Only when you get home, you open it up to
smoke it and you find that you got nothing but soap. Now what you
going to do?

It's circumstances like that that lead to violence and killing. The
dude that got beat is going to go back and pay the hustler a visit,
and when he comes back he's going to have his gun. Standing on
the street, I've been witness to people getting shot and killed because
of rip-offs. I've seen more than five people get shot, and I've seen
more than five people die.

Stuff like that messes with your mind. It gets to where you can't
sleep, because the shit you've seen haunts you at night. You lying
in bed, and all you seeing is people dropping.

I even had a relative die in my arms. It was my uncle. He got stabbed by a female in an argument over some powder cocaine. After they exchanged words, my uncle came out of the house and was hanging out on the street, and this woman came looking for him. She had a knife, and she walked up behind him and started going crazy stabbing him. My uncle had a cast on his leg, so he couldn't defend himself too good. The cast was weighing him down, and she kept stabbing him and stabbing him.

I come up, and I can see what's happening. I see that it's my uncle. By the time I got to him, he's just laying there. Blood was pouring out of his back and his chest. I took him in my arms, but I didn't want him talking to me, because when he tried to talk the blood would rush out of his chest like a geyser. Every time he opened his mouth the blood would be gushing out. The blood would squirt in the air.

He died before the ambulance came, and it took me a long time to get over it. We was real close, living in the same house. After he was dead, there'd be times when I'd walk into a room, and I'd swear I could smell him. He wasn't alive no more, but I was still feeling him in the air. I could sense his presence inside the house.

TONY: This violence wave is butchering the hustling process. It don't make no sense. When I first started dealing heroin back in 1978 it wasn't like that. There wasn't so much unnecessary violence.

If I gave a dude a hundred quarters [small plastic bags of heroin], I'd expect him to give me three thousand dollars after he's been out selling. If I come to get my money and he says, "Man, I took some shorts. And some people who came by was sick, so I gave 'em some quarters because they was sick. I ain't got all your money. But here's a thousand dollars," I'd say, "No problem."

I'd give the dude forty more quarters and tell him he's got to make my money up. If I come around a second time, and he's been taking more shorts and still ain't got my money, I'd pull out my baseball bat. I'd beat the dude all up. I'd whop him across the ribs, and I'd bust his kneecaps. I'd make sure he was sore for a month. After that bat whopping, I'd *know* the dude was going to make my money up. I'd know he wasn't going to be taking no more shorts.

But these days, the young kids out hustling don't understand that. They don't understand the importance of fear. The only thing they care about is gold chains and fancy cars. If some dude smokes up some dealer's money, the dealer don't go back with a baseball bat and put the fear in the dude. He thinks he's got to save face, so he goes back with his gun and kills the dude straight off the top.

That to me is stupid. That's just butcherin'. It don't make no business sense.

THOMAS: Before I went to prison, I used to sell heroin in the neighborhood where I grew up, but when I got out everything had changed. Drugs had come out onto the street. These days, crack is where all the action is. So I started selling rock—which is a whole different world.

The thing that makes selling crack different is there's a lot more terror on the streets. I've seen dudes get shot and killed just because they didn't pay their cocaine bills. When you're selling heroin and come up short, the dude you're working for is going to give you a chance to work off what you owe him. But that can't happen with crack.

Once you start hitting the pipe instead of selling the product, you goin' to mess up big time. You might tell yourself, "I'm gonna get away for a minute. I'm gonna take a break." So you sit down and smoke a rock. The first taste of that high makes you say, "Damn, that was good." So you smokes you another rock. And another one. The next thing you know, you done smoked up three fourths of the man's product. At that point, the only thought goin' through your mind is "Well fuck, I done messed up this much of it, I might as well smoke the rest."

After that, you got to be running to duck the man. It ain't like no heroin bill. Your body can only absorb so much heroin, and by takin' shorts you might run up a five-hundred- or six-hundred-dollar bill. That ain't nothing. But with crack you can smoke up two thousand dollars' worth in a single afternoon. I've seen plenty of dudes do it. I've even done it myself. Now the average cocaine addict can't work off a two-thousand-dollar bill.

You can take a heroin addict, give him one shot just to keep the sickness off him, and tell him to go make his bill up and he'll go do it. But you can't tell a crack addict that he can have just one rock, and that he's got to sell the rest of the product to make his bill up, because after one hit on the pipe he's going to smoke up everything he's got.

The only way the dealers can control the sellers is by putting fear in them. If they shoot a dude for smoking up product, then the other sellers won't be messing up.

JEROME: When a dude messed my money up, I'd cut him with a knife or I'd shoot him. I did that lots of times. You know, I had bills to pay. I was buying weight, and I had to pay the dude that was fronting me. That's one of the things about the drug business—everybody's always owing somebody. I was buying thirty thousand or forty thousand dollars' worth of dope, cutting it myself, and then putting hustlers on the street to sell it. If I didn't pay the dude fronting me, he'd send his people out to knock me off. I'd be dead before I even realized what they was doing. In the drug business these are the things you got to worry about. It's the reason you got to be focused on your money.

Usually, the only people you're gonna find to sell drugs on the street are drug abusers. A dude that's shooting drugs will do damn near anything to maintain his habit. So you got to use him. If a dude messes my money up, I'll give him a second chance. I'll let him make it up, because I'm a fair dude. I treat the brothers good. But if a brother takes my kindness for weakness, then I got to put my mark on him. I got to get out the knife or the gun or the baseball bat.

I'm a good person. I never want to hurt nobody. But if I got to cut a dude or beat him about the head with a baseball bat, I never feel bad about it. That's because in the position I'm in, I can't afford to let nobody steal from me. The way I look at it is a person that steals from me don't care about who I owe or what might happen to me. The drug scene is violent, man. Very violent. If a dude messes up my money, he's putting my life on the line. Now how can I care about a dude like that?

A lot of dope fiends will be taking shorts, getting high, and giving dope to their girlfriends. Then they'll run away because they know they messed up. They owe me, but they ain't got no money. One thing about a dope fiend, though, is they're never hard to find. Even when they're hiding from you, they gonna be trying to get some dope. They're gonna show up somewhere. On the street, people know that I'm a good dude. If I'm trying to find somebody they'll tell me where he's at because they know I'll give 'em a bag of dope for the information.

If a dude is hiding from me, when I find out where he's at I'll show up with my knife and my people. He'll see me and know what I'm there for. I don't have to say nothin'. As soon as he sees me he'll start lying. Every time you go after a dude, they lie to you. They tell you, "Man, jump-out came by and took my stash. I been tryin' to get in contact with you, man. I been tryin' to find you." I don't go for that kind of shit. I don't waste no time listening. I just tell 'em, "You messed my money up, and it ain't going to happen no more." Then I make 'em bleed. I stab 'em in the stomach or beat 'em about the head. I don't do no talking, man. Everybody on the street knows what I'm doing. They know my money ain't to be messed with.

I try not to go through cycles where I got to cut dudes. I take care of business right away. If I let one dude get away with stealing my drugs and coming up short, the other dudes selling for me will think I'm soft. They'll do the same thing, and then I'll have five or six people coming up short. But if they see me take a stand with a knife, they'll say, "Bullshit on that. I ain't fucking around with Jerome's money. I ain't going to be bleeding on the floor like that dude there."

That's the way it is in the drug game. You've got to make your mark. You've got to let people know that you're serious about your money.

ALONZO: I remember one time I got jumped for messin' this dude's money up. I was working the street, doing hand-to-hand, and this dude I was working for come around and give me some coke. He said, "Look, man, I'll be back in two hours. If you don't have my money I'll blow your motherfuckin' brains out." That's because I'd messed his money up once before. He was giving me a second chance.

But as soon as the dude walked away, I run off again. See, when you messin' with crack you do crazy things. The dude just finished telling me he was gonna blow my fuckin' brains out, and I heard him. I believed him, 'cause he'd done it to other dudes. But when you got the craving, the coke'll talk to you. I heard the coke sayin', "Fuck that shit! Let's smoke and get high." The pipe was calling me, man. The pipe was sayin', "C'mon! C'mon! Let's get out of here!"

I run off to this girl's house. My intention was to screw this girl, 'cause I knew she liked to smoke. So me and her started in on these rocks. After we started smoking, I lost interest in sex. I was thinking,

"You can keep your drawers on, bitch. We'll just smoke." A lotta girls will do that. If you come to trick, they'll try to get you to smoke first, because they know you'll just want to keep smoking. You should always make 'em trick first. But that's not what I done this time.

Me and this girl smoked up *all* the dude's product. We just smoked and smoked and smoked 'til it was gone. I didn't have no money to give the dude, so I was ducking and hiding, trying to avoid him. But they found me going into a crack house. Eight dudes run up from behind and jumped me on the street. They got my arms pinned up over my head, and were carrying me by my arms and legs. They were taking me back around to this alley, and beating me with sticks and bottles. The dude whose money I messed up was there. He was yelling, "Didn't I tell you not to fuck my money up? I been good to you! And you keep fuckin' my money up!"

All the people in the neighborhood was looking out their windows, watching to see what was happening. The dudes carried me back in the alley, and I thought they was gonna kill me, because that's what the dude told me he was gonna do. But they just gave me a beating, man. They knocked me down, and whipped me with bottles and sticks. They whipped me bad. Kicking me in the ribs, and kicking me in the head, and beating me with these big ole two-by-fours. I was lying there all bloody, and the whole time they was whipping me I was thinking, "I wish they'd stop. I wish they'd let me go, so I can get a hit of 'caine, man. I *need* a hit."

And that's exactly what I did. When they finally stopped, I went upstairs to the crack house. People in there took pity on me. This dude said, "Man, we seen what happened to you." And he gave me a rock. Another dude gave me some heroin. I wasn't sitting in there two minutes before I had a hypodermic in my arm and the crack pipe in my hand.

DOUGLAS: I first started robbing to support my drug habit when I was a teenage kid. My partner and I was robbing people on the street, and we was stickin' up convenience stores and gas stations. We always got away, but there was never much money in it. You know, you rob some woman on the street and you might get fifty bucks and a couple of credit cards. You rob some store and you might get two hundred bucks.

We started robbing for bigger money when we began stickin' up people who were engaged in criminal activity. There are always a lot of hustlers out on the street doing hand-to-hand combat, and my partner and I started robbing them because they carried a lot of cash. Sometimes we could take two thousand or three thousand dollars off a single hustler. You watch the street and hit five or six hustlers a night, man, you makin' some serious money. When I robbed a hustler, I always made it a point to never hurt the dude as long as he didn't buck. And I'd never raise my voice. I'd just walk up to the dude, put my gun in his face, and tell him to keep quiet. I'd keep my voice normal, because I didn't want no scene, man. I didn't want no attention. I just wanted to get the dude's money and get the fuck out of the area.

But the street is violent, man. Hustlers is always looking out for stickup boys. When you're making a living robbing drug dealers, there are going to be times when you're ducking bullets, and there are going to be times when you've got to use your gun.

The first time I had to shoot a dude, it was a traumatic experience for me. This guy was a hustler out selling hand-to-hand. I put a gun on him and said, "Don't move, man! Just keep real still! Do not move!" But the dude bucked, and reached for his vest pocket. I didn't know if he had a gun or not, but I was watching his hands. When he went for his vest, I thought, "Holy shit! This guy has a weapon!" So I shot him. When I fired, it was like the whole world was moving in slow motion. I could see the bullet go into the dude's chest, and the force of the blast lifted the dude off his feet and knocked him to the ground.

I saw the dude lying on the sidewalk, and I ran like hell. It was broad daylight and I was shooting this guy on the street. That scared me. I thought maybe some of his buddies was gonna come after me. When I finally stopped running, my knees were knocking and my hands were shaking. It was very emotional, 'cause I'd never had to shoot nobody before. I thought maybe the dude was dead. That maybe I'd killed him. The next morning I read the newspaper real close, looking to see if there was anything in there about a murder on Cicero Street. I figure the dude must've lived, because I never saw nothin' in the paper about no murder.

JOHN: I worked the street as a runner for this dealer named Sammy for about four or five months. Then I took up with another dude across the street. Sammy didn't like that. He thought this guy was invading his turf. He saw me on the street a couple of times, but he never said nothin'.

Then one day he come right up to me and put his gun in my face. He was waving it in front of me, and he fired a shot right past my ear.

I started running. I ran toward the crack house I was working for, because I knew those guys in there had guns too. I thought maybe they would protect me. Sammy was chasing me, and yelling curse words. When I got in front of the apartment, I turned and looked back to see how close he was. That's when he shot me. He hit me in the leg. I crawled into the crack house, and told the dude I was working for that I'd been shot. He called the ambulance and I went back outside. I laid down in the street and waited for the ambulance to come.

MOHAMMED: I've been in prison three years now, and in the time I've been here, five of my close associates have been killed out on the street. These are buddies that I used to run with. They've had their brains blown out, or they've been stabbed. One of 'em was found beaten to death in a trash can. All of 'em due to retaliation. All of 'em was killed for messin' some dude's money up.

One time, before I come in here, I was standing with a dude when he was killed. Me and him used to go hustling together. He'd just beat some dude, and this dude had his people out looking for my friend. We was standing on the street corner, and this guy drove up in a car, jumped out with a shotgun, and blew my buddy's head off. I seen the guy's car, but I didn't know the dude that done it.

There was a lot of people on the street, and everybody got all excited. They was screamin' and hollerin', and running up. They want to see what's happening. The motherfucker's body is lying there, and they see that. His head is splattered all over the place, and they look at that. Everybody's all around, pushing to get a look. Then the police come, and everybody's runnin'. Ain't nobody want to get involved with that shit.

You'd think that after you see your buddy get his head blown off it would make you stop messin' with crack. But your craving overrides your caring and your concern. You want to know what you do when something like that happens? You reach down in your dead buddy's pocket, and take whatever drugs he's got left. Then you go get high with it.

That's what I done. I went up to this crack house. Everybody was passing the pipe and tellin' each other what they seen. They was all excited, talking real fast. "Damn, did you see that shit, man? That dude's head was over on the sidewalk, man. I mean, his ear was way over there, man, and his eyeball was way over here." The whole time they're talking, they're taking hits. They're saying, "Pass me the pipe, man. C'mon, pass it over here." I was in there smoking, listening to 'em talk. "Damn, man, did you see that dude's head?"

ROBERT: I had one instance where these older dudes who were well established in the drug business tried to beat me and my partner. They thought they could beat us because we were young. They sold us some bad dope—some heroin that had been cut with rubber.

My partner and I were looking at it, saying, "This is bullshit. I ain't going for this." I've got a raw habit, and I've got to have my dope. My partner is doing all the talking, and he tells the dudes, "You've got to straighten this out. This is not what we paid for. You make it right, or you give us our twenty-five hundred dollars back."

The dude jumps up and says, "Young motherfucker, this is what you paid for! This is your dope!"

I said, "Wait a minute." And I put my gun on the table. I said, "Man, this gun ain't young."

The dude sees that we're serious, and he says okay, okay he'll come back and make it right. So my partner and me are sitting there in the projects waiting on this dude. We're there all afternoon and into the night. We're standing at the window looking out at the parking lot, and about six-thirty my partner says, "They ain't coming back." I said, "Man, I ain't going for this. They done got all our money."

Two days later I see one of the dudes pull into the parking lot and he goes up into another apartment in the projects. I take my nine-millimeter and put it into my shoulder holster and pick my shotgun up off the table. My partner grabs his gun and the two of us go down and hide in the parking lot to wait for the dude.

I'm ready to hurt someone. This is business, and I'm strapped down for action. There's no doubt in my mind that if this dude don't get things straight, then he's going to die. Pretty soon, he comes walking back and gets into his car. I jump up, put my shotgun to his head, and say, "Man, don't move. Whatever you do, don't move." I said, "Where is my money? Where is my dope? If you don't have mine, you'd better be prepared to meet your maker."

The dude is saying, "Don't hurt me, man. Please don't hurt me."

I pulled him out of the car, and said, "I want mine. And I want it right now."

He said, "I ain't got but five hundred dollars and a couple quarters of this dope here."

I said, "Man, that ain't going to get it. I want all of mine."

My partner and I took him over to our car, shoved him in, and went driving over to the other dude's house who was with this guy when they ripped us off. I've got a shotgun to his back, and he goes up and knocks on the door. The dude's wife looks out the little peep hole, sees his face there, so she opens the door. The other dude is in the bedroom. I run back there, smack him with my shotgun real hard, and tell him, "I want mine." We tie both these dudes up, take five thousand dollars in cash and twice the amount of dope we paid for. And it's *good* dope. This dude is mad, mad, mad at me, because I'm tying him up in front of his wife and children. I tell him, "You shouldn't fuck with me, motherfucker!" Then me and my partner walk out the door.

I wasn't there to hurt the dude. I was just there to get mine.

I'm out on the street, and I hear that these two dudes have a contract out on me. They want me dead. But I'm wild. I figure that's right down my alley, and I cover my backside. I keep my nine-millimeter in my holster, and I carry my shotgun on a shoulder sling under my coat. My weapons go wherever I go.

One day when I'm getting out of my car, this dude calls out my name, and as I turn around he opens fire with a twenty-five automatic. He shoots me in the hip. I bring my shotgun up and pull out the nine-millimeter. I'm working with both hands. I'm all automatic. It's boom-boom-boom-boom-boom! He's got three dudes with him, and they all hit the ground. They're all hiding under a car. Those dudes all got hurt. I don't think any of them died, but they all got hit. I wasn't shooting to kill them. I was just trying to get them off my back.

I went home, got my machine gun, and went over to the dude's house that put the contract out on me. I stood out in front of that dude's house and just opened up. I blew out the front windows and the front door with about fifty rounds.

After that, these two dudes realized, "Hey, this young motherfucker is crazy!" They said they wanted to make peace, and that they wanted to hire me. I said, "No way, man. I'm independent. If you want to make peace, that's cool. But I ain't doing none of that other stuff. I ain't working for you motherfuckers."

*   *   *

JEROME: I got two younger brothers, Ben and Darrin. They could
see how much money I was making selling drugs, and one day Ben
came to me and told me he wanted to get into hustling. He wanted
me to front him drugs to sell. But I told him, "No. It's too violent.
The stickup boys be robbing and shooting. Buddies be killing buddies." I told him, "The game's got way out of shape." It used to be
you could be relaxed when you was selling. You didn't have to worry
too much. But these days the people you grew up with will kill you.
You got all these young bucks coming into the game, and they be
shooting everybody up. I told Ben that, but he didn't pay no attention. He got into hustling. And he was doing real good too. He
bought a Nine–twenty-eight Porsche and a brand-new condo.

Then in 1988 I got locked up on a drug distribution charge. My
brother Darrin, who's even younger than Ben, he used to come over
and see me in maximum security. I'd tell him, "Darrin, don't get
involved in selling drugs." He was working a job, and I'd tell him,
"Man, I love the way you got that job." But he knew how much
money Ben was making, and he told me, "Man, I'm gonna get me
some money together. I can't do that working this job."

So Darrin started selling drugs too. The way it is now, if you got
the best dope on the street, people will be jealous of you. If they cut
their dope all to shit, they going to try to get you away from their
territory because your dope be better than theirs. Darrin used to tell
me about that. He'd say, "Man, those dudes are jealous because I'm
selling all my dope, but they ain't making no money." Darrin never
done nothing to hurt nobody. He didn't even carry no pistol to put
fear in dudes or send them on the run. He was just out there selling
'caine.

One day Darrin was walking down the street where we live, and
this dude came up to him to slow him down. He started talking to
him, and this other dude with a gun came up from behind a building. Darrin tried to run, but the first dude clipped him and knocked
him down, and the other dude ran up and shot him from behind.
He shot him twice in the back, once in the neck, and once in the
hand. My sister Terri heard all the screaming and shooting, and she
went running out to Darrin. He was trying to get up, and she said,
"No, Darrin, stay there. Stay there." He was lying on the ground
telling her, "It was Everett that shot me. Tell Ben. Tell Ben that
Everett shot me." I guess he could feel himself going into uncon-
sciousness, so he hollered out the name of the dude that shot him.

The police came and they took Darrin to the hospital on a Med-Star helicopter. My sister Terri was right there the whole time.

I was in prison. I didn't know about none of this, but that night I called a friend of mine, and she told me, "Did you know that Darrin got shot?" I said, "No!" I hung up the phone and called home. This lady was there that was a friend of my mother's. She answered the phone and she was crying. I said, "What's happened?"

She told me, "Darrin's been shot. Everett did it."

"How bad is he?"

"The doctor is saying he might not make it until tomorrow. If he can make it to tomorrow, the doctor says he'll have a good chance."

That night I prayed and prayed. Man, I prayed. Then in the morning I called home again, and my neighbor told me, "Darrin's dead. He died a couple hours ago."

Man, I can't tell you how bad that made me feel. I was just standing there holding the phone, thinking, "Damn! Darrin never done nothing to nobody. They set him up just because his clientele was good. They was jealous and they killed him." I know the dudes that done it. They thought they could get away with it.

After they killed Darrin they knew they had to do something about my brother Ben. They thought there'd be revenge. They was afraid Ben would retaliate, and they paid somebody to kill Ben. This young dude, nineteen years old, came up and shot Ben in the head. So now both my brothers is dead.

I really miss them. The best way to put it is to say that I grieve a lot—I grieve for my mother and my family. My sister Terri, she was pregnant when Darrin was shot, and because of the stress she had her baby one month early. A little baby boy, and that boy died too.

Emergency Rooms

SUSAN O'NEILL [nurse]: I had a sheltered upbringing. I mean, I knew there were drugs in the world, and I knew people were using them, but I never experienced any of it directly. Then I came to work in the hospital, and the first drug victim I saw was a little child. Her father got high, and then he raped her and threw her off the roof. I remember looking down at this little girl, thinking, "My God, I'm not going to be able to handle this job."

*   *   *

DR. PAUL ORIAFO [surgeon]: Up until the end of 1987 the trauma unit only saw an occasional gunshot wound. Most of the patients brought in had injuries that resulted from a serious automobile accident or a fall from heights—that sort of thing. The injuries that were caused by violence tended to involve the use of a baseball bat, a lead pipe, or a knife.

We'd see an occasional gunshot wound, but not more than maybe two or three a week. But in 1988 that changed dramatically. All of a sudden we began seeing two or three gunshot wounds *every day*. And right now, our unit is averaging five gunshot wounds a day.

Prior to 1988, when a serious trauma was announced people would say, "Oh my God, there's a gunshot wound in the ER!" They'd be very curious and would want to see what a gunshot victim looked like. Not anymore. When we have a serious trauma now, and are working under the Code Yellow alarm, nobody pays too much attention. They just shrug their shoulders and say, "Oh, another gunshot wound."

DR. SANDRA EZELL [surgeon]: In 1988 the type of patient we received in the emergency room started to change. We started seeing more and more multiple gunshot wounds, with the wounds located in the areas where there are vital organs—the head, the chest, the abdomen. Which means we're seeing a lot more patients who die.

Even those who are lucky enough to be shot in the extremities tend to be much more seriously wounded. In the old days, if a healthy young male was shot in the thigh, chances are the bullet would either lodge in the muscle or pass on through without doing any serious damage. But now the bullets are so big that they fracture arms and legs. These days, if a healthy young kid gets shot in the thigh, there's a good chance that he'll be brought in with a completely shattered leg.

DR. MICHAEL LIPPE [surgeon]: One Saturday night the fire department called saying they had an ambulance on the way with three gunshot victims, one with CPR in progress. I immediately organized the triage. Because we're literally seeing battlefield conditions, our triage is like a military system—you take the people who are dead or certain to die, and put them to one side. You focus your resources on the living. Someone with half his head blown off and an agonal pulse is not going to make it, and to dump twenty-four units of blood into him would just deplete valuable resources.

On this night, the ambulance came in and I took one look at the kid under CPR and I knew he was not going to make it. "He's dead," I said. "Get him off to the side." The other two victims had multiple abdominal wounds. We put them into surgery and went right to work on them. Eventually, one of them died, but the other survived and spent a long convalescence in the intensive care unit.

After everything settled down, I went back with a nurse to write up a chart and categorize the guy we'd left in triage. We took his shirt off, and there was a gunshot wound in his shoulder, two in his upper chest, and another in the center of his chest. This guy had wounds all over him. We counted seventeen holes in him. This was the first automatic weapon injury I'd seen, and I could see where the stream of bullets had chewed him to pieces. Somebody must've waved a machine gun back and forth across him, because the pattern of his wounds was like a Z across his torso.

DR. KENNETH LARSEN, JR. [surgeon]: One time a guy came driving up to the ambulance bay in a Mercedes. He had six kids in his car, and they'd *all* been shot. He parked the Mercedes in the ambulance entrance, walked in, and said, "Okay, I need one stretcher and three wheelchairs. The other two can still walk."

The crew went out to get the kids, and he's telling them, "Be careful pulling them out of the car. I don't want any blood on the upholstery."

At least this guy had the decency to walk in. Usually what happens when there's been a drug shooting is they'll drive up to the ambulance entrance, open the door, push the victim out of the car onto the pavement, blow the horn, and drive away. Whenever we hear a horn blow, we know what we've got. We don't even walk to the ambulance area without a stretcher now.

On one occasion some guy drove up, rolled his buddy out, and left without blowing the horn. A little while later another patient came in and said, "By the way, did you know you had someone lying in a pool of blood in your ambulance bay?"

DR. MICHAEL LIPPE: We had one case where some people drove up, pulled a guy out of the car, stuck him in a wheelchair, and wheeled him into the hospital lobby. Then they took off. The guy they'd left had OD'd, and was stone-cold dead. His buddies didn't want to get into any trouble so they disappeared. This guy had been sitting there about twenty minutes when a security guard walked over to see if he was going to register or leave. He nudged him to wake him, and the guy slumped over. The guard comes in and tells us, "Hey, you've got a dead person sitting in the lobby."

DR. SANDRA EZELL: Cops like to complain about repeat offenders—guys that they bust four or five times a year. Well, in the emergency room we see repeat offenders too. After I'd been working on the trauma team for a while, I realized I was patching up gunshot wounds in guys who'd been shot two, three, or four times before.

When the repeaters come in, I never recognize their names or faces. As a surgeon operating in an emergency situation, I don't pay too much attention to who I'm working on. I'm too busy trying to stop the bleeding, assess the damage, and take whatever steps are necessary to save the life or stabilize the patient. Sometimes I'll cut away bloody clothing and recognize a scar from a previous wound—a wound that I treated. One time I tore open a guy's shirt and saw stitches that were the result of a bullet hole in the abdomen. I'd sewn those stitches into that guy only a few nights before. It gives you a strange damn feeling to be looking at fresh wounds and remembering the bullet you just pulled out of the guy. But it happens—it happens a lot more often than you'd think.

A lot of the repeaters will talk quite nonchalantly about their scars. You ask them, and they'll say, "Oh, yeah, I got this scar back when I was shot in January. And this one here is from when I got stabbed a year ago."

They'll have big nasty scars all over their torsos, and they'll be talking about them as if they were nicks they got from their morning shave.

DR. PAUL ORIAFO: The weekends are unbelievable. The hallways are always packed with patients. It starts on Friday and doesn't let up until Monday. It's not uncommon to have three, four, or five gunshot wounds come in within a span of an hour or two. They'll descend all at once. Then, on top of that, the police are bringing in overdose cases and people who've gone psychotic from PCP.

The police are all part of the mix. They'll be in the halls trying to restrain patients, and plainclothes detectives will be asking victims

questions. Some guy might be lying there dying, and the police will
want to know who shot him. So it's an incredibly chaotic environment in which to try and practice medicine.

I remember one weekend not too long ago when I had seven major
trauma patients come in between midnight and two A.M. One guy
was brought in who had been shot in the left temple. The bullet was
lodged behind his right eye, and the eyeball was hanging down about
to drop out completely. Another guy was brought in right after that
who'd been shot in the chest at point-blank range with a forty-five-
caliber bullet. I could see the bullet and the path it had traveled on
the X ray. The bullet had gone from one side of his rib cage to the
other, and he was paralyzed from the waist down.

We went right to work on the guy who'd been shot in the temple.
He was drowning in his own blood and couldn't breathe. The anes-
thesiologist couldn't intubate him through the nose because the bullet had ripped out all the bones in his nasal area, and she couldn't
intubate him in the mouth because he was bleeding so profusely she
couldn't see inside his oral cavity. We had to perform a tracheotomy
and cut through his throat just so he could breathe.

While we were doing all this, the guy who'd been shot in the chest
was starting to bleed to death. He was dying from exsanguination.
He started asking us, "Am I going to die?" We told him we were
doing the best we could, and we would keep doing the best we could.
He was perfectly aware of what was happening. Then he asked,
"Doc, am I ever going to walk again?" We said we didn't think so.
Once again, he asked, "Am I going to die?" He asked us that several
times. Then he started having short breaths, agonal breathing, and
that's when we knew he wasn't going to make it.

I opened his chest up to try to save him. There were holes everywhere. He had a big hole in his heart, a big hole in his aorta, and
a big hole in his vena cava. I took one look and knew it was not a
salvageable case. He was twenty-one years old, and he died within
thirty minutes of arrival.

While we were working on these two guys, three more gunshot
wounds came in along with a couple of overdose cases. One kid was
seventeen years old. He'd been shot just above the navel. He was
vomiting copious amounts of blood, and he'd *walked* in. His uncle
was with him, and he'd been shot too. As if that wasn't enough,
an ambulance brought in a big fat guy that had been shot in the
buttocks.

By this time, we had seven major trauma patients. Then we get a call saying three more are on the way. Law enforcement officers were all over the place trying to get statements from the victims. I remember standing in the middle of all that chaos, overwhelmed with major trauma cases—all of them gunshot wounds and overdoses. I couldn't help but wonder, "Hey, what's going on here? Are we experiencing a total breakdown of law and order?"

DR. KENNETH LARSEN: The kids really run the gamut. They range from a lot of macho bluster to crying for mommy. You meet very few genuine tough guys on the operating table. I've had a lot that plead with me, "Don't let me die! Please, don't let me die!"

I can't let that get to me. I just tell them, "Be quiet and do what you're told, and you'll live." You want to get the patients to use their own energy and apply it to helping in their own care. You want them to concentrate on what you want them to do, and keep them from thinking that they're going to die. It's generally a bad sign when they say they're going to die, because about eighty-five percent of the time they're right. What you want is to get them to will themselves to live.

DR. MICHAEL LIPPE: There are times when a patient who has been shot will say, "I want to talk to a priest. I'm going to die. Let me see a priest." Obviously, the patient needs emotional support, but it's also the time that is most crucial for us—when we're doing everything we can to save him. Frequently, we'll try to push those fears aside by telling him, "You're not going to die. Just cooperate with us and you won't die."

I've had some that keep on saying they're going to die. They'll start calling out for their mother. That gets to you, but you try to ignore it and keep on working—keep your attention focused on getting the IV in, on getting their blood pressure up, on stopping the bleeding. Still, you hear them, and it gets to you.

DR. PAUL ORIAFO: A young man in his early twenties was rushed in, and his mouth was in shreds. It looked as if something had exploded inside his mouth. His tongue was hanging out, the kid's eyeballs were popping out of his head. His face was very red, his mouth drooling saliva and blood, and the tongue shattered.

I'd never seen anything like it. It was very hard to work with him.

There was another doctor there, and I told him that maybe he should handle it because it was too hard for me to look at. But it bothered the other doctor too.

Naturally, this kid couldn't talk. He could only make sounds. We asked him what happened to him, and he indicated with his hands that some people had forced him to kneel down and put a gun in his mouth. He made a gun with his finger and thumb, pointed it in his mouth, and pulled the trigger.

He was gurgling terribly and we had trouble intubating him. We had to open his neck for breathing, and his face was swelling by the minute. He made it out of the ER, though. We kept him alive, and got him into intensive care. Oral surgeons worked on him, and the ear, nose, and throat people worked on him. But his wounds were just impossible, and he died four days later.

In the last few minutes he kept gurgling at us, trying to speak. I could understand him, and he was saying, "Doc, I don't want to die, Doc."

I don't care how hardened you are, that gets to you.

DR. SANDRA EZELL: About a month or so ago a kid came in that I can't forget. A fifteen-year-old boy who had been shot in the chest four times with large-caliber bullets.

I opened his chest, and there was a very large tear in his aorta. It looked like a hole you might tear in a sheet. His chest was full of blood, and there were bullet and fragment holes in his heart. The heart is supposed to be firm and muscular, but his heart was flat as a pancake, which meant all the blood had leaked out. It wasn't pumping anything.

What struck me was that his lungs were nice and pink and clean. It was obvious he wasn't a smoker, and I thought, "My goodness, he took care of that part of his life. He took care of his health." It just underscored the fact that this boy was so young and fresh. He had lungs like a baby's—as pink as bubble gum. And look what happened to him. He died in the ER. I remember asking myself, "For what? He died for what?"

DR. MICHAEL LIPPE: Opening a chest requires a genuinely heroic effort. What we're usually trying to do in these drug-related shootings is get a clamp on the aorta and sew up a hole in the heart.

Under normal circumstances chest openings don't happen very often. I did my emergency medicine residency at a hospital with an active trauma center, and in three years I saw a total of three chest openings. In two years at this hospital I have personally opened twenty-eight chests—an average of more than one a month.

Anyone involved in drug dealing should know what's waiting for him in the emergency room. We have a routine procedure that we follow. When a patient is being brought in with a penetrating wound such as a gunshot or stab wound to the chest, we ask the emergency medical technicians if any vital signs were present when he was found in the field—a pulse, an audible moan. Anything. Because if he arrives with no signs, odds are it's too late. He's already as good as dead.

If only the lungs have been hit, you can correct that with a tube. The procedure requires an incision under the ribs where you insert a tube that drains whatever has collected in the chest area. If there's bleeding in the chest, then blood collects around the lungs, and the lungs collapse because of the weight surrounding them. Once you drain the blood, the lungs will be able to expand.

In some cases you'll insert a chest tube, get a *massive* amount of blood, but the vital signs fail to return. In those cases, you don't have time to go to the operating room. You've got to open the guy's chest right on the spot, right there in the emergency department, and hope that you can stop the bleeding. Emergency physicians are constantly forced to make split-second decisions that have major consequences. Hopefully, you make the right decision most of the time. In these drug-related shootings we're seeing today, you'll be looking at a patient whose life is sinking in front of you. You're standing there thinking, "He's gonna be dead if I don't do something drastic. I've got to go for broke."

To open a chest, you make an incision on the left side of the torso just below the nipple, and wind the incision down around the side all the way to the tip of the left shoulder blade. You do this with a standard scalpel, slicing along the fourth rib. Then you come back and slice again, this time a little deeper so that you cut right down to the rib. Then you pick up a pair of scissors, and puncture a hole through the chest wall. If you keep the scissors close to the rib you can strip the muscles away and get the chest open from there. In less than thirty seconds—*wham*, you pop through, and *bam*, the chest is open.

Then you take the rib spreaders, which have two flanges and a crank, and you fit the flanges between the third and fourth ribs. You crank it so that it separates the ribs, and you have enough room to get your hands inside.

Usually, there's a rush of blood, a huge clot that just falls out. A gush of blood will fall onto the floor. I've had to throw away three or four pairs of shoes since I started working here because they've been soaked with blood. I've had to shower after opening chests because blood will be flying all over the place. We've moved our trauma resuscitation room from the back of the emergency department to the front, because getting one of these people to the resuscitation room meant carrying them on a stretcher, and there was a constant trail of blood through the length of the department.

Once you've cleaned the blood from the chest cavity, you reach for the pericardium sack, which encases the heart. You make an incision in the sack, because it will frequently be filled with blood, and the blood is pressing in on the heart. You drain the blood in the sack, put your hand inside, find the hole in the heart, and plug it with your finger. Doing that *can* save somebody's life.

I had one guy with a single gunshot wound to the left ventricle, and I was able to plug the hole and get his vital signs back. I was standing there like the little Dutch boy with my finger in the dike. There have been other times when I walked from the emergency room with my hand inside somebody's chest giving them open-heart massage while we're wheeling the patient to the operating room.

After you've opened the pericardium, you want to cross-clamp the aorta, which is the main blood vessel feeding blood to the rest of the body. Most of these people have lost half to three quarters of their total blood volume so they're in *profound* shock, and it becomes a waste of time and a waste of whatever's left of the body's capabilities to keep pumping blood to the legs or arms. Those areas can do without blood for a while, but the brain and the heart and the kidneys can't. So you cross-clamp the aorta so the blood supply is forced to the upper part of the body where it's needed. Then you go about repairing whatever damage you can, and replacing lost blood.

Obviously, chest opening is an extreme measure, a last-ditch thing, and most of these patients don't survive. Of the twenty-eight chests I've opened only two have survived long enough to get to the operating room, and neither of those two left the hospital alive. You know when you begin that the patient is probably going to die, but you're doing everything you can. Occasionally, you'll save a life, but most of the time you're not going to succeed. That's especially true these days with the caliber of ammunition that is being used on the street in these drug shootings. If the heart is hit, it's going to be destroyed, and there's no way the victim is going to survive.

Rivers of Blood

THOMAS: I got stabbed real bad one time. I was working for this dude and I left the scene and didn't come back for several hours. The dude thought I was trying to rip him off. Actually, I was just trying to hide from the jump-out squad. There had been a couple of busts nearby, so I split. I got high, and came back a few hours later.

Anytime you're working for a drug organization, you're supposed to inform your people whenever you leave your post. I failed to do that. When I went back out on the street to start selling again, one of the higher-ups came around and told me that I had violated the rules. Him and another guy took me around behind a building and they pushed me around a little bit. They were telling me that I had to stick to the rules. I didn't like that and I pushed back. I was trying to defend myself. Then this dude pulled a knife, and he stabbed me three times. Real quick.

It happened so fast I didn't even know how bad I was cut until I got halfway down the street. My finger had almost been cut off, and that was all I was worried about. I was running down the street to get help, and all of a sudden I felt faint. I stopped running and reached down to touch my stomach, and I was all wet. I was bleeding like crazy and feeling real hot. When I fainted I thought it was all over. I thought I was dying.

An ambulance came and got me and took me to the hospital. A couple of days later the police started asking me questions. They wanted to know "Who did it? Who stabbed you?" I was lying in my hospital bed thinking, "I ain't dead. But if I start talking I'll end up dead." So I told the police that I didn't know nothing. I said I didn't see who stabbed me.

This cop knew I was lying. He knew what the game was all about. But there wasn't much he could do. He wrote down what I said so he could put it in his report, and then he left.

ALONZO: I don't have a problem with shooting somebody, as long as it's for the right reasons. If somebody violates you, man, you got to take a stand.

This one dude I know messed up this other dude's money, and to keep hisself from a beating, he told the dude that I stole the money. Which wasn't true. He'd done smoked up all the man's product, then blamed it on me. Now I had a reputation for fucking up people's money, so the dude believed him. He sent his people out, and they jumped me and whopped me real bad. They paid me a star whipping. One of 'em had a baseball bat, and somebody stopped him from doing my head. Otherwise I'd be dead right now.

I ain't never had a problem with getting whopped up on for something I done. I can handle that. I'll just crawl away and lick my wounds. But I thought these dudes was whipping me for no reason. After they was through, I was lying there dazed, and they told me why they done it. They told me what this guy said I done.

Well, that ain't right. I figured I had to give the guy what was coming to him. I went and borrowed a gun from a friend of mine, and I caught up with the dude on the front porch of a crack house. I asked him, "Why'd you do that, man?"

He said, "I didn't do it. It wasn't like that."

I said, "I took a terrible beating, man. I took a beating because of what you done."

He was going, "No, no, man. I didn't say nothing like that."

I wasn't going to listen to them lies. The dude knew what he done. So I shot him. I shot him in the leg. I didn't want to kill him or nothing, I just wanted to make him pay for what he done. I wanted to let him know he couldn't violate me.

The ambulance came and took him away, but he didn't tell the police who shot him. He didn't tell 'em nothing. The next time I saw the dude on the street, I spoke to him. I said, "Hey, man, what's happening?"

He nodded at me, and said, "What's happening?" And we kept going on. He knew what he'd done. He knew he'd started something, and I'd finished it. After that we left it behind. If I see him, I'll talk with him. I ain't got no more beef with the dude.

BARRY ANFANG [detective]: When I was working uniform patrol my partner and I got an assault call. We went into the tenement where the disturbance was reported, and when we went inside the first thing I saw was blood spattered all along the hallway. This was my first big bloodbath.

We found this lady lying on the floor. What had happened was she was a junkie, and she'd gone to bed with a dealer to get some dope. Her boyfriend figured out what was going on, and went to town on her. He hit her over the head with a baseball bat, and then took a knife and slit her open. He cut a big cross into her chest—slit her from her throat all the way down her belly, then he slashed a deep cut across her breasts.

What amazed me was that after all the blood I'd seen on the walls and in the hall and on the ambulance sheets the lady lived. She lived because the heroin had depressed her system and that prevented her from bleeding to death. Basically, she was too high to die.

JERRY [homicide detective]: We got a call over the radio informing us that there had been a shooting out on the old Meredith Highway near the Baptist church. We went racing out there with the siren blaring. When we arrived at the scene the victim was still in his car. He was a teenage kid, and he was in the front seat sitting behind the steering wheel. He'd been shot right between the eyes at point-blank range.

This was an obvious drug assassination. This kid had been driving a brand-new 300 Z and he was wearing all kinds of gold. He had a beeper on his belt, and when the ambulance technicians lifted him forward a wad of about three thousand dollars in cash fell from his coat pocket. One look at that bullet hole, and I knew he wasn't going to make it. But he was still alive, and he could still talk.

After we got him into the ambulance I leaned real close to him and said, "This is serious. You've been shot, and I don't think you're going to survive. Do you understand what I'm telling you?"

He nodded yes.

"Before you die," I said, "do you want to tell me who shot you?"

He looked me square in the face, and in a voice husky with blood, said, "No."

JOE SCHWARTZ [homicide detective]: Nobody wants to get involved in a drug murder case. Witnesses are extremely reluctant. They're afraid. They think that if they testify they're going to get killed. Which is true a lot of times. Witnesses get threatened. They get hurt. They get killed.

Last night I went over to the Twenty-four-hundred block of Fourteenth Street, where a guy had been shot in the chest. The victim was a drug dealer, and he was still conscious when we arrived on the scene. One of our detectives interviewed him, and he told the detective, "Fuck you. I ain't telling you shit. I'll take care of it myself."

Half an hour later that guy died. So we had a homicide on our hands. We tried to interview his friends and relatives, but they all told us the same thing: "Fuck you. We'll take care of it ourselves."

That's the sort of thing a homicide detective deals with constantly. It never ends. I've had family members who are witnesses to the murder of their uncle or their son, and they won't tell me anything, except to go fuck off.

You can't help but get disgusted at people. When you're involved in situations where it's drug dealers shooting drug dealers, and none of the witnesses will talk, you feel like taking the case and putting it on the shelf. Saying, "To hell with it. Let 'em kill each other."

And if you want to know the truth, more and more cases are being handled that way.

DR. PAUL ORIAFO: A nineteen-year-old kid was brought into the emergency room recently, and we were told he was one of the big drug kingpins in the city. He was shot in the right side, but the bullet didn't do much damage. We treated him, kept him one night, did all the tests we needed, determined it was nothing serious, and decided to release him.

Naturally, there were investigating police officers asking him what had happened. They wanted to know when it happened, where, who it was, and if he wanted to press charges. He kept saying, "Don't worry about it, man. I'll take care of it myself."

That caught everybody's attention. The man says he's going to take care of it himself. I said, "Hold on. You're telling me we're going to have another customer here soon?" Because that's what he meant.

Well, we've heard a lot of tough talk before, so we released him and nobody thought too much about it. Six days later this same guy was brought back into the hospital with three bullet holes in his head. By the time he gets to us he's already brain-dead.

That was the guy that was going to take care of it himself.

MONTY SUDER [homicide detective]: We're getting more and more cases, and we have less and less information to work with. Witnesses refuse to cooperate, and when they do talk, they lie. Relatives of the victim will look you in the face and lie to you about what happened to their son or daughter, husband or wife.

Not too long ago we had a case where a kid who was a runner owed a dealer fifty bucks. The dealer grabbed the kid off the street, put a gun to his head, and told him he was going to kill him on the spot. The kid was begging for his life, "Don't kill me, man! Please don't kill me! I can get the money. Let me make a phone call, and I'll get the money." So the dealer let him make a phone call. The kid called his mother and told her that he needed fifty bucks or this son of a bitch was going to kill him. Mom knows all about her son's drug-running, and asks to talk to the dealer. He gets on the phone, and Mom promises that she'll get the money. She tells him, "Let's all meet at McDonald's in an hour, and I'll give you the fifty bucks."

Mom has a junkie boyfriend, and instead of getting the fifty bucks together, she gets her boyfriend and two of his drug addict buddies, and they all pile into the car and drive down to McDonald's. The dealer is there waiting with the son. When Mom pulls up, the dealer starts walking to the car. Now, it's a busy day at Mickey D's—the parking lot is full of cars coming and going, and people are walking around everywhere. All of a sudden, these two guys jump out of Mom's car and shoot the piss out of the dealer. They've got automatic weapons, and rounds are flying everywhere. The dealer doesn't have a prayer. He's killed on the spot, and an innocent bystander is hit and wounded in the cross fire. The two gunmen grab Mom's son, and they all haul ass out of there.

The shooters know the heat is going to be on. They're afraid the dealer's gang will retaliate, so they decide to head south. Mom and her junkie boyfriend promise them, "Don't worry, we'll send you money while you're laying low." Well, Mom and her boyfriend never send the promised cash. So these two guys return to the city with the intention of taking care of Mom and her asshole boyfriend. On Christmas Day they bust into her apartment, and shoot the place up. Mom is wounded, and the son—the kid these two guys had just saved a few weeks earlier—is shot and killed.

Our investigator shows up at the crime scene, and sees the kid is being carried out on a stretcher with a sheet over his face. The investigator asks Mom, "Who's the dead boy?" She gives a phony name. Lies right in the investigator's face. Her son is dead, she knows who killed him, and she still won't tell the truth.

Meanwhile, the kid's father comes blowing into town from out of the blue. He'd never wanted to have anything to do with the kid when he was alive, but he comes flying into the city after the kid is dead because he wants to know where the kid's possessions are. He stakes a claim to half the possessions, and *gets* half the possessions. But he leaves town before the morgue has released the body. He doesn't even wait around for the funeral, and doesn't contribute to help bury his own son. He's got a New Year's party to go to. When you see stuff like that, there's not much you can do except shrug you shoulders and say, "Happy New Year."

What you feel is frustration. Tremendous frustration. Anytime you've got a witness that knows who the shooters are, and that witness won't talk, it's frustrating. It drives you crazy. It disgusts you.

Most homicide detectives are self-motivated, and we'll bust our asses to close a drug-related murder, but not because we believe somebody should be brought to justice. It's mostly for the personal pride you take in your job, and the fact that you're proud of the closure rate your department maintains. *That's* what motivates me on a drug homicide. Because when you go out there you find that the family doesn't give a fuck, and the neighbors don't give a fuck. Ain't nobody that gives a fuck about these bastards getting killed. The media would like to pin us down to saying something like, "Now, I don't give a fuck about these people either." The truth is, we probably don't. I know I don't. When I see a junkie kill another junkie, or a dealer kill another dealer, my only thought is "Hey, we got two birds with one stone. We've got one dead and another one we can lock up. That's two of 'em off the streets."

GEORGE LAW [crime scene investigator]: One night I was working the midnight shift, following up on a burglary, when a homicide call came in. I drove out to this duplex apartment where five people had been shot. When I walked in, the bodies were lying there on the floor. The victims had been bound and gagged and then seated around this coffee table before they were shot. The guy who did the shooting had to have used an Uzi—or some automatic weapon that held at least a thirty-round clip. There were shell casings all over the place, and it was obvious that this guy had just unloaded and riddled the victims with bullets.

One look and I knew it was drug-related. Whenever you see a victim who has been bound and gagged before getting shot, you know it's drugs because domestic violence never has that premeditated execution-style look.

In this case we dusted the victims' bodies for fingerprints. There have been a couple of times when we've been successful in getting prints off of bodies, and because these people had been bound and gagged it was obvious that the killers had touched them before they blew 'em away. We dusted those areas near where the gags and ropes were—that is around their mouths, the backs of their heads, and their arms and wrists.

I remember looking down at all the carnage and mess and thinking, "Wow, some guy shot five people at once." But I wasn't shocked. I mean, it's not like this sort of thing is unexpected.

RICHARD BOHAN [homicide detective]: Not too long ago we had a case where four people—a girl and three guys—were preying on the elderly. This gang was on crack, and they'd break into the homes and apartments of senior citizens who were living alone. Most of their victims were women, and they'd steal from them without ever worrying about getting captured or being held responsible for their actions. These women would be in their beds at night, and they'd wake up to find this group of strange people standing over them. The women would be terrorized and robbed. Then two or three weeks later this gang would return and rob the same victims a second or third time.

They were getting worse and worse, and finally one night they ended up killing an elderly woman. Early in the morning a neighbor on his way to work happened to see a black male walk out of this white woman's home. He knew something was wrong and he immediately called the police.

When the police arrived they discovered that the woman inside had been beaten to death. The cops set up a perimeter and caught one of the gang members. He was a juvenile, sixteen years old, and he'd been smoking crack all night. We brought him in for interrogation, and right away the homicide detective handling the case learned that this woman wasn't their only victim. They'd terrorized, robbed, and shot one other elderly female.

For all we knew, the other victim might still be alive, and we were trying to get this guy to tell us the exact address so we could get to the house. If the woman was alive we wanted to get her whatever emergency medical attention might be necessary. But our suspect didn't know any addresses. They were all so high and cracked out of their minds that he didn't remember where they'd been. He did, however, remember being on Seventy-ninth Street. So we took him out on location and started driving up and down streets hoping he'd recognize the neighborhood or the house. After driving around for about ninety minutes we got a call from the county police. They'd found the woman we were looking for, and she was dead.

That made two murders in the same night. We brought this kid back to the police station and told him we were going to continue the interrogation. Not wanting to put both confessions into one statement, we wanted to get two statements from him. Two separate confessions. But this guy kept dozing off in the middle of our questions. At one point we woke him and said, "Hey, this is important. Would you mind staying awake?"

He looked at us and said, "C'mon man, I was up all night." Like it was only natural that he'd want to get some sleep. It's true he'd been up all night—he was up robbing, terrorizing, and murdering senior citizens. But his thought process was such that he had no concern over what he'd done. No remorse for the victim, no worries about what was going to happen to him now that he'd been caught. The consumption of crack cocaine had turned him into a total crack animal.

Even though there are other addictive drugs that cause people to do bad things, I've never seen a drug like crack that so totally consumes a person. A heroin addict who's been involved in a homicide will always show some emotion. He'll cry and say, "Man, it's the heroin! I want to get off it! I can't! I've got to steal. I didn't want to murder the old lady. I just wanted to tie her up and steal. I didn't mean to do it!" But crack addicts are a totally different breed. There's no remorse, no fear, no anger—all emotion is totally gone. These people will sit there, just like this guy, and tell you, "Yes, I was out robbing to get some money to buy crack last night. Yes, two old ladies were killed along the way."

JOE SCHWARTZ: Crack addicts are a different breed. They have no values. No morals. The drug is cheap, easy to get on the street, and it makes you do things you normally wouldn't do.

Right now I'm working on a case where this guy kidnapped a nineteen-year-old girl at gunpoint. She was a college student, and she'd been out to a nightclub. She was walking back to her car when this guy stuck a sawed-off shotgun in her face.

The guy was high on crack and he'd been drinking heavily. He forced her into her car, where he raped her. He forced her to have sex with him, and she gave him everything he wanted—pleading with him, begging for mercy. "Please, don't hurt me! Don't hurt me!" But after he'd raped her, he was afraid she'd call the police. So he took her out of the car, put the shotgun to the back of her head, and blew her brains out. She was begging for mercy, but he killed her in cold blood.

When you see a young woman who's been murdered like that, you picture your wife or daughter being caught in the same situation, because this could've happened to anybody. This girl wasn't doing anything wrong. She was just out to have a good time. After spending some time with her friends, she was going home. A totally innocent victim. When you see an innocent victim like that, you really want to catch the guy who did it. It's not like your everyday drug assassination. You relate to the victim, and the victim's family. You want to get that guy off the street.

Fortunately, most criminals are stupid. That's how we catch them. They do stupid things, and this guy was no exception. The next day he was driving around *in her car!* The police pulled him over, and that's how we got him.

Eventually, he confessed. He told us exactly what had happened. Now that it's over, and he's got a level head again, he feels a great deal of remorse over what he did. He's genuinely sorry that he killed this girl.

But it's too late for that now.

GARLAND PRICE [homicide detective]: In 1987 the impact of crack cocaine was just beginning to be felt in homicide. We were getting the first hint of what crack could do. Since then, we've begun to see murders that are qualitatively different from anything we'd ever seen before, and it's all attributable to crack.

For example, in the last year alone I've had three separate cases where a son has killed his mother. In each case the son had been smoking crack, or was using crack in combination with PCP. All of them have been brutal murders—stabbings and beatings. We had a lot of brutal murders before crack, but nothing like this.

The first case involved a kid by the name of Phillip Clemens. He was twenty years old, and living at home with his mother in a nice middle-class neighborhood. He was heavily involved in drug use, and was experimenting with PCP and crack cocaine together. By itself, PCP is a tough drug to handle. It's a real burner. But in combination with crack cocaine it's even worse. It made this kid paranoid, short-tempered, and very violent. His behavior was very bizarre.

The mother was worried and told her friends that she was having problems with him—that he'd even tried to have sex with her. She'd be in the shower, and he'd come in high on drugs, pull the curtain back, and stand there looking at her naked. He'd grab her breasts, and would feel her up. She'd fight him off, and would scream and holler, "I'm your mother! Don't do this to me! Why are you doing this?"

She was very upset, but didn't know what to do. On the day she died, the mother was on the phone with one of her friends when the boy came in high on crack cocaine and PCP. He started bothering her again, trying to feel her up while she was on the phone. She told her friend, "This boy is messing with me again!"

She chased him off, and he went downstairs to work out with his weights. He had these single-hand barbells that he liked to lift in front of the bathroom mirror. He liked to look at himself as he was lifting the weights. While he was doing this, he dropped the barbell on the sink and cracked the porcelain basin.

When the mother hung up the phone, she came down and saw that he'd broken the sink. That got her upset, and the two of them had an argument—which just set this kid off. He went absolutely berserk, and beat her over the head with the barbells. He killed her by smashing her skull in.

As a detective, you see things like this and you just can't believe a son would do that to his mother. But pretty soon, the phone will ring, and you'll find out the same thing has happened again.

Just last week we had another crack/PCP murder that involved a family by the name of McBride. The circumstances were somewhat similar, and I'll tell you how I solved the case. On the night of August twenty-second, the son came up to his mother's apartment, carrying a white gym bag. When he got there, he saw his two sisters knocking on the door, but not getting any answer. He asked them, "What's going on?" They told him they were worried because they hadn't heard from their mother, and asked him, "Have you heard from her?"

He says, "No, I haven't."

The sisters ran over to the rental office, where they got the residential manager and the maintenance man, telling them, "Something must be wrong!" They all went back over to the apartment, and the maintenance man forced the lock on the door. As soon as the door opened, the son bolts inside, runs straight back to the bedroom, and screams and cries, "Oh, my God! Oh, my God!" The two sisters hurry back and see that their mother has been murdered. She's lying on the bedroom floor after having been stabbed to death. The brother is crying and carrying on like he's all shocked and hurt.

The police are called and as soon as we arrive on the scene, we transport everybody down to the police station to get statements from them. After they were gone, I checked around the apartment for evidence. The bedroom had pretty much been destroyed. There was broken glass and a couple of broken lamps on the floor. It was obvious that a big struggle had taken place. There were also signs of a smaller struggle in the living room and kitchen that somebody had tried to straighten up. As I walked around, it became apparent to me that the mother was a very religious woman. She had a table that she used on a daily basis to read her Bible, and the Bible was sitting open where she'd been studying it. In the kitchen, there was an open drawer where the murder weapon came from. The weapon was a large butcher knife with a twelve-inch blade. There were trails of blood from the living room to the bedroom, and huge amounts of blood in the bedroom. The mother had been stabbed so often, and with such tremendous force that this butcher knife had been broken into three or four pieces. I mean, that knife had just shattered. The medical examiner counted seventy-five stab wounds to this woman's head and body. So we're talking about an extraordinarily brutal murder.

While I was looking around, I found a white gym bag by the door. I picked it up and checked through it. Inside was a pair of pants, a shirt, a pair of bloody socks, and a bag of potato chips. I went through the pant pockets and found a set of keys. My first thought was "I wonder if these keys will open the front door?" I stuck a key in the door, and sure enough, it worked the lock. Immediately, I called the police station, where we'd taken the residential manager, and I got her on the line and asked her, "Was anybody in that group of two sisters and the brother carrying anything with them when you went over to the apartment?" She said, "Yeah, the son was carrying a white gym bag. I remember he put it down when he went into the apartment."

As soon as I heard that, the son became my primary suspect. Why would he go through the charade of getting the residential manager and the maintenance man to come open the door when he had a set of keys in his bag? He was just trying to deflect suspicion away from himself. He got so wrapped up in playing that role, in crying and screaming, that he forgot all about the gym bag and left it lying there for me to find. That was his big mistake.

I drove back down to the police station, where one of our investigators was interviewing this kid in the office. I called the investigator out, and apprised him of what I'd found in the gym bag. Based on that information the investigator went back in and continued to interview the kid, but the son kept insisting that he didn't do it. He was putting up a big front, saying he was innocent. So I went into the interview room and told him, "Look, I *know* you did it. I know you killed your mother." He gave me this startled, wild-eyed look, and I told him, "You can't continue to deny the facts. You're going to have to tell the truth. If you don't tell this investigator the truth, I'm going to come in and you're going to have to deal with me."

After that, he confessed. He told the investigator that he'd gone out on the strip and bought a couple bags of PCP and three or four rocks of cocaine. He'd freebased the cocaine, smoked the PCP, and then went home, where he got into an argument with his mother. He said he didn't actually remember killing her—which I don't believe—but that he remembers waking up in the morning, finding himself covered with blood, and finding his mother dead on the floor. He washed the blood off of himself, straightened up the living room, and then spent the rest of the day trying to establish an alibi. So he was very conscious of what he'd done. There's no doubt he knew he was guilty.

One of the strange things I've noticed about these crack/PCP homicides is that when people confess there's no remorse. That was true for both of these guys who murdered their mothers. They don't break down when they talk about the crime. They don't cry. Instead, they talk in a very matter-of-fact, unemotional way. It gives you an eerie feeling that they could easily do it again. That they don't care. All they want is to get back out on the street, back into the swing and flow of the nightlife.

RICHARD BOHAN: When you're working homicide, and you see a case where one dope dealer shoots another dope dealer, that's business. Or if some guy tries to rip off a dope dealer and gets stabbed and killed trying to steal the guy's crack, there's involvement there.

You can tell yourself, "If he hadn't been messing with drugs, then he wouldn't haven't gotten himself killed." It's not what you'd call an innocent victim. Emotionally, those cases are the easiest to handle. You tend to remain detached and get on with the business of doing your job—which is to solve the case.

It's the innocent victims that are tougher on your emotions. We had one just recently. It was a case where an aunt was baby-sitting a three-year-old boy. The parents of this child were hardworking, decent people. They both had jobs, and every morning on their way to work they'd drop their little son off with his aunt. She took care of this boy and a couple of other kids on a regular basis.

This family lived in the inner city, and unfortunately the aunt had a crack problem. She used it and she sold it. But she always watched the kids and seemed to take care of them as best she could.

The street she lived on was controlled by a drug dealer who operated it as an open-air market, and he had his street sellers distributing drugs from her front yard. All day and all night long the traffic would pull up, and a seller would be there to make the transaction. This went on day in and day out. And the guy who controlled the street paid her in crack for letting him and his people work from her property. One day she decided she wanted a higher rate of pay. She wanted more crack cocaine, and she got into an argument with the dealer. He said no, she couldn't have more, and she told him, "Alright then, you can't sell from my front yard. Get your people away from my house."

Well, in order to maintain control over the street, the dealer felt he needed to teach her a lesson. He couldn't let her get away with talking to him like that in front of the neighbors and sellers. So he followed her into the house with the intention of giving her a beating. He didn't have a weapon. He was just going to use his fists.

He was a big boy, but she was a big girl. There was some pushing and shoving, and a lot of screaming and yelling. From the street the dope sellers were watching, the customers were watching, neighbors were watching, and, of course, the children were watching. He picked up a chair, and she picked up a baseball bat. He threw the chair. She swung the bat. He stood there looking at her, and she was just like a mean bull with that bat. He wasn't about to take that. So he told her, "I'm coming back, and when I get here I'm going to light this place up." Then he walked out of the house, got into his car, and drove off.

Ten minutes later he was back, and when he got out of the car he had a gun. One of his dope dealers was with him, and he had a gun too. The children were playing in the front yard, and when she saw him pull up, this woman grabbed the kids and ran into the house.

Unfortunately, she lived in a wood frame house. In broad daylight on a residential street in front of everyone in the neighborhood this drug dealer and his buddy did just what he'd promised he'd do. They lit up the house. Eighteen rounds were fired, and those rounds penetrated the wood walls. Inside, the aunt was lucky. She wasn't hit. But one child was shot in the face. The bullet passed through his cheek without causing any serious damage. But the little boy, her three-year-old nephew, was shot in the head and killed instantly.

For me that was a tough case. Not in the sense of solving it. It didn't take us long to figure out who did it, and even though it took us a while, we arrested both shooters. They're in jail on murder charges. What made the case tough was the senselessness of that child's death. That little boy never had any idea of what was going on, and I couldn't help but feel for the loss of his life and the grief of his parents.

And what did the people in the community do when they learned that this three-year-old child had been killed by a crack dealer who was trying to maintain control over his open-air street market? Did they rise up and march? Did they rise up and say, "No more!"? Did they demand an end to the drug menace in their neighborhood? Did they demand an end to the senseless killing?

No. They remained silent. Except for a couple of newspaper articles and editorials, not a single voice was raised in protest. Right now, on the street where this took place, dope dealers are selling drugs. It's business as usual. Meanwhile, the good, decent citizens are sitting behind locked doors, looking out the windows, asking, "When is this going to end?"

The answer, of course, is that it isn't going to end.

GERALD: I was convicted of murder, and I attribute that killing to drugs, because when I committed the crime I was way beyond high. I had mixed and mixed my drugs, and then mixed them some more. I went way beyond my limit.

I was with this dude, and the two of us smoked some PCP, smoked some marijuana, and drank some sixteen-ounce beers. I'd shot up from ten o'clock that morning until eight o'clock that night. I shot up nine or ten times that day. Then we snorted some cocaine, and smoked some more PCP. Like I say, I'd exceeded my limit.

We were at a crap house and a fight broke out over a crap game. Gunshots were fired. The dude I was with was involved in the fight, and he ran out the door. I responded by running out after him. We ran down an alley until we came to the back of a house. When we stopped running, there was this dude at the end of the fence. Someone was screaming and hollering, saying he was the guy who had shot the dude in the crap house. I didn't know where he came from. I didn't have no argument with him. Like I said, I'd consumed all these drugs, and I reacted to the situation without thinking—without even realizing what was going down.

I don't know if the dude thought we were coming after him or what, but he kicked out at me. That brought the anger out in me. I had a pocket knife and I grabbed that and stabbed him. I stabbed him three times. And he died from those wounds.

I regret the fact that I took someone else's life with my own hands. I didn't have no beef with the dude. No argument with him. I just reacted like a damn fool. I should have shook his hand. That's what I should have done.

It's scary, because I want to be a right individual. I don't want to be thought of as vicious and coldhearted. I want to be a caring, loving person. When I look at myself, I know deep down that I don't have that much violence in me. That was the drugs working on me. I know I committed the crime, but I just can't see myself being that violent.

A lot of nights I lay in my bed, and when I wake up in the morning my covers will be wet and my shirt will be wet. I'll know I've been dreaming about the crime. That fear is going to be with me for the rest of my life. Sometimes I fear that my life is going to be taken in the same manner, or that my son's life will be taken because of what I've done.

No matter when I get out of this prison, I'm always going to have to remember that in June of 1983 a man died at my hands. I've got to carry that with me for the rest of my life. The only thing I know how to do is ask God to forgive me. Once He forgives me, I don't worry about no other man.

CHAPTER 7

PROSECUTION, PRISON, AND PUNISHMENT

One of the drug war's more appalling statistics is that 95 percent of everyone arrested for distribution or possession of illegal narcotics never go to court on the original charges. "Plea bargaining," a judge said recently, "is as necessary to this system as breathing and eating is to a human being."

The costs of taking a single case to court are much higher than most people realize. Arresting officers have to come in off the street at public expense, numerous assistants have to help the district attorney prepare evidence at public expense, and more often than not the defendant has an attorney hired to represent him at public expense. Multiply those factors a thousand times over, and you begin to get a feel for how the cost of prosecution guarantees the failure of the courts as a weapon in this war—especially since even without the burden of drug cases, the criminal justice system is already bogged down by the weight of crowded court dockets, overflowing prisons, and overworked prosecutors.

"I'd never try to bust anyone for simple possession of cocaine," says an undercover narcotics cop. "It's not worth the trouble. Sometimes you can threaten an individual with a possession charge and turn him into an informant so you can go after the dealer who sold him the stuff, but that's about as far as you can go. To actually prosecute on simple possession is a waste of time. If you're going to go to court, there's got to be something more involved."

"There have been times," says another detective who works in an inner-city area, "when we've raided crack houses in the morning, and that same afternoon we'll see the people we arrested back on the streets. They've already begun dealing drugs again, but there's nothing we can do about it because we have no control over the court system. Sometimes we'll arrest the same person three, four, or five times in the same year. Obviously, the guy can't be doing any serious time. He'll have repeatedly been caught dealing drugs, but no one is willing to treat it as a serious crime. All we can do is hope that if we arrest five drug dealers, maybe one of them will have enough prior convictions so that a judge finally says, 'Enough,' and gives the guy some prison time. Most cops who stay in narcotics do it because we enjoy police work, not because we believe in the court system. The truth is, we don't."

Prosecution

JEROME: I was running my own heroin and cocaine organization. I was buying weight and paid hustlers to go out on the street selling. Plus I had people holding, and I had lookouts on the corners with walkie-talkies. They was there to let the hustlers know if the jump-out squad was in the area. So it was just like running a corporation. There was lots of people I had to pay.

One time I had to stab a dude. The dude kept messing my money up. Taking shorts. I told him I didn't go for that. Then I gave him another chance, but he messed up again. So I stabbed him up. I cut all around his stomach. I seen that his stomach was bleeding bad.

The ambulance took him to the hospital. The dude had eighteen thousand dollars' worth of damage done to his stomach because they had to take out some of the intestines. And they had to stop the bleeding. That blood was overflowing in his system.

The police went to the hospital and asked him who cut him. He wouldn't tell them nothing, but his sister did. She told the police that it was me. After she did that he agreed. He said I was the one that did it.

I knew the police was looking for me, so I turned myself in. I told 'em I didn't do nothing. Made bond. And when I got out of jail I went and talked to this dude's sister's boyfriend. He was on drugs too, and I told him, "Look man, tell the dude I'll give him some money and some dope if he don't come to court." The boyfriend was game for that. He knows my dope's good, and he was thinking, "Shit, I can stay high." So he talked to the dude in the hospital and said, "Hey man, keep on blackmailing Jerome. You can keep getting dope from him."

The dude thought that was a good idea, and he said he wouldn't testify against me. After he got out of the hospital I gave him twenty quarters and a hundred fifty dollars. I told him, "Look, this is just the start. I'll give you more later." He was living with his sister in the same neighborhood where I was at. But I told him to move out. I said, "Go stay where the police can't find you, and I'll take care of you."

I had to go be in a lineup, and this dude was supposed to be there to identify me as the person who stabbed him. I showed up with my lawyer, and when the police came in they were laughing and joking. They knew they had me. But my lawyer kept telling me, "You alright. So far the dude ain't showed up yet." The police waited and waited and waited, but the dude never showed.

That made the police mad. When I left I went straight home. About ten minutes later I see the police knocking on the dude's sister's door, trying to figure out why he didn't come to the lineup. They left him a note saying, "You'd better come next time. We're putting a warrant out for you." They scheduled a second lineup, but he didn't show for that one neither. The police came back to his sister's house again, asking questions. They wanted to know, "Has Jerome been threatening y'all? Is that why the dude ain't showing up?" They were asking those kinds of things, and they scheduled a third lineup. When he didn't show for the third time the judge threw the charge out. See, that dude was the only witness the police had. Without him they didn't have any evidence against me. They couldn't prosecute without a witness.

Man, that pissed the cops off. They knew I done it, and they hated seeing me beat that charge.

ERNIE: When I was in high school somebody got busted with some dope, and he told the cops that I was the one who sold it to him. So I was arrested, and had to go to court on a distribution charge. I was sixteen at the time, and the worst thing about it was I had to cut my hair. I had a ponytail, and my father wouldn't let me go to court with hair like that. I also had to pay five hundred dollars to hire a lawyer, which was no big deal, because when you're selling dope it's easy to come up with five hundred bucks.

The lawyer gave the judge this big sob story about how I was from a military family, and how pressures are put on a child that has to move all the time. Then he went into his bit about how this was my first offense. All that stuff. The judge put me on probation, and made me write a five-hundred-word report on distribution laws. You know, big deal. I've got to write a dumb fucking report.

The first thing I learned when I started going through the court system was that I could get off real light. When I went back to school I was still selling dope. Getting busted had just made me that much of a bigger man. It gave me something to brag about—you know, another battle ribbon on my chest.

Politicians and policemen like to talk tough, and pretend that selling drugs is a big, bad crime. But the court system doesn't treat it that way. After you've been arrested, the first thing the DA does is reduce the charges. You can get busted three, four, five times, and never spend more than a couple hours in jail. Unless you're holding serious weight, or committing violent crimes, the court is going to look at you as a petty offender. The way plea bargains are structured, you start to think, "Hey, I own the court system. I'm invincible. These assholes aren't going to do anything to me."

ROBERT SILBERING [assistant district attorney]: Everybody knows there's a drug problem in New York, but for me the magnitude of the problem didn't sink in until 1986 when the office of the special narcotics prosecutor, where I work, really started jumping. Nineteen eighty-six was when crack cocaine hit the streets, and the city responded by establishing a special drug task force which more than doubled the size of the police department narcotics unit. But I don't know what good it did. Before we knew it we had an avalanche of cases coming in. An explosion in numbers. The narcotics officers are making tons of arrests—more than tripling our caseload—and yet, we did not get any significant increase in judges or prison space. Now, how is the criminal justice system supposed to handle that kind of an increase when we're already understaffed to begin with?

*   *   *

GARY HANKINS [police officer]: We make thousands and thousands of felony arrests every year. Last year we made over sixteen thousand felony arrests in Washington, D.C., but the courts here are only capable of handling seven hundred fifty-nine felony trials. *That* is the problem. The criminal justice system is not a justice system, it's a criminal management system. No matter how perfect our cases are, we can only try a small percentage of them. The goal of the system is not to prosecute criminals, but to avoid trials. That's why the smallest flaw in an otherwise perfect case will get that case thrown out. That's why criminal defendants find that it's so easy to plea-bargain to lesser charges.

When you're making sixteen thousand felony arrests and most of them are good cases, but less than one thousand go to trial, it's obvious that a lot of guilty people are getting breaks. They know they're guilty, their friends know they're guilty, and they know we have them cold—but they also know the odds are against their ever being prosecuted. So they go back to the community, and say, "Yeah, I got arrested for selling crack cocaine, but nothing happened to me." There's a perception on the street that the system is too backed up to try anybody, and the more drug dealers we have clogging the system, the more accurate that perception becomes.

SOL WACHTLER [judge]: In addressing the drug problem, legislative and executive leaders have concentrated a great deal on the front end—that is, police and arrests—while devoting little attention to the courts.

For every person who goes to jail, eight to ten people pass through the court system. In New York City, we had seventy-five thousand drug cases come before criminal courts last year, and are projecting one hundred ten thousand for this year. In the city we have a total of seventy-five criminal court judges. That means that each judge is permitted an average of four and a half minutes per case. Given these circumstances, judges are only able to negotiate pleas. They don't even wield the *threat* of trying these people. The bargaining power lies with the defendants, and not with the courts. The plea bargain has replaced the indictment in our system. The word on the street is, it doesn't matter what you've done or been arrested for, the courts won't be able to prosecute you.

The fact that our resources are stretched beyond our ability to cope is evident just by walking in the building. In Suffolk County they're using basements for courtrooms. The building's pipes and plumbing are exposed overhead, and every time a toilet flushes in the building they have to stop the trial because you can't hear over the rushing water. In other basements the jurors have to wear overcoats because there isn't any heat. There are pretrial examinations being conducted in hallways, and attorney conferences are taking place at Burger King and McDonald's.

There's an administrative judge who used to have nice chambers—about thirteen feet by fifteen feet. He's been forced out because his chambers are now being used as a courtroom. The judge has no office. He's got a couple of desks in the clerks' pool. You've got to see this makeshift courtroom to appreciate it—a judge in robes behind a desk with a chair on a low platform in front of a window and the jury crammed into one side of the office. It looks like something out of a cartoon.

We're seeing the impact of drugs everywhere in the system. That's especially true in the family courts because of the increase in child-abuse and child-neglect cases. There's been a one-hundred-forty-five-percent increase in child-abuse cases in the past year, and they are almost all drug-related. The family court in the Bronx reminds you of Calcutta in the bazaar days. People are jammed in the halls so tightly that you cannot walk through. You have people standing there filling up every possible inch of space. On rainy days people are actually lined up outside the door holding their umbrellas waiting to get in.

That is our justice system.

CARL [customs inspector]: The first drug seizure I made was when I was working as a regular inspector at the airport in Los Angeles. I was clearing passengers through Customs as they came in from overseas.

This one couple was returning to the United States from Switzerland after having traveled to Thailand, and I looked through their carry-on baggage and saw this lady had a box of Maxithin pads in her travel kit. The reason I looked in that box was because I knew they probably figured I'd be too embarrassed to run my hands through those Maxithins. I opened the box from the bottom, and out drops a syringe. That made it obvious to me that they were carrying heroin. So I took them back into one of our interrogation rooms and did a very thorough search. Sure enough, I found fifty grams of heroin in the bottom of a jar of cream. It seemed odd that I could only find fifty grams. I thought that if they were going to go all the way to Thailand and back, they'd try to bring in more than that. But fifty grams was all I found.

At the L.A. airport we're in a situation where there are three jurisdictions that can make a formal arrest and prosecute for drug smuggling. The first is the DEA, and we called them to see if they wanted to come over and arrest this couple. They said no, it was too small of an amount for them to prosecute. So then we called the L.A. Police, and they declined on the same grounds. The third authority was the L.A. County Sheriff's Department. I called them and explained the situation, and they didn't want to prosecute either. I told the deputy that they were our last chance, that the DEA and the LAPD didn't want to make the arrest either. The deputy was sympathetic and understood why I wanted these people arrested, but he was also very up-front. He said, "Look, it's too small of an amount. We can put them in jail for a couple of nights at public expense, but even if we do, nothing will ever come of it. The DA will never go to court over something that small. If you want us to come all the way out there and make an arrest, then you need to find enough heroin to make it worth our trouble."

That really surprised me. I thought those people should have been put in jail for bringing heroin into the United States. But there wasn't much I could do. I asked my supervisor what I should do, and he told me to confiscate the heroin and write out a citation. So that's what I did. I made them pay a fine and then sent them on their way.

RAY CHENEY [detective]: What you've got to understand is the criminal justice system is a big game. The drug dealers know it, the attorneys know it, and the cops know it.

I went through a routine with a defense attorney just the other day. We'd arrested a guy on a buy-bust operation. An undercover officer had made a buy, then described the two individuals that participated in the transaction. We converged in our cars, and I grabbed one of the suspects. As I did that, some third guy that's just standing there takes off running. I watch him reach into his pocket and pull out a plastic bag, which he tosses on the ground as he's running

away. He ran for several blocks, and was eventually caught by another officer. We retrieved the bag he'd thrown away, and it had
eight or nine rocks in it.

He was charged with possession of cocaine and resisting arrest
without violence. I was called in to give a deposition to this public
defender, and she got on a kick about the resisting arrest stuff. She
said, "Who told him he was under arrest?"

"I don't know," I said. "I wasn't there when he was apprehended.
So I can't tell you."

"Yeah, but how can you charge him with resisting arrest when he
didn't know he was under arrest?"

Finally, I tell the stenographer to stop recording things. I look at
the attorney and say, "Hey, why are you asking me these questions?
You know how the game is played. He's got two charges, possession
and resisting-without. If you want to get rid of the resisting-without,
take a plea when it's time for court—say that if we drop the resisting-
without you'll take the possession. You know that's how it's played.
So stop wasting my time with technical questions on a charge we
both know you're going to plead out."

That put an end to the deposition.

JULIO MOREJON [detective]: As cops, one of the problems we routinely encounter with the court system is whenever we take a dealer
who has made good money into court, he has a private attorney
representing him who has had plenty of experience defending dopers.
The defendant's attorney might have forty or fifty drug trials under
his belt. But our prosecuting attorney will invariably be fresh out
of law school and just learning the ropes. It's like putting a high
school ballplayer up against a professional. Who do you think is going to win?

Even though you've never been to law school, you'll sit there
knowing that you know more about how to prosecute a case than the
state's attorney. That's something that's happened to every cop who
has ever been to court. We coach them when we can—tell them
what charges to bring and what charges to plead out. But once a trial
begins there's not much we can do. Because of the salary structure
involved, it's the big-time drug dealers who have the best attorneys.
That can be very frustrating. There's nothing more demoralizing
than to sit there and watch a perfectly good case go down the drain,
because some young attorney is making mistakes in court.

*   *   *

ROBERT BEATY [detective]: The Constitution guarantees every defendant the right to a fair trial before a jury of his peers. I don't have any problem with that, except for the fact that it means a lot of drug users and abusers are sitting on juries in judgment of people arrested on drug offenses. The epidemic is so large that it's inevitable. A certain percentage of the population is using drugs, and a certain number of juries are tainted by the presence of drug users. Sometimes you can look at a jury and just sense that no matter how solid your case is, you won't be able to get a conviction. That's because there will be two or three dopers in the jury box who will *never* vote "guilty."

JOSEPH R. GOULET [marine supervisor, U.S. Customs Service]: During my first couple weeks on the job, I had a case that we ended up taking to court for a jury trial. What happened was at about six-thirty one morning, one of the guys I work with went out flying with the [Customs] air branch looking for boat targets. After a while he starts yelling on the radio. He's about twenty-five miles out, and says he's picked up what looks like a go-fast out of Bimini headed toward the Hallover area around Miami. I say, "Okay," and I go down and get an outboard 30-footer. I know the go-fast is probably going to beat me there by about two or three miles, but I decide to give it a go anyway.

Well, for some reason these guys had stopped dead in the water for a few minutes, and by the time I got to Hallover I could see them pulling into the inlet and taking the first left up Indian Creek. I was flying down Indian Creek chasing them, but I had to stop a couple times to drop my antennas to get under bridges. The bad guys didn't have to make any stops, so they opened up about a three-quarter-mile lead.

Then they stopped again, and I could see them throwing something over the side. Man, I'm hauling ass now. Instead of stopping to find the contraband, I'm tearing after them. It took me about thirty minutes to catch them.

I board their boat and say, "Okay, where'd you come from?"

"Just out testing the boat about five, six miles out," the pilot says, all innocent-sounding.

The officer in the airplane who spotted them is overhead, and I get on the radio and ask if this is definitely the boat he saw out of Bimini. He says, "Yeah, no question."

We get a Coast Guard helicopter to come in and check the area where we saw them throw the shit over the side, and the chopper finds a bag with twenty-two pounds of coke in it floating near Indian River golf course.

I arrest the guys on the go-fast, and when we go to trial their story is they never threw any dope over the side—they were throwing "garbage" over. Just cleaning up. The coke must've belonged to somebody else, they say. Now, the jury is in a coma. They're knitting and looking around, not listening to a fucking thing. You can feel it in your gut—these guys are going to walk because the jury doesn't give a shit.

The U.S. attorney is asking one of the defendants, "Did you see the Customs boat come from behind you?"

"Yeah."

"Did you hear the siren?"

"No, never did."

"Did you see the blue light?"

"Yeah, saw that."

"When you were turning around looking over your shoulder, were you looking out for Customs? You were worried they might catch you with dope, right?"

"No, no! That's not why I was looking over my shoulder!"

"Then why were you?"

And the guy says, "Because I like to look at the wake the boat makes."

Everyone cracks up at this. But the thing is, the wake is beautiful. A lot of people who go out on boats like to watch the wake. It's true! The jury's in a coma until the guy says this, at which point they break up laughing, thinking, "Oh, you lying motherfucker! Now we're going to convict your ass." And they do. The one truthful statement the guy makes in twenty minutes of testimony is the fucking thing that gets him hung. Talk about justice working for all the wrong reasons. Dopers may or may not end up going to jail, but justice has nothing to do with it.

JULIO MOREJON [detective]: I had a case about four years ago that really pissed me off. What happened was one morning I got a call referencing a possible burglary. So my partner and I hurried out to the scene and we saw two guys come running out of this house, one of them holding a gun. We arrest them, and in their pockets we find some handcuff keys, four thousand dollars in cash, a watch, and a gold chain. We take them back into the house and find a victim handcuffed inside. The cuff key that we found inside this guy's pocket fits perfectly, and the victim identifies the two guys we just arrested as having robbed him. The watch, the money, and the gold chains are his.

The victim was Haitian, and he apparently practiced voodoo. Under the kitchen counter I found a plastic bag full of what looked like ashes. I confiscated it and sent it to the lab, and the lab report came back saying, yeah, it's ashes. Nothing but ashes.

We go to court and the defense attorney makes a big deal out of this plastic bag. He says there was really cocaine in the bag, but that I stole it and replaced it with ashes. That was totally untrue, but at this time the River Cops investigation was going on in Miami. That investigation involved a group of police officers that had been ripping off dopers and selling the drugs themselves. That was big in the news at the time, and the defense attorney's allegations were consistent with the daily newspaper headlines. So the jury bought it, and these two guys that we'd caught red-handed were acquitted. We had all the necessary physical evidence, and a victim who positively ID'd the people who had robbed him, and we couldn't get a conviction.

The fact that we had some crooked cops on the force completely destroyed my credibility. My testimony meant nothing to the jury.

JOE SCHWARTZ [homicide detective]: Nobody wants to get involved in a drug murder case. Witnesses are extremely reluctant. They're afraid. They think that if they testify they're going to get killed. Which is true a lot of times. Witnesses get threatened. They get hurt. They get killed.

One of the cases I'm working on right now, for example, is a drug murder. What happened is the original victim owed a dealer some money so the dealer had him killed. Two people participated in the murder. One of the codefendants was a guy by the name of Damon Chase, and Damon was later murdered by his buddy because he was going to flip and testify against the shooter. That gives me another murder to solve. We know that the other codefendant, the shooter, has been soliciting people to kill other witnesses—all of whom were dealers working for him. Now, they're scared to death because they're afraid he's going to have them killed. Nobody wants to testify.

When we go to court we never know what our witnesses are actually going to say, because they're scared. They'll tell us one thing in private, and then become reluctant, afraid to take the stand. A lot of times a drug-murder defendant will get his drug-dealing buddies to come in and pack the gallery. Their presence will intimidate witnesses. These are the guys the witness is going to have to face on the street after the trial is over.

There's nothing we can do about it. As a consequence, a lot of the people we arrest for murder get off when their cases go to trial. I'd say about half the people we arrest and charge with murder end up being set free. These are people that we *know* are guilty. We put them back on the street every day. Keep in mind, that's half of the people we arrest—and we only make arrests in about fifty percent of our cases. So, realistically you're looking at a twenty-five-percent closure rate. For every one hundred murders that take place in Washington, D.C., twenty-five will end with an arrest and a conviction. That tells you that people are getting away with murder all the time.

About three months ago we had a drug murder case where our two main witnesses never showed up. We couldn't find them. The trial ended with a verdict of not guilty. Later, we learned that the defendant's brother kidnapped our two witnesses and held them in a hotel against their will. When the not-guilty verdict was announced, he let them go. We're charging the brother with kidnapping now, but let's face it, that's not the same as a murder charge. He'll probably do some prison time, but the brother who committed the murder has been set free. He's back on the street, and there's nothing we can do about it. We can't retry the case, because you can't prosecute twice on the same charges. Criminal procedure laws are written to favor the bad guys, not the victim who's been murdered.

ESTELLE: The guy I was dealing with, I used to hold a lot of his weapons, ammunition, drugs, and money. I'd keep 'em inside my apartment so he never had nothing on him. In return for my holding his stuff, he'd pay my bills and spot me with drugs.

I was holding sawed-off shotguns, pump-action shotguns, rifles, pistols, automatic weapons—he had all that stuff, and he used it. Sometimes he'd be shooting people. He'd shoot 'em for drug reasons. Maybe somebody'd mess his money up. Instead of getting their bill straight, they might talk shit. That draws anger, because that's a couple thousand dollars of his loss. I always knew when he got upset about something, because he'd come to me to get his guns and bullets. I'd know he'd be out there doing some type of shooting, and that he wasn't going to be at no pistol range. His bullets were meant for people.

Him and another drug dealer was beefing. They had lots of arguments over turf. They was both big. They both had runners and lieutenants, and they controlled different streets in the city. Then when they started beefing over turf, people was getting shot. People was getting killed.

I'd known the guy I was with for a long time, and there was nothing under God's creation that I wouldn't do for that man. I liked him that much. I even got him off a murder charge by going before the judge and jury and lying under oath. See, there's a bond that forms between drug dealers and drug users. People that's out there doing criminal activity, they have a bond. If you can help a brother, you do it, because there might come a day when he can help you.

In the case I'm telling you about, there had been a drug murder that took place right behind my apartment, and my friend got arrested. He was charged with murder. His trial had been going three weeks when his attorney brought me into court as a surprise witness. I gave him an alibi. I said him and me was standing on the street together, that we saw this group of people, and then we heard some gunshots fired. I said he couldn't possibly have fired the gun, because he was standing right by me when the bullets was fired. The people on the jury bought what I was saying, when the truth is I had no knowledge of that incident whatsoever. I was nowhere around. Everything I was telling the jury was a lie. That's how he beat that murder charge.

Even though I know he done killed people, it can't change the way I feel for this man. I don't care if he killed fifty people, my feelings will never change. Him and me been tight too long.

He has a little brother, and I helped his brother get off a murder charge too. I did it the same way. They put me up to testify, and when I get up there on the stand people believe what I'm saying. Even though I'm not telling the truth, I'm talking like I've got something really important to say, something they *need* to hear.

After I went to court for the little brother and got him off the murder charge, he wasn't home a week when he got shot eight times. The brother was shot in retaliation, because these two dudes was beefing. His little brother is still alive, but he's paralyzed from the waist down. That really got to me. He's going to be paralyzed for the rest of his life. He'd be much better off in prison having his health and his strength, than he is being free and paralyzed. But I can't turn back the hands of time. I can't take back nothing I said.

That kind of stuff happens all the time. If a drug dealer kills somebody, he'll find a witness to go to court and lie. That's all part of the game. It's part of survival. I don't feel bad about taking the stand and lying to the jury, because I know this man would do the same for me.

Doing Time

ALEXA: I grew up in Amarillo listening to country music. After I moved to Oklahoma I started hanging out in this country-western bar where live bands would play. I had a whole group of friends that would show up there regularly—especially on Thursday nights. Thursday was our shit-kickin' dance night.

One night this guy came up to one of my friends and asked about me, saying, "I find her attractive." A couple weeks later he bought me a beer, and we chatted for a while. Then he asked if I wanted to toot some coke. I liked coke, and we went out into the parking lot to do a few lines.

Eventually, I got to know this guy really well. His name was Walter. He dealt coke, and did so exclusively in large volumes. He'd grown up in west Texas, and was a real country kind of guy. Basically, a good old boy with a southern accent and a big hearty laugh. I really liked Walter, and it wasn't long before the two of us became tight.

Even though we were never lovers, we spent a lot of time together. I saw Walter six, seven nights a week. My friends were blown away by the way we became inseparable. That was because Walter had an endless supply of coke.

That was a fun time. Every day after work I'd go down to the country-western bar, meet Walter and some other friends, drink, dance, and snort coke. We'd usually stay there until one or two in the morning, then go back to his house, sit up chatting, and do more coke. That was a tough pace. All day at work I'd feel groggy and tired, but at night, after a line of coke everything seemed euphoric and wonderful. No matter how exhausted I'd been during the day, I never had any trouble staying up and partying all night long.

Walter sold to a wealthy, yuppie crowd. He knew a lot of attorneys and businessmen who were into coke, and every now and then I'd make deliveries for him. I wasn't dealing it myself. I was just helping Walter out. Everything was cool until this one guy that was one of Walter's best customers got busted. The police had been monitoring him for a while, and were using a friend of his as an informant. After he was arrested he called to tell me that the police were asking about me. Apparently, the informant had been present a couple of times when I'd made deliveries and had identified me as the guy's supplier.

That was an incredible shock. I didn't know how much the police knew, but I was nervous and scared, and immediately talked to an attorney. He checked into it, and then called me back and confirmed that there was an investigation in progress and that I was a target in that investigation.

That had me scared to death. I thought the police would come and arrest me at any moment. I had all of the blinds pulled down in my apartment, and I was constantly peeking out the window expecting to see a police car. But instead of arresting me, the police called my attorney and he arranged to have us go in and see them. So we went down to the police station and met with this undercover detective by the name of Tom Casey. I was nervous as hell, but he was real nice. Real cordial. Instead of treating me like scum, he asked me if I wanted a cup of coffee, and he was joking around with my attorney. When we got down to business, what he told me was very straightforward. He said, "We know you've made cocaine deliveries on several different occasions to at least three different people. We're prepared to arrest you on cocaine-trafficking charges, but you're not the person we're really interested in. We want the guy that gave you the coke. If you're willing to cooperate with us, we won't press any charges and you'll never spend a day in jail. But if you refuse to help you're going to be placed under arrest this afternoon." Then he got up, walked out, and left me alone with my attorney.

I was confused, frightened, and tearful. Walter was my best friend. I cared a lot about him. We'd had a lot of fun together, and he was always very good to me. I couldn't see myself turning him in, but my attorney didn't have any doubts about what I should do. He kept telling me, "Look, Alexa, you sold cocaine in the presence of a police informant. And there are at least three witnesses who are willing to testify against you. Probably more. You've got no choice. You've *got* to cooperate."

No matter how much I liked Walter, I knew I didn't want to go to jail. That absolutely terrified me. I mean, what would my mother and father think? How could I face them with something like that? All these thoughts were going through my head, and my attorney kept telling me I had no choice. Finally, I agreed to cooperate. Casey came back in, and the deal he spelled out was that I had to reveal the name of my source and help obtain evidence against him. In other words, I had to set Walter up.

Casey said, "Okay, here's what we're going to do. You're going to call Walter right now and tell him that you've got this friend from high school in town." Then he thumped his chest and said, "That's me. I'm the friend from Amarillo. You tell Walter that I want to make a buy, and that it's too big for you to handle. Tell him that I want to meet him. See if he'll have dinner with us tonight. If I can get Walter to deal directly with me, you'll be out of the picture."

I made the phone call, and hearing Walter's voice on the other end of the line almost broke my heart. I was hoping he wouldn't answer. He had no idea what I was doing to him. He was real cheerful, and agreed to meet us that night. The three of us met at this restaurant, and I introduced Walter to Casey. I was real uncomfortable, real tense. Just horribly guilty. But Tom Casey was a great actor and he put Walter at ease. The two of them had a great time talking and laughing. In the next two or three days, Casey made a couple of small buys from Walter just to build up his trust. Then he told him that he wanted a kilo to take back to Amarillo. Walter said, "No problem. When do you want it?"

They set up a Friday night meeting, and that's when the bust went down. They arrested Walter at his house. That night Casey called me at about one A.M. and said, "It's happened." Then about three or four in the morning my phone rang again. It was Walter. He said, "Your friend from Amarillo is a narc." I said, "You're kidding! What makes you say that?" Walter said, "The bastard just arrested me. I'm calling from jail." I said, "That's terrible! I can't believe it!" I was putting up this big facade. I was so ashamed of what I'd done. I didn't want Walter to know. I felt so guilty and cared about him so much. But after a couple of days Walter put the pieces together and figured out what happened. He knew it was me that set him up, and I never talked to him again after that.

Unfortunately, Walter had a huge amount of cocaine at his house when Casey arrested him. We're talking three or four kilos hidden in the closet, so the arrest was big news. The local television and radio stations all made a big deal out of it, and Walter was sentenced to ten years in prison.

Right now, he's at Leavenworth in the third year of his sentence. I think about him all the time. I have days when I walk around horribly depressed. I know I was a rotten friend. I turned Walter in to save my own skin. Sometimes I ask myself, "What could the police have done if I'd kept my mouth shut and refused to cooperate?" Sure, they could've arrested me. But I was small potatoes. There's no way they could've sent me to prison for ten years. I was making nickel-and-dime deliveries.

There are days when I'm feeling guilty and I'll wonder about divine retribution. I'll be driving down the road and I'll think, "Walter is in prison. Am I going to be punished because of what I did to put him there? Is something terrible going to happen to me?" I'll feel this incredible guilt and remorse, and I'll say to myself, "God, Walter, I'm sorry. I hope you don't hate me for what I've done."

JOHN: On my last binge, I got drunk in a bar and went outside to get a cab. I ended up walking toward some residential area, and I was waiting there. The next thing I know, two squad cars pull up and two cops get out. They had me spread-eagled and were patting me down. I'm protesting, saying, "Hey, what's going on? I'm just waiting for a cab!"

But what had happened was I'd been standing in someone's private doorway banging my head against their door—*without even knowing it*! The people in the house were scared and they called the cops.

The police arrested me, and it was the first time I'd ever been arrested for anything. I spent two nights in jail, and that was an eye-opener to say the least. Here I am, a forty-two-year-old professionial businessman, locked up with all these eighteen-, nineteen-year-old kids who are pissed about being taken off the street. For those two days and nights in jail, there was nothing for me to do but sit there and think about what had brought me to that point. Well, there was no doubt in my mind that it was my drinking and drugging—my cocaine and alcohol abuse.

The total degradation of being booked, fingerprinted, and thrown in jail was very humiliating. But for me, the absolute low point of my forty-two years in this life was being brought into the courtroom in manacles, and having my wife sitting there watching me. When I remember it, I feel this wretched embarrassment for her.

*   *   *

DR. WALTER L. FAGGETT [drug treatment director]: One of my first patients was a guy named Darrin. He came to the hospital strung out on PCP. He was two credits away from graduating from high school, but he'd started lunching out on Boat, and was one of the worst PCP addicts I've ever seen. He'd smoke and smoke and smoke all the PCP he could get. He had some terrible psychotic reactions, and his EEG was abnormal as well. Darrin was seventeen, and once the PCP caused cognitive impairment he was never able to get his two credits. He never graduated.

He jumped out of a couple windows and got himself shot, but the real tragedy was getting a call from his lawyer one day. A young lady friend of his had set him up, and he had sold thirty-two ounces of PCP to a DEA agent—which meant he was looking at a twenty-year minimum. The DEA had tapes of the whole deal, and Darrin's slurred speech was easily heard on the tapes. I had to testify at his trial, and I testified that the slurred speech indicated severe cognitive impairment. PCP can duplicate schizophrenia, and there were times when I'd seen Darrin psychotic. I tried to explain to the jury that Darrin had literally been crazy since his addiction to PCP began. That wasn't an exaggeration, it was fact. Darrin had had fifteen admissions into treatment programs over a two-year period and had been diagnosed as having drug-induced organic brain syndrome. His judgment was severely impaired.

I was surprised when the jury convicted him, and he was sent to prison. I thought, "Wait a minute. John Hinckley can shoot the President, claim insanity, and live a nice life in a mental hospital, but you're telling me my patient is *not* crazy?" I couldn't believe it. Darrin belongs in a hospital, not a prison. But let's face it, our prisons are packed full of people like Darrin—people who have severe mental disorders brought on by drug addiction.

MERILEE: I've been arrested lots of times, and driving down to face the judge, I'd be smoking cocaine in my car. My attorney told me not to do that, not to come to court high, but I didn't pay him no mind. I'd carry my coke and my pipe right into court with me. The police would be all about the courthouse, and I wouldn't care. I'd be sitting there waiting for my trial, smoking, smoking, smoking. Getting high, high, high. Even then, I still enjoyed the high. Even though I knew the judge was gonna throw my ass in jail, I enjoyed it. I had the craving, man. I had to have it.

Finally, this one judge, he looked down at me and said that I was "a danger to society." He gave me some serious time. He sentenced me to seven years in the penitentiary.

NEIL: For me one of the most difficult things about going to prison was having to face my parents the first time they came to visit me. That was really hard. When I was growing up they were constantly talking to me about drugs, and telling me I should stay in school. They gave me everything they had. My father taught me a good trade, and we worked together doing construction for a couple of years. Then to see me go astray hurt them real bad.

When they came in the prison to see me, they had to be patted down by a corrections officer, and they heard the iron gate slam behind them. Then they had to look at me standing there in prison clothes. I wanted to see them bad as hell, because I love them—but not right then. Not like that.

CHRISTOPHER: I've been incarcerated for the past five years on armed robbery charges. It was because of my drug addiction that I turned to crime. Drugs was my big downfall. Basically, I've been in and out of prison for the past ten years, and it ain't no life for anyone.

My mother's had three strokes since I been incarcerated, and it hurts that I ain't able to be by her bedside and show my concern. I know that my coming back and forth through prison has played a big part in her illness. It's a sad situation, man. I think about it constantly.

I talk to her on the phone, and try to explain how I feel. Let her know that even though I messed up in life, I've got concern for her. I got caring in my heart. But talking on the phone ain't the same as being by her bedside.

One thing about being in prison is it gives you plenty of time to analyze the mistakes you made in life. It gives you plenty of time to feel your absence from your loved ones.

RICK: As far as drugs are concerned being in prison is no different from being on the street. Most of the people in here are still getting high. People who have been out on the street dealing drugs keep their connections. They come into prison and they can pull favors. They've still got their bank accounts that they established on the outside. They can sign a slip for a money order and say it's for their mother's rent, but nobody knows where that money is really going to end up. Being incarcerated doesn't end your access to money, and it doesn't end your access to drugs.

Anything you want, you can get on a prison compound. You can get marijuana, cocaine, crack, PCP, heroin—a prison compound is just another open-air market.

PHILIP: Going from the streets to prison is moving from one drug-infested place to another drug-infested place. When a dope fiend wants his dope, he'll take whatever measures are necessary to get it. You'd be amazed at how easy it is to smuggle drugs into this penitentiary.

Probably the most common way is to have a guest bring it in. If you've got a baby, your woman can hide the drugs in the baby's diaper, and when you're holding your little baby you know where to look. In this prison, we're allowed to have contact visits, so another way is to have your girlfriend stick some drugs up her pussy. When the two of you are alone on the bed, all you got to do is reach between her legs and pull the drugs out. To get past the shakedown when your visit is over, you pack the drugs into a balloon and swallow it or stick it up your anus. It's as easy as that.

I've been locked up for nine years, and I've never had any trouble getting drugs.

ESTELLE: When my oldest brother was incarcerated, I kept him supplied with drugs while he was in prison. He was selling on the inside, and he'd call me on the phone every week and tell me what he needed. Every Sunday I'd visit him, and pass him some heroin and cocaine.

There'd be a prison guard there that pats you down when you go in the facility to visit. To get by the guard, I put the drugs inside a balloon, and then inserted the balloon in my vagina or in my bowels. Once I got past the guard, I'd go to the visiting hall, and after being there awhile, I'd tell the officer that I needed to go to the bathroom. In the bathroom, I'd take the balloon out of my vagina and wrap it in a piece of tissue.

My brother would be in the visiting hall waiting for me, and I'd be sitting face-to-face in the chair across from him. The officers can't watch every move you make. There's too many people in the visiting hall. While we were sitting there talking, I'd give him the tissue. He'd unzip his pants, reach down, and stick the balloon inside his butt. If I had more than one balloon, he'd stick one up his butt and swallow the others. That way when the guards patted him down, it would be like he had nothing on him.

After he got back on the compound, he'd have enough drugs for himself—he could support his habit for a week—and he'd have enough drugs to sell. He was making good money the whole time he was in prison.

MIKE YEE [corrections officer]: I was a prison guard for several years. One of the first things I learned was there was always some kind of constant scheming going on among the inmates, because once you're in prison most of your activity is centered around trying to get alcohol or drugs. It's amazing how successful they are. Even in our high-security detention center—"the hole"—we'd do periodic shakedowns and find black tar heroin. I was surprised that the stuff had gotten into the prison at all, let alone the high-security area. But the inmates are really ingenious.

One time one of our guards was patrolling the recreation yard. He looks up, and an arrow comes whizzing by his head. Then another arrow, and another. Each arrow had seven or eight Thai sticks tied to it. The inmates had their buddies outside shooting arrows over the prison walls into the yard.

The guards always had a lot of fun when we found dope that was meant for one of the inmates. One of the favorite ways they had of sneaking dope into the prison was to use tennis balls. Their friends on the outside would slice the tennis ball in half, load it up with dope, and tape it back together with duct tape. At night, they'd launch these tennis balls over the prison walls with slingshots. Sometimes we'd find them before the inmates did. One of the games we played was to cut the ball open, dump the dope out, and put a little note inside saying, "Fuck you, buddy, you've been screwed."

RANDY SHARKEY [corrections officer]: For two years, I worked in a state penitentiary as a prison guard. We had both minimum and maximum security prisoners. The minimum security guys would go outside during the day and work on the road gangs. They'd cut weeds and pick up litter for the Department of Transportation, and they'd work in the public parks. That gave them access to the civilian population. At night, they could make telephone calls from inside the prison, and they'd tell their friends and family members where they were going to be working the next day. Then their friends could go out and hide drugs or alcohol for them at a prearranged location.

When the trucks returned to the compound, these guys would have their drugs hidden inside tennis balls wrapped with duct tape, and they'd throw the tennis balls over the prison fence to the inmates on the compound inside. They'd also do a lot of body cavity packing. So there was no practical way to stop the drugs from getting in.

Part of my job as a guard was to strip-search the guys who had been out working on the road crews when they returned to the prison.

On one occasion, the road crew had been out to Tamiami Park, and a couple of guys had been drinking booze and smoking crack inside the men's room at the park. One of the prisoners was also trying to smuggle some crack back into the prison. I brought him up for the strip search, and he was standing there naked, hiding the crack in his mouth. I asked him to lift his tongue, and he just kind of did it halfway. I could tell that he was stoned, and that he was hiding something, so I got on the radio and speaking in code asked for help to be sent. When you ask for help it's a Ten–thirty-three emergency, but the inmates all know the codes, so this guy knew I was calling to get help. He went nuts. He attacked me, and took off running stark naked across the compound.

It took five of us to finally catch the guy and subdue him, but before we could, he'd swallowed the crack. So we had to send him over to the hospital's jail ward for observation. When you swallow cocaine, there's always the potential for death. Crack doesn't break down in the system the same way cocaine hydrochloride does, but if you swallow enough of it it will cause death. It can also make you very, very sick.

Anyway, we did manage to get this naked maniac over to the hospital where he was treated and kept under observation. As a prison guard, you'd get involved in that kind of nonsense almost every day. Crack is such an addictive drug that people will do all sorts of crazy, desperate things to get it. In the prison environment, that addictive behavior leads to an endless series of physical confrontations between the prisoners and the guards. I can honestly say I hated working in that penitentiary. I wanted to work in law enforcement, and being a corrections officer was a way of testing the waters, but I hated every minute of it. Eventually I was hired by the police department, and I'm currently working as a narcotics detective, and I resort to the use of force a lot less frequently on the street than I did in the prison. As a cop, use of force is reasonably rare, but in the prison it was constant.

PHILIP: The easiest way to smuggle drugs in is to hire a corrections officer. A lot of the prison guards grow up in the same neighborhoods as the inmates, so it's only natural that there are some inmates and guards who know each other. They'll have established a bond on the outside, and then choose to keep the relationship going on the inside.

The guards know there's a lot of money floating around, and they want in on the action. Every now and then some dude will be sitting on his bunk with a big, huge quantity of drugs. There's only one way you can get a huge quantity of drugs into the prison, and that's through a corrections officer. That's something that is happening all the time.

BARRY: When I came into prison, I decided I was gonna abstain from using drugs. But there are a lot of forces surrounding you that you can't control. After I came in, I was sitting on my bunk reading a book, and I look over this way and there's a dude sitting on his bunk rolling a joint. Then I look over the other way, and a dude's sitting there hitting the coke pipe. Dudes is doing it right out in the open. They ain't even trying to hide it. They know the corrections officers ain't gonna mess with 'em. The corrections officers don't want to get caught up in no beefs. They don't come messing around in the dorms unless they have to. As long as everything's cool, they stay on the perimeter. When you're in that kind of environment, you're gonna mix and mingle, and you're gonna get back up in doing drugs.

There was this one guard here that I used to talk to all the time. I thought he was the squarest dude in the world. Then one day about a month ago I opened the newspaper, and I see this dude's picture. He'd been busted for running a cocaine ring in the prison. Him and another guard would come in with cocaine strapped all up and down their legs. Now I was talking with this guy for a year, and like I said, I thought he was the squarest guy around. I thought I knew everything that was going on, but I come to find out he was *the man*. I couldn't believe it. I knew that guards was dropping off packages and stuff, but I never would have suspected this guy. He was a sergeant, and he was up for promotion. He was going to be a lieutenant. But like everybody else, he got caught up chasing the money.

DOUGLAS: When I got thrown in prison, I reverted back to the life I'd known on the street. I was vicious. I was mean. I tried to put forth a macho image. If some dude looked at me funny, I'd whip his ass. Immediately, I got into the prison drug scene. I had someone on the outside smuggle some drugs in, and I was dealing drugs from my prison bed.

After a while, I got a job in the kitchen, and I learned how to make jailhouse wine. Every ingredient you need to make wine you can find in the prison kitchen. We had yeast that comes right out of Safeway, and we had twenty-five-pound bags of sugar and tons of potatoes. We had all the juice in the world, and big cans of peaches and cherries. Because we had all the materials right there, we could make wine better than most people can make it out on the street. And we could make any flavor we wanted.

What we'd do was take two big fifteen-gallon trash cans, fill them with all the necessary ingredients, and then hide them up in the ceiling. We'd let them sit up there for a couple of days to ferment. Then we'd take them down and start selling wine to the inmates. I mean, it was an open concession. Everybody knew we were open for business, and because of that I never had to worry about money. I had enough money to buy all the drugs I needed.

RANDY SHARKEY: Prison is violent—very violent. You have a lot of stabbings and jail rapes and things of that nature. The inmates do a lot of body cavity packing, and have every kind of drug imaginable inside the prison. They also mix their own alcohol, which they call "buck." They bury it in the ground or hide it in the rafters to let it ferment. When they drink buck they get crazy, they get violent. The homemade alcohol and crack cocaine were the biggest problems, because they make people go crazy. They lead to fights and all kinds of violence.

In order to survive as a corrections officer, you can't show any fear. If the inmates see fear in you, they'll eat you alive. I'm only five-six and I weigh about one hundred twenty-five pounds, so naturally, when I first started working at the prison I had to prove myself. I've trained in martial arts all my life, and I'm very good at defending myself. In my two years at the prison, I've been involved in over seventy incidents that required the use of force. It's not that I'm a bad-ass guy, it's just that in order to survive you have to be prepared to defend yourself.

Inside the prison there's a place we call "the box." That's where the inmates are sent if they mess up. They're locked inside separate rooms, and are not allowed to mix with the general population. Of course, they have to be fed every day, and one of my duties as a guard was to take them their food. We had this one guy being kept there named Kruder. We called him "Crazy Kruder," because the guy used to pace back and forth all day long talking to himself.

One time I went inside his confinement room to give him his food, and as soon as I walked in, he slammed the door shut behind me. He's a strong, stocky guy—about five-ten, two hundred twenty pounds. I'm standing there with his food tray, and he pulls out a toothbrush that has a razor blade melted into it. He takes that and starts slashing his wrists. After he cuts himself, he says, "Now I'm gonna cut you!"

He came rushing at me, slashing with the toothbrush. Because of my martial arts background, I was able to block the razor blade and kick the guy. I knocked him back against his locker. He got up, and tried to cut me again. I kicked him, and he fell against the locker onto the floor. He's lying there with his wrists bleeding, and he starts to cry, singing some stupid, crazy song.

That was it. I was able to get out and get some help. But I couldn't sleep for three days after that. I thought the guy was going to kill me. When you're working in that kind of an environment, it's inevitable that the violence, the drugs, and the insanity are going to get to you. You start to think and act like a criminal. You have to know your enemy in order to survive. The prisoners all talk about "EOS"—end of sentence. Every day, I'd find myself saying, "This evening I EOS at five o'clock." I wasn't thinking of it as a job—each day was a separate sentence.

DUSTY: I didn't get involved with drugs until I was in prison. I'd seen what they do, and I was too scared to use them.

Then one day I was depressed. I'd been arrested on an armed robbery charge and sentenced to fifteen years. The thought of doing all that time had me all fucked up. I was mad at myself for putting myself in that position. I couldn't believe it was happening.

A friend of mine had some heroin. He cooked it up in the bathroom, showed it to me, and gave me the needle. I was so depressed that I went ahead and shot it. I did it again the next day and the day after that. Heroin was the only way I could beat my depression.

For the next seven years, I shot up every day that I was in prison. After a while, heroin was all I lived for. I'd do whatever I had to do to get it. One time my wife brought me a new pair of tennis shoes and I sold them to get some heroin. I sold almost all of my clothes, and then I started stealing from the other inmates. If I knew a guy had some drugs, I'd rob him. I had a homemade knife and a hatchet that I used to rob people.

That got me into a lot of trouble. I got stabbed one time, and got my head busted open another. In between I got my ass whipped plenty of times. The way I look at it, it's a miracle that I'm still alive. Messing with drugs is a ticket to death. If you don't kill yourself, then somebody is bound to do it for you.

TONY: The first thing you learn when you come into prison is that if someone looks at you wrong, or says something to you wrong, then you fight them. If you don't fight them everybody is going to know you're a punk. They're going to take advantage of you. People in here like to prey on the weak.

Another thing you learn is that you never take nothing from nobody. That's the way the buttfuckers work. Some dude might come up to you like he's trying to be your friend, and he gives you a Twinkie. So you eat it. Pretty soon he comes back and says, "Hey, I'm hungry. Can I have my Twinkie back?" You say, "No. I ate it." He says, "You ate my Twinkie? What are you going to give me?" He wants sex in return for his Twinkie. His buddies will gather around, and that Twinkie you ate is damn sure going to cost you a piece of your ass.

GEORGE: Rape is a definite problem for those who are weak. If you're a good-looking guy, and you don't know how to protect yourself, you're going to have trouble.

I seen one new guy come in with long hair. On his first day in here, he was walking behind one of the dorms on the compound, and this dude threw a sheet over his head. Four guys jumped on him and raped him. He never knew who did it, because they kept the sheet wrapped around his head the whole time they were fucking him.

I seen that and I felt bad for the guy. I wanted to help him, but that's the kind of thing you don't get involved in. In prison there's a code that says you don't mess in nobody's business. You either live by the code, or you die.

TONY: You get all kinds of violence in prison. It's more than just fistfights. People have all kinds of weapons. They've got knifes, hatchets, crowbars, glass bottles. They've got all kinds of shit, and they use it. People get killed in prison a lot more often than you'd think. If somebody gets murdered in prison, nobody cares. It's not the sort of thing that gets in newspapers or makes the evening news.

One day we had a shutdown, and the guards found enough weapons to fill the back of a long-bed pickup truck. That tells you what kind of weapons we got in here.

HARRY: You always hear people talk about how violent prison is, but I think the street is more violent now. At one time it wasn't that way. At one time prison was more violent. But you get into a beef in this here prison, and you goin' to fight with fists or knives. Even if some dude comes at you with a knife, you still got at least a fifty-fifty chance of living. But on the street you ain't got no fifty-fifty chance. A dude will shoot you down over a twenty-dollar cocaine bill. These young 'uns don't believe they can end up in a box. They say, "It ain't goin' to happen to me. I ain't goin' to get shot as long as I do the right thing." Well, you can be doing the right thing and still get blown away. It's crazy out there—with the wars for turf and the stickup boys. It's got to the point where drug dealers don't even respect each other. And when there's no honor among thieves, there's no honor at all. I figure it's got to be a lot safer in this here prison, man.

THEODORE ZIEGLER [drug treatment administrator]: Prisons are not the answer to addiction. We have one treatment facility called Raymar. It's a nice place—individual rooms, a complete staff, VCRs, stereo, movies, and a great cook. I should have it so nice in my own home. We have prisoners brought to us in chains. They've been remanded for treatment. They've been told they've got to play the game for at least ninety days. In the first week a lot of these people elect to go back to prison. They choose prison over treatment because if you drag your ass back into prison you don't have to change anything about your life. If you stay at Raymar, the staff is going to make you bathe. They're going to make you brush your teeth. They're going to make you launder your clothes. They're going to make you examine your life and talk about what's wrong and make you confront that. They'll bring your family in, and you'll have to deal with them too. Then at the end, they're going to get you a job. You'll actually have to work eight hours a day. In short, treatment is very difficult. It takes a lot of hard work and commitment. In prison you don't have to do any of that. Consequently, a lot of addicts choose prison. It's a lot easier than coming clean.

CHAPTER 8

TREATMENT

"Medicine is oftentimes a very primitive science," says a research psychiatrist experienced in treating a wide range of drug dependencies. "This is particularly true when we try to talk about drug addiction and how it operates on the brain. Because our knowledge is limited, treatment tends to be primitive. In most cases the best we can do is put the patient in a counseling environment where he can begin to *talk* about the problem. The medical side of the disease can't be dealt with except on a very short-term basis."

It is true that current medicine has no cure for addiction. It's also true that even the best treatment programs can save only about 25 percent of the addicts they treat from the recidivism that plagues them. Still, the fact that some people do rise above their addiction proves that there is hope. "For some reason," says a former addict who works as a drug treatment counselor, "drug addicts and alcoholics never get cured alone. They get cured in groups. By coming together with other addicts they form a fellowship that gives them strength and insight and wisdom. The process is a mystery to me—all I know is that the twelve steps of AA and NA have worked for millions of people who are currently in recovery."

Yet, after years of success, most recovered addicts are vulnerable to temptation. Though they may be far from the drug war's front lines, they continue to fight private battles daily. As one former addict, five years into recovery, said, "I can talk about my previous life and feel okay. I can tell you all of these things and still feel alright. Except for one thing—I would *love* to do some cocaine right now. Just *love* to."

———

WAYNE: Seeking help and getting treatment is very difficult, because it means admitting something you've been denying for a long, long time. That's hard. That's very hard to do.

I remember on June twenty-second my boss told me that she thought I had a drinking problem, and that I had to quit drinking or find a new job. That came as quite a shock. I was drinking at least a case of beer a day, plus all the drugs I was doing on top of it. I didn't think I was that bad, but I did start going to AA meetings. I quit drinking to save my job, but my drugging continued. I was telling myself, "Maybe I have a problem with alcohol, but I don't have a problem with drugs. I'm not doing that much cocaine." At AA meetings people would tell me that I couldn't do *any* drugs, but I thought they were full of shit. I kept insisting that my drugging wasn't a problem. You know, a little pot, a little acid, a little cocaine—what's the big deal?

The truth is, I was drugging five, six, seven days a week. I honestly can't tell you how much cocaine I was putting up my nose. All I can tell you is that it was a lot. I was using more drugs than I'd ever used before, and insisting that I didn't have a drug problem.

What made it tough for me is we all have visions of what a drug addict is. I thought a drug addict was someone who was strung out in a shooting gallery. You know, some hollow-faced, dirty, scroungy guy who looks like he hasn't eaten in a couple of months. That was my stereotype of a drug addict, and it certainly wasn't the way I pictured myself. I had a nice place to live, a job, and I bathed regularly. I wasn't a bum on the street. I wasn't wearing dirty clothes. I wasn't sleeping in cardboard boxes. So how could I be a drug addict?

Getting beyond my stereotype, and coming to terms with the fact that the stereotype wasn't the reality, was difficult. The reality was, and is, that *I* am a drug addict. That was very hard to admit, and it was very hard to say. To call myself a drug addict seemed like such a cruel, ruthless, nasty thing to do. But to get help and deal with my problem, I didn't have any choice. Not only did I have to say it, I had to believe it.

STEPHANIE: I'd been doing cocaine for a couple of years, and I kept telling myself that I was going to quit. You know, every week or so I'd say, "Hey, this is getting too expensive. You're doing too much of this stuff. It's time to quit." But I never did. I just kept on, thinking I could quit whenever I wanted to. Thinking that I didn't have a serious problem.

I was miserable because my life was so fucked up. I was going to work hung over. I was getting drunk every weekend, and sleeping with strange men. I wasn't eating right. And I was spending a lot of money on cocaine.

After promising myself I was going to quit for about the zillionth time, and then not doing it, it finally dawned on me, "Hey, I've got a problem here. I can't quit. I'm addicted to this stuff." You'd think that realization would cause me to seek out treatment, but it had just the opposite effect. It gave me an excuse to really let go, and the amount of cocaine I was using absolutely skyrocketed. That was when I started using every day. I'd tell myself, "Hey, I can't help it. I don't have any control."

Every evening I'd come home from work, go up to my room, close the door, and sit there and do coke. I'd be all alone, because I was ashamed. I didn't want anyone else to see me. My voice was real shaky, my hands were real shaky. I'd lost a lot of weight, and when I looked in the mirror my eyes were bloodshot and wired. My life was pitiful. Really, it was no life at all. I'd do a line, and immediately I'd want more. That's all I wanted—more.

I had a really bad job record at work. At night, I'd get just a little bit of sleep, then in the morning I'd do a few lines to help me wake up. When I first started doing coke it made me real talkative and fun and stuff, but not anymore. Now it was dragging me down. I was always tired, always feeling sick. At work, I kept getting up from my desk to go to the rest room, where I'd do a few lines in the privacy stall. Every fifteen, twenty minutes I was running to the rest room. Other times I'd just do it at my desk. It was impossible for me to do a good job, because I was so coked up.

I was amazed at the way I was spending money. It got so bad that I just quit paying my bills. The more I worried about money, the more I'd spend. Sometimes I'd go on compulsive shopping binges, buying clothes and running up huge bills on my credit cards. Then when the bills came in the mail, I'd just toss them into the trash can. The *only* things I was spending money on were rent and cocaine.

I had a couple days off over the Fourth of July weekend, and I flew back to the town where I grew up to visit my parents. All I wanted to do was go home and *not* do any drugs. I stayed sober down there for three days, and after flying back here the first thing I did when I got to my apartment was call my mother. I said, "Mom, I'm going through a really rough time, and I want you to pray for me."

She said, "Why? What's wrong?"

I said, "I can't tell you. I just need you to pray for me."

The next morning, the first thing I did was go out and buy some cocaine. I didn't want to, but I couldn't help myself. I went on a three-day binge where all I did was cocaine. It was so depressing. I shut myself up in my apartment, unplugged the phone, and snorted line after line after line. I didn't even bother calling in sick at work, because I was sure I was going to be fired. After three days, I was dizzy, shaky, and nervous. I had an upset stomach, and a terrible headache. I felt like absolute shit, and spent the next couple days in bed.

That Sunday I called my mom, and she was crazy with worry. She'd been trying to call me, but hadn't been able to get through because I'd unplugged the phone. She said, "Stephanie, tell me what's wrong!"

I couldn't tell her. We were on the phone for twenty minutes, and I kept crying, saying, "I can't tell you. I can't tell you." She was really worried, and kept asking, "What's wrong?" Finally, I said, "Mom, it's cocaine. I'm addicted to cocaine."

I thought she was going to be mad at me, and get upset. There was this long silence, and the first thing she said was, "Well, you need to get into treatment."

As soon as she said that, I knew it was what I wanted to do. It was the first time I'd even thought of treatment as being a viable option. But my situation had become impossible to deal with. I'd hit bottom. Everything seemed so overwhelming.

My parents flew up the next day, and made all the arrangements for me to enter this twenty-eight-day inpatient treatment program. I cleaned myself up, and they drove me down to the hospital. I remember when I checked in it was real scary. I couldn't believe it was happening. In a way, I was glad because I felt this huge weight being lifted off my shoulders. But I was also thinking, "God, I can't believe this is happening to me. I can't believe I'm so sick that I need to be put in this hospital for a month." There's something very ominous, very frightening, about actually facing up to your addiction, facing up to the fact that you have this disease.

JIMMY: I was arrested twice in the same week. I'd been addicted to heroin for right around eleven years, but managed to get by because I always had a steady job. I'd work all day and shoot up in the evenings. I was earning union wages, and could afford to spend three hundred or four hundred dollars on heroin every month—the same way an alcoholic can afford to run up a hundred dollars a week in bar bills.

Gradually, my habit got worse. Instead of shooting up two or three times a week, I was shooting up every day. Then I started taking off from work at two or three o'clock in the afternoon, because all I could think about was the needle. My boss couldn't understand why I was always disappearing, and I got fired.

So I started shoplifting to support my habit. That's something I'd never, ever done before. I'd always considered myself an honest person, but I had a couple of friends who were fencing hot items and I needed the money. I'd steal clothes and jewelry from department stores, and I'd break into warehouses to steal from distributors. That was the easiest, because there was so much merchandise just sitting there, and you never had to sneak past any checkout counters. Once you'd fouled the alarm system, whatever was in the warehouse was yours for the taking.

Then one day a plainclothes security officer caught me trying to steal some jewelry from a department store, and he detained me until a policeman came down and made the arrest. Two days later I was caught trying to steal food from a grocery store. The cop who answered that call recognized me from the previous arrest. He'd just thrown me in jail two days earlier. He put handcuffs on me and was being real tough, saying, "Hey man, what the fuck is wrong with you? Why are you ripping these people off?"

He shoved me in the back of his squad car, and was treating me like dirt—like white trash that he was tired of looking at. He was saying, "You're a real dumb fuck, you know that? What the hell's the matter with you?"

So I told him. I said, "I'm a junkie."

Now, that's the first time in my life I ever admitted that to anyone, and this incredible transformation came over that cop's face. The look of venom and disgust disappeared, and was replaced by this look of pity and sorrow.

He started asking me a bunch of questions. "What are you addicted to? How long have you been addicted?" He sat down in the back of the squad car with me, and the two of us talked for maybe twenty to thirty minutes right there in the parking lot. I told him how long I'd been using heroin, how I'd lost my job, what all I'd stolen and where. At one point, I broke down crying because I'd never told the truth to anyone before. That was very emotional—to put my life into words like that. I'd always tried to maintain the outward appearance of a decent, law-abiding citizen.

This cop was very understanding. He said, "Man, you got to get off the horse. Are you ready to quit? Do you want to quit?"

I told him that was what I wanted more than anything in the world. He told me that I had to tell the judge that I was a junkie, and that maybe I could get into a drug treatment program. He drove me down to the station, and before he booked me on the shoplifting charge, he gave me his telephone number and told me to have my attorney call him. He said he'd talk to the DA personally if that would help. Sure enough, a plea bargain was arranged where I wouldn't have to serve any jail time contingent on my enrollment in this drug treatment program.

That was nine months ago, and I'm still in treatment. I'm going to the clinic on an outpatient basis. Right now, I'd have to say that cop saved my life. If he'd just booked me and thrown me in jail, I'd still be out on the street robbing and stealing and doing whatever I had to do to support my habit. If he hadn't gone to bat for me with the DA, and made all the necessary arrangements, there's no way I could have been admitted to the rehab program on my own.

I credit him with saving my life. Since then, I've come to learn that he's got a sixteen-year-old daughter who is a cocaine addict. That's why he was so understanding. He *knows* what the hell of addiction is all about. He knows more than your average cop.

THEODORE ZIEGLER [drug treatment administrator]: Treatment facilities are operating at levels way *over* capacity. The bodies are piling up.

Our facility is staffed to treat a maximum of three hundred fifty patients. We're currently treating well over seven hundred. Last year, for the first time in the history of our organization, we shut down the intake process. We just don't have the space. But that is only part of our problem. The fact is, we live in the most litigious country in the world, and that makes things all the more difficult.

To illustrate what we're dealing with, let me give you a hypothetical scenario. Say you come to my front door and want treatment. I say okay, and we take you in. As part of the intake process we diagnose you, and develop a preliminary treatment plan. Then we explain, "Okay, you're a cocaine addict. Unfortunately, our staff is carrying twice their maximum load. They're not going to be able to start with you for two or three months. We'll put you on a waiting list, and begin treatment as soon as we can." You leave, and while you're waiting for your appointment you overdose and die. But before you do, you've told your family you were waiting to see us. The family finds the preliminary documentation and discovers that, yes, we diagnosed you as an addict in need of treatment, but no, we didn't take any immediate medical action. Never mind that it was impossible to fit you in. When a family sees a diagnosis like that, what do you think they're going to do? They're going to sue the ass off us—and they're going to win.

To deal with the potential legal action we're facing, I had to go to our board of directors and say, "Listen, we're exposing ourselves to a horrendous amount of litigation. The only way we can protect ourselves is to *not recognize* that these people have a problem when they come to our door. If we simply refuse to recognize them, and do not even diagnose them, then we can't be sued."

BARRY: A lot of people out there want help. They know they got a problem, and they seriously want help. Trouble is, you always meet the drug before you meet help—and a drug addict ain't never going to understand addiction. What drugs do to you can't never be explained. As long your mind is fogged with drugs, the drug will control you and manipulate you. Now that I'm straight, I look back on the things I done when I was on the shit—the robbing, the lying, the stealing—and I don't understand how *anybody* could do that stuff, much less how I done it myself. I honestly believe that if I hadn't been arrested and put in jail I'd be dead right now. If the drugs hadn't killed me, somebody's bullet would've.

*   *   *

DOUGLAS: A lot of the treatment programs you go to is nothing but cons and ex-cons. The judge'll put you on probation with the requirement that you got to go to group meetings or some other kind of program. So you start going to these meetings 'cause you don't want your parole revoked. But what happens is you just end up gettin' deeper into a life of crime. All of the dudes at these meetings is drug addicts, man. Most of 'em just tryin' to stay out of prison. They ain't tryin' to stay clean. They ain't got jobs, and they scheming for ways to get ahold of some money. The meetings just give you a new peer group, a new social set. You hang out with these dudes, do drugs, and engage in more criminal activity. Armed robberies, burglaries, banks—that's the kind of shit you get into. When I was in treatment, it was a pretty sure bet that I was going to violate my parole.

DR. WALTER L. FAGGETT [drug treatment administrator]: My training was in adolescent medicine, and that's where I first got interested in drug abuse. I was taking care of teenage methadone and heroin addicts as early as 1971. I felt pretty good, like I was doing something positive. I had thirteen- and fourteen-year-olds coming to group meetings all strung out. I'd take them places, and even took them to my apartment complex and let them swim in the pool. I also took them to the Army hospital where I was working to show them there was a different life—that they could get out. The one thing I learned right away was, to be effective you have to be involved.

To fulfill my obligation to the Army, I went down to Texas for a couple years, and when I left I felt pretty good. I thought I'd done some good, constructive things with the kids I was leaving behind. After getting my discharge from the Army, I returned to the area and I followed up on some of my patients. I discovered that I had a ninety-five-percent failure rate. That was depressing. I'd hoped the results of treatment and intervention would have been much better, so it was tough to take.

One day I received a letter from a former patient by the name of Greg. He had been an IV heroin addict at the age of fourteen. I'd had serious doubts about his ever being able to make it to adulthood. He was in prison, and in the letter he said he'd been incarcerated for ten years. He was, however, drug-free, and explained that he wanted to do some work in drug treatment upon his release. He wanted to share his experiences so that maybe he could save someone else from drugs. I said great, and sent word to the physicians working at the prison to let me know what I could do to help Greg. Well, Greg was released, but I never heard about it. The next time I saw him was in the hospital emergency room, and he was strung out on heroin again. He was terribly embarrassed to see me, and he signed out against medical advice and left. He didn't even try to stay for the treatment process.

I had another patient from that same group of young kids named Carol. She called me not long ago and invited me to a party celebrating the third anniversary of her being drug-free. She has a job and an apartment, and it was really great to see her. I was thinking, "Yes, I must've had some positive impact. She's been drug-free for three years now. She's kicked the needle. That's really great." The sad thing, however, is that Carol had AIDS. I thought it was going to be really good to see her and congratulate her on her third anniversary, but it was a real downer.

Then, I had a third patient by the name of Tony. He was a good kid—a high school graduate who got himself a job as an electrician's apprentice. He had come looking for help with a PCP problem, and once he got into treatment he was extremely cooperative. Tony really worked hard in the program. I got to know him, and felt a fondness for him. He was one of my favorite patients, and I thought his prospects were better than most. When he left he had a job, a good family, and he was feeling good about himself. He wanted to share what he'd learned in treatment with his buddies on the street. He tried to get them to stop using dope. One day he was in a car with a couple of his friends, and a dealer came up to the window and tried to sell them some dope. Tony told his friends not to buy it. "You don't need it," he said, and some words were exchanged. The dealer was carrying a weapon, and he opened fire on Tony. The other kids in the car were wounded, but Tony was killed. When I heard about that I was crushed. The unfortunate reality of a job like this one is you're constantly coming face-to-face with tragedy. Relapse, violence, and AIDS are all part of the mix. To be effective you have to be involved, and you have to care. But being involved also means you get a lot taken out of you. Patients you think are making progress don't survive.

*   *   *

WAYNE: For me, the early part of treatment was the worst, because
I was going through withdrawal and experiencing a lot of physical
discomfort. I was in an outpatient program, and I didn't go through
medical detox. I was still going to work and continuing with my daily
routine. I'd been drinking and drugging to excess for fifteen years,
and then all of a sudden I stopped. No more booze, no more pot,
no more cocaine, no more Valium. No uppers, no downers. Nothing
that would alter my mood or help me with my anxiety. Before treatment it was always easy for me to say, "I'm stressed out, I need a
drink"; "I'm stressed out, I need a Valium"; "I'm depressed, I think
I'll do a few lines of cocaine." I always knew that there was some
chemical substance out there that would make me feel "better." I
was used to having that crutch, and then all of a sudden it was gone.
Not having it scared the shit out of me.

Once I got into treatment, I couldn't reach for that magical "feel
better" substance anymore. I had to deal with whatever was bothering
me by staying clean and sober. That task was made doubly difficult
by the physical symptoms of withdrawal that I was going through. I
had prolonged periods of insomnia, and periods where I was exhausted all the time. My skin would itch, and I'd feel drug cravings.
There are many different sorts of physical withdrawal that you go
through, and all of them are unpleasant.

The great advantage of being in treatment during that period of
withdrawal was that there were professional people there who could
explain to me why I was experiencing so much discomfort. They
were able to say this is why you can't sleep, this is why you're irritable, this is why you're experiencing such extreme exhaustion. From
a physiological standpoint, I understood that I was supposed to be
going through what I was going through. Without that knowledge,
I'm not sure I would've been able to make it.

STEPHANIE: I feel like I'm an intelligent person, but I can't believe
I let myself suffer as long as I did without *seeing* what the problem
was. All of the experiences I had with drugs, the getting fired from
my job, the waking up with strange men, the blackouts, the fights
with my family, all of those things were red flags telling me, Stop!
Get help! Get into treatment! But I didn't see it. I was so heavily
into denial that I let myself go on and on doing terrible things to
myself and others.

As difficult as it was, it's a blessing that I finally hit bottom, and was forced to get help. At the hospital, the first thing they did was put me through detox. The medical staff had me do a drug history. In addition to cocaine and alcohol, I'd been taking Xanax as a prescription drug for years. The doctor said he was going to take me off Xanax, and that really scared me. I remember telling him, "You don't understand! I *need* my Xanax!" You know, here I am, the drug addict, telling the doctor what to do.

During those first couple weeks, when I was withdrawing from cocaine and Xanax, I was constantly trying to finagle Valiums from the medical staff. Even in treatment, I thought I *needed* drugs to survive, and being deprived of them had me feeling very panicky, very scared. At first, I didn't like the medical personnel, because they were making me take responsibility for my drug addiction, which is something I didn't want to do.

DR. WALTER L. FAGGETT: The typical group experience here is we bring a new patient in and introduce him or her to all the other patients, and we encourage them to think of the group as their new "family." They are all here for each other, and we strongly promote the idea that if one of them hurts, then the whole group hurts. Each of them needs to get their pain out so that everyone can discuss it. For most patients, this is the only support structure they've ever had in their lives, and it takes a minimum of six months to build that base. It doesn't happen overnight.

When the group meets we discuss issues that arise as a consequence of the patients' drug use and addiction. One of the recent issues we discussed was the way women are giving sex to any man they can find in a crack house in return for a rock. We discussed how crack destroys the will, how crack is one of the most powerfully addictive drugs we have ever seen, and how crack destroys a mother's maternal instincts. We talked about abused and abandoned babies—how getting crack is more important than taking care of your child. We also discussed how the medical community is seeing more and more AIDS among crack-addicted women because of the sex-for-crack phenomenon.

One of the patients participating in that discussion was a young woman who was four months pregnant. In the middle of the discussion she started cramping, and I immediately called for another physician to come in and evaluate her. My fear, of course, was for the possibility of a miscarriage, which is common among addicted women. She was cramping so bad she started crying, and she was taken out of the group for medical care. After she left, the rest of the group continued the discussion. One of the other young women remarked that she'd been carrying twins when she started cramping like that, and the pregnancy aborted. So we talked about that issue—drugs and pregnancy. After a while, the young woman who'd left us came back in. She still had tears in her eyes, but she'd been given medication for the pain. She said she'd had to beg and plead with the physician to let her come back. She said she didn't feel good enough to participate in the discussion, but that it was important for her to be there. She wanted to listen to what was being said.

To me, that was a positive sign. I think it reflected the strength of what you can do for people when you show them how things *can* be—things such as a strong sense of unity and belonging without the aid or illusion of drugs. If you show them a positive, supportive environment, and do your best to give them the tools to replicate that environment on the outside when they leave, then they have a much better chance of making it. To see that little glimmer of fight, to see that woman return to the group because she was fighting to get well—that's a victory. That's the sort of thing that keeps me going and gives me hope.

To see people getting better, to see a team mature, and to know that you've helped a few patients along the way, that gives me a great feeling. I was down at the bank the other day and one of the guards approached me and said, "Dr. Faggett, don't you recognize me?" It was one of my patients. He was clean and had a job, and he looked super. For me, that was terrific. A wonderful success. Basically, I feel that if I can help keep a patient drug-free for even one hour, then I've done some good. That's one hour they had to feel differently. That's one hour they had where they weren't trapped in the hell of addiction and substance abuse.

LARRY: The main thing about treatment is it gives you a bubble to be clean in. When you check into a twenty-eight-day inpatient program, you're not on your own. You're in a controlled environment. There are doctors and nurses and counselors there. As long as you don't go AMA [against medical advice], then you've got four weeks of being clean right off the bat. That's something I'd *never* done before.

While you're in treatment you analyze your feelings, and you're forced to confront what it was that drove you to addiction. A lot of people are biologically predisposed—they have a history of drug or alcohol abuse in the family. But that's not true for me. I grew into my addiction because I liked it. I think a lot of that was because I'm dyslexic. I've always had low self-esteem because I have this learning disability. When I was a kid in school, I used to go into these blind angry rages. Being dyslexic made it impossible for me to be like the other kids. I was always angry, always mad. Then when I started using drugs, I discovered this nice feeling. I never found anything to calm me down like I did with drugs.

For a long, long time I enjoyed getting high. Marijuana, codeine, PCP—I'd do anything. And I enjoyed it right through the last several years of my addiction. My idea of life was to get married, have a family, buy a house—that whole bit. But it wasn't happening. Because of my addiction, I was stealing a lot. My finances were in terrible shape. I wasn't paying the rent. I wasn't buying groceries. I wasn't acting right. There was a lot of animosity between me and my wife. A lot of addicts put their families through hell, and here I was putting my wife and my daughter through hell. I was making them go through addiction with me.

Crack is the drug that really brought me to my knees. I could go through two hundred dollars a day, easy. Sitting here now, I feel bad about all the stealing I did. I stole from my parents a lot, and that haunts me. If my father left his wallet on his bedroom dresser, I'd sneak in and steal money out of it. If he left his clothes on the bed while he was taking a shower, I'd go through his pockets and take however much money he had. He doesn't make that much to begin with, and here I was stealing from him. That created a lot of hate and discontent between us. I feel bad about that. Even if I could give back all the money I stole, I could never make up for all the hate and anguish.

Being in treatment and talking about these things has helped me a lot. In order to overcome addiction, you need to understand it. You need to come to terms with the things that motivate your drug use so that you can control those impulses and urges. Then you need to make amends for the things you have done, the people you have harmed. Treatment has definitely helped me with my family. Even though I can't erase the past, or take away any of the bad things I did, at least I can talk about it. That was impossible when I was living in addiction. I wasn't even aware of all the pain I was causing

until I went into treatment, and took time out for some sober reflec-
tion. Fortunately, my wife is very understanding. She's very supportive. My father is an intelligent person, and he has some
understanding too. We're not talking about changing the past, but we
are talking—we're talking about building a future that makes sense.

WAYNE: When I first started going to NA meetings I was amazed
by the incredible tales people were telling when they described what
they did in addiction. They were talking about embezzling money,
beating their wives, beating their children, prostitution, and theft.
They'd talk about how they were living on the street, homeless because of their addiction. I'd listen to these really horrid stories in
total amazement. I'd think, "Nothing like that ever happened to me!
I was never that bad!"

At first, that made it hard for me to identify with some of the other
addicts. But after a while, I realized that even though our experiences
were different, the feelings were the same. The morning after a great
night of using coke, I'd wake up feeling lonely and unloved. I'd feel
guilty for spending so much money, or for sleeping with a stranger,
or for having had an alcohol-induced blackout. I'd feel like a totally
worthless person. Which is the exact same emotion these people felt
when they described the terrible things they'd done. Even though my
bottom wasn't as low as theirs, on an emotional level I could relate.
That realization helped me get through the horror of what they had
done. The common bond we all share is we know what it *feels* like
to be a drug addict.

ERNIE: When people first start coming to NA meetings they're very
vulnerable. They feel guilty. That's something that we all share at
the early stages of recovery. We think we're *bad* people. The beauty
of group meetings is that once we begin to express our remorse, we
come to realize that we're not alone. That there are a lot of folks out
there who understand, and they understand because they've been in
the same boat.

When new people come into the program, I look them in the eye
when I speak to them and I'm not ashamed to tell them about the
things I've done—the robbings, the muggings, the violence. I tell
'em how I used to inject teenage kids when I was shooting up, because they wanted to try it for the first time. I tell 'em how a lot of
the guys I used to run with are dead now. I don't try to hide my

criminal past, because I want them to know that a lot of people have experienced pain and regret. A lot of us carry a heavy burden of guilt. But it doesn't have to be that way forever. You can give that burden away by talking about it, by being honest and sharing at meetings.

A lot of the younger addicts don't stay with the program. After a couple days, weeks, or months, they go back out and are never heard from again. Most of them end up in prison. So I always make it a point to talk with the younger kids, to tell them, "Hey, you don't need to sink any lower than you already have. You don't need to waste years of your life in prison. You don't need to die of an overdose, and you don't need to kill anyone. You're lucky, because you don't need to sink as low as I did. It's your choice. If you really want to, you can stop right now."

ANTOINE: Crack cocaine is scary, man. I've been in prison two years, and I'm in a voluntary drug program at the penitentiary. I could've been out on the streets six months ago, but I stayed in prison because I wanted to obtain the benefits of this program. I didn't feel I was ready for the street. I have a fear of going back out, because I don't want to get caught up in the drug scene again.

Here in prison I've seen friends do two or three years, get out, and in less than a month they come back on a new charge. All it takes is one hit, man. If you believe "I can handle this one hit," then you've got a serious problem. Because you can't handle that shit. Ain't nobody can handle crack 'caine for long. I don't care what anybody says. You can't handle it.

Me and this other dude I was locked up with got to be tight. He did six years. He was a Muslim, and he prayed with me all the time. He was real sincere. He was saying that when he got out he was going to get his life together. He swore he wasn't gonna go back to drugs. He was lifting weights, and his physique was cut out. He was a strong dude, and he was pumping a lot of iron.

After doing his time he got out, but he only stayed out for two months. They brought him back in on a cocaine charge. The first thing he did when he got back in that environment was start hitting the pipe. When they brought him back, the dude was so skinny I almost didn't recognize him. I couldn't believe a dude that strong could lose that much weight in such a short time. His whole body had deteriorated.

That's why I'm afraid of going back. A lot of people probably don't understand a dude saying he has a fear of leaving prison. But if you'd lived the life I did, you'd understand. When I was hitting the pipe, I'd have to hide from my daughter so she wouldn't see me. Right now, I weigh two hundred eighteen pounds, but when I got arrested I was only weighing one-fifty. I was walking around like a ghost. My jaw was sucked in. My eyes were sucked in. I didn't even look like the same person. Every day, I pray to God to never let me live like that again.

DR. MARK GOLD [medical doctor]: The art form of treatment is in a very primitive state. The kinds of treatment that are utilized for cocaine addiction tend to be borrowed in part from successful treatment of alcoholics. But, by and large, the treatment is a long, difficult process.

The data show that relapse is now so common that it's being included in the definition of cocaine addiction, and is being studied as a newly acquired drive. As we have the drive for food, there may be, over time, with cocaine a new drive—the drive to readdiction. The national data suggests that no matter how quickly we treat people, other people relapse. It's not just that there are new people joining the cocaine epidemic, there is also this internal recycling going on.

LARRY: Staying clean is hard. It's very hard. I've been clean for eight months now, and I think about getting high every day. At one time or another, I've gotten high almost everywhere in this city. No matter where I go I have memories. Those memories trigger the urge to use. Lots of things trigger the urge. If I see somebody strike a match, I'm automatically thinking about the crack pipe. When I go to work in the morning, I pass within a couple blocks of the drug strip, and I'm thinking about getting high. When I'm sitting at home alone watching the TV, I'm thinking about getting high. There are times when it's an obsession. Even though I'm clean, my disease is alive in my fantasies. It's hard being in recovery, because an addict in recovery is still an addict.

The temptation to relapse is always present. Since coming out of the hospital, I've relapsed once. My wife and I were in the process of getting things back together—straightening our finances out and paying a lot of overdue bills. Because I was doing so good, I got an instant teller card, and my wife sent me out to buy some diapers and milk. As I was walking down to the store, I saw a buddy of mine who I used to get high with. He said, "Hey man, what's going on?" He was heading off to get high, and something inside me clicked. I told myself, "You'll be okay. You haven't done anything in six months. This one time won't hurt, because you can obviously handle it."

My wife and I only had sixty dollars in the bank, and instead of taking out ten dollars to buy diapers and milk, I took out all sixty dollars and spent it on crack. I picked up right where I left off. I was right back in addiction, smoking up every penny I had. The only thing was, I didn't enjoy the high. The whole time I was smoking, I knew I was wrong. I was thinking, "Aw shit, man, I shouldn't be doing this."

I was lucky. My relapse could've been a lot worse. If we'd had more money in the bank, I would've kept on going. I would've smoked up two hundred, three hundred, four hundred dollars—whatever we had. This time, instead of going out stealing to get more crack, I was able to pull myself together. I was able to go home and face the music. Which is what I did. I went home and told my wife what I'd done. Then the next day I went to my aftercare meeting, and I told the group what I'd done.

Some people in the program say that relapse is a part of recovery. But I don't believe that's true. It doesn't need to be a part of recovery. It's only part of recovery because it's a statistic, it happens. You don't have to relapse to recover. What you need is to be totally honest with yourself. You need to understand that you're a drug addict, and because you're a drug addict you're going to have memories, cravings, and desires. You're going to want to use. Nothing can change that. So you've got to accept the fact that recovery is hard—it's very hard. It's the battle you have to fight every day.

STEPHANIE: There was this guy in treatment with me by the name of Bill, and the two of us had an attraction for each other. We went through a twenty-eight-day inpatient program that was followed by outpatient aftercare and meetings. Bill got out a week before I did, and he relapsed immediately. When I got out, I started seeing him. I was hoping he'd come back to the outpatient meetings and get his life in order. Everybody who went through the program with us was telling me I was crazy, that I should stay away from him. They were saying, "Stephanie, don't be stupid. Seeing Bill after he's relapsed is dangerous. It's foolish."

Of course, I didn't listen. We wanted to go out with each other, so that's what we did. Exactly one week after I'd been released from the hospital I was over at his place, and we decided to go out and get something to eat. The restaurant we wanted to go to was closed, so we drove into Annapolis and went to this place on the waterfront. They had an outdoor patio where a live band was playing. It was a really beautiful Sunday afternoon, and this band was playing great songs. When the waiter came by, Bill said, "I want a beer." And I said, "Me too. I'll have a beer."

When I ordered, I knew I wasn't going to have just one beer. I knew I was going to get drunk. Which is exactly what I did. The two of us sat there and drank all day.

From our treatment sessions, I knew that Bill's drug of choice was crack. Even though I was a cocaine addict, I'd never tried crack. I'd only used powder. After I was good and drunk, I said to him, "Let's get some crack. I want to try it."

Bill was game for that, and we took off to get some crack. Bill lives in this very rural area of Maryland, and we went driving along these winding backcountry roads. It was really beautiful. There was nothing but rolling farmland for miles and miles. Just as the sun was setting, we pulled up in front of this little grocery store that stood in front of a couple of run-down shacks. As soon as we pulled in, these little black boys came running over to the car to sell us crack. I couldn't believe it: Here we were in the middle of nowhere, and they have this open-air market. It was just like being in the city. These little black boys were competing with each other to sell us crack.

We bought a couple rocks, then drove down the road to a nice wooded area to smoke it. Bill made a makeshift pipe out of a beer can, and as soon as I took a hit I could feel it expanding in my lungs. I felt the high right away. It was a lot like powder cocaine, only better—a bit more euphoric. Even before I exhaled, it gave me this really good feeling. Right away, I wanted more. So Bill drove back and we bought a few more rocks, and smoked everything we had that night.

A couple days later, I went out with a friend, and as I was driving home I stopped and bought some beer. I drank a couple beers, and thought, "Hey, I want some crack."

I've got this shitty little car, and I'm a young white girl, and off I go, driving into the worst black area of the city to buy some crack. Looking back, I'd have to say that was an insane thing to do. This neighborhood is very violent, and I was putting myself in a dangerous situation by going in there all alone in the middle of the night. But when you're doing drugs you feel immortal, and it didn't bother me a bit at the time. Fortunately, I didn't have any problems. I just bought my crack and went on my merry way.

I couldn't even wait to get home to smoke it. I lit up in the car, smoked everything I had, and then went back to get some more. Once I got back to my apartment, I remember sitting there thinking, "This is ridiculous! Is this what I went through twenty-eight days of treatment for?" I was thinking that as I was sitting there smoking crack. I *knew* what I was doing was absolutely crazy! This time, I couldn't fool myself into thinking that I could control my addiction. I knew exactly what I was getting into. I'd been through enough hell to know what was going to happen.

The next day I made a conscious decision. I went to my aftercare group and told them everything that had happened. I admitted it all. At the time, I felt like a horrible failure. I thought everything had gone down the drain. But I talked to a doctor, and he told me that relapse is common. Oftentimes, it's a phase that people go through. So for the next couple months I worked on turning my relapse into a positive learning experience. That was eleven months ago, and I've been clean and sober ever since. Looking back, I'd have to say that I'm glad I relapsed, because it taught me a valuable lesson about myself. Even after all I'd been through prior to treatment, and all I'd been told in treatment, I thought I could "get well." One of the crazier things is I thought it would be okay for me to drink again after treatment. You know, I told myself that my problem was cocaine, not alcohol. All the doctors and nurses told me that was nonsense, but I had to learn the hard way. I had to learn for myself. After my relapse, I know beyond the shadow of a doubt that I have this disease—I'm an alcoholic and a drug addict. Even if I stay sober for the next twenty or thirty years—which I fully intend to do—I'll still be an alcoholic and a drug addict. I'm comfortable with the fact that there's no cure, and that I'll never be a social drinker or a recreational cocaine user. For me, that was an important lesson to learn.

I've been clean for eleven months now, and I'm actually starting to feel comfortable about myself. I've got a routine and a job, and I feel safe. Which I never felt before. When I first got sober I was always teetering on the fence. I never knew if I was going to relapse or not. I'd feel cravings and urges, and I was afraid of what I might do. But I'm starting to trust myself now. I'm starting to believe that it really is possible to go through life without doing drugs.

One of the things they always tell you in meetings is to self-diagnose. To remind yourself that you have a disease, and to remember how bad it was so that you won't go back. I've been doing that, even though it is very distasteful for me to remember, because some of the things I did were so gross. I'm sad that so many years of my life were wasted. But when I look back, I realize that I never liked drugs anyway. I *hated* the life I was living in addiction. It's kind of funny. Giving up drugs feels like such a major sacrifice, and yet, it's really no sacrifice at all. I'm finally getting to a point where I don't miss drugs, and that is setting me free to live a safe, happy life.

JOE: Relapse is not at all uncommon. For some people it's the missing link between recovery and addiction. I was a drug addict and alcoholic for the better portion of twenty, twenty-five years. I was so hard-core that I spent a couple years living on the street as a homeless person. Finally, in 1977, I checked into the VA hospital, and went through their treatment program. After being released from the hospital, I kept up with the AA meetings, and stayed sober for eleven years. During that time, I went back to college and got my degree and established myself within my profession, which is engineering. I'd completely transformed myself from a homeless street drunk to a working professional who commands the respect of his peers. Working full time, and getting into a couple other outside activities, I found that my attendance at AA meetings began to taper off after a few years. I told myself that I didn't have time, which is a total bullshit excuse. But the important thing was that I was staying sober. Even though I'd quit going to AA meetings, I still wasn't drinking.

Then in March of 1988, I went up to my hometown—which is a small town about ninety miles from where I live now—for a short visit. A friend and I went out to see a movie. He'd been doing some painting for this guy who owned a bar, and after the movie he wanted to stop by the bar to pick up his paycheck. I said, "Fine. No problem." So we went inside, sat down at the bar, and while we were waiting for the owner my friend ordered a beer.

That did it. As soon as he said, "I'll have a beer," my reflex was to say, "I'll have one too." Here I'd gone *eleven years* without injesting a single drop of alcohol, and all of a sudden I'm ordering a beer. My friend looked at me like I was crazy. He and I had grown up together and he knew what the score was. The bartender set the beers down in front of us, and my friend grabbed my wrist and said, "Are you going to drink that?"

I said, "Yeah, I'm going to drink it."

He was incredulous. "Why?"

"Because I want to."

My friend knew better than to argue with me, because I would've knocked him off his fucking stool. So we drank our beers and ordered some more. And then some more after that. The whole time I was sitting there drinking, I felt like I was two completely different people. I was the guy on the barstool drinking beer, and I was another guy watching myself with disbelief. I was carrying on a schizophrenic conversation inside my head: "What the fuck are you doing?" "It's none of your business. Stay out of this. I know what I'm doing." "You're an alcoholic. You've got no business messing with this shit." "Shut the fuck up. I know what I'm doing. I can handle it. I want another beer." "No, you can't have another beer!" "Fuck you. I'm going to have another beer." You know, that kind of conversation was going on inside my head.

My friend and I sat there and drank six beers each. Then we stopped. I didn't get drunk, and after six, I didn't want any more. I just went home to bed. Which was very curious. Before, I'd always drink myself to complete oblivion. I *couldn't* stop. But the scary thing about this night was that I didn't have any trouble stopping. Going home to bed seemed like the most natural thing in the world. It was like I was a "normal" person. Getting up the next morning was no problem. I didn't sleep till noon, and I didn't have a hangover.

After the weekend was over, I returned to the city where I live and got right back into my routine. I didn't have another drink for a solid three months, when I went back to my hometown for another visit. Once again, I got in touch with my friend and we went out for a few beers. We'd go out, have six, seven beers, and that would be it. So automatically I started thinking, "Hey, I don't have a problem anymore. I can handle this shit."

This time, when I came back to the city, I stopped off at a grocery store, bought a six-pack of Budweiser, and took it home and drank all six beers. Pretty soon, I started doing that on a regular basis. I'd buy a six-pack on my way home from work, and drink my beer in front of the TV. A pattern was beginning to form, and all the while I was telling myself, "Hey, I can handle it. I'm a different person now. I've got a good job, a nice home, a new truck. All these responsibilities have changed everything. I'm not going to let this shit get the best of me."

Well, my favorite drink wasn't beer, it was Jack Daniel's. One Friday night, instead of stopping at the grocery store for a six-pack, I stopped at the liquor store and bought a fifth of Jack Daniel's. I polished that off over the weekend, and once again my pattern changed. Instead of drinking beer every night, I was drinking bourbon. I was starting to have hangovers in the morning, but I was still managing to get to work without any real problem.

Pretty soon, I stopped buying fifths, and started buying half gallons of Jack Daniel's, because I was running to the liquor store too often. When I'd go out to dinner with friends, I'd have four or five drinks before dinner, a couple of drinks with the meal, and a couple more bourbons after dinner. Then I'd go home and have a few more drinks before bed. And I was still bullshitting myself. I'd gone well beyond the point of social drinking, but I'd be telling myself, "Hey, what's a few drinks with friends? It's no big deal. I can handle it. No way am I going to let this shit get control of me. I'm a different person now."

The strange thing was, I knew better. I'd been through treatment. I'd been to thousands of AA meetings. I knew I was an alcoholic. I knew what it was like to live on the street as a drunk who couldn't hold a job. And once again, I was experiencing all of the classic symptoms. I was irritable at work. I was having hangovers in the morning. I had blackouts. The quality of my work suffered on the job. I wasn't getting along with people. But in spite of all that, I chose to believe my voice of self-delusion. As the bottles piled up in the garbage can behind the house, I chose to believe my denial. I kept telling myself that I didn't have a problem, that I was a better person now.

This went on for about ten, twelve weeks, and during this time I was seeing a lady friend. One night she and I got into an argument, and that set me off. After I hung up the phone, I started drinking with a vengeance. That night I polished off a fifth of bourbon and a six-pack of beer. The next morning I got up and lit into a half gallon. Before I even realized it, the entire half gallon was gone. So I opened up a bottle of Canadian whiskey that someone had given me as a gift, and went to work on that. I'm talking about serious nonstop binge drinking. I'm sure I blacked out on a lot of it, but after about twenty-four hours I do remember getting into this routine where I'd lie down and sleep for a couple hours, and then wake up in incredible pain because I'd be going into withdrawal. So I'd have a few drinks, and then I'd lie back down and try to go to sleep. Then I'd have to pop back up for more booze. I was thinking, "You've got to stop. You can't keep doing this. But if I stop I'm going into dt's. What am I supposed to do about that?" I'd had dt's before, and didn't want any part of that. So I thought, "Well, I'll get some beer and taper myself off with beer." Of course, that didn't work either.

This went on for five full days. Nonstop binge drinking followed by a couple hours of sleep, and more binge drinking. That was five days of absolute hell. And I ended up exactly where I belonged—in the hospital. I was admitted to the addiction treatment center on an emergency basis. I had to go through medical detox, and then start treatment all over again. That was terrible. I felt so fucking guilty, because I knew better. After eleven years of sobriety, I'd let it happen again. It's embarrassing to think about, and embarrassing to admit. Of all the people who should have known better, I let the bottle get the best of me, and I damn near drank myself to death.

Fortunately, the hospital had a first-class treatment program, and I was able to get myself back into a reasonable semblance of shape fairly quickly. I've been out of the hospital for about six months now, and I can assure you that I'm not missing my AA meetings anymore. Those meetings are what I use to treat my disease. Even though my relapse was very painful, and I'd never recommend it to anybody, I feel like I learned a lot as a consequence of having gone through it. For me, going through treatment a second time was like learning to walk all over again. Now that I'm back in the swing of things, and over the initial shock, I feel like there's one thing in this world that I'm entirely sure of, and that is, I'll never be able to bullshit myself again. I'll never be able to tell myself, "Hey, you've changed. You're a big boy now. You've got responsibilities. You can handle a drink."

The truth is, I can't. Unfortunately, that's a lesson a lot of us are forced to learn the hard way. Drug addicts and alcoholics are among the most stubborn, hardheaded people in the world. We don't believe what we're told, but only what we experience, and in that sense, as painful as it may be, relapse can be therapeutic.

ERNIE: The last time I went to jail it was on an assault-with-a-deadly-weapon charge. My deadly weapon was a Seagram's Seven bottle. What happened is I was downtown drinking and drugging the way I did every night, and I ran into this guy who'd pulled a knife on me a couple weeks before. He was talking trash, wanting to fight, and he had a couple friends there with him. He was telling me to come on, and he had his knife out. That's when I picked up the bottle. I broke the end off so it had a jagged edge, and I was ready to go upside this guy's head. A crowd gathered, and we were standing in the middle of the street getting ready to rumble when the cops showed up.

They hauled both of us off to jail. The guy with the knife was back on the street inn about half an hour, because his friends bailed him out. But no one came for me. I sat in jail two days waiting to go before the judge. I had a couple other charges outstanding, and my lawyer was talking penitentiary because the DA was tired of seeing me come through the system. I'm only five-five, and I honestly didn't know if I could survive in the penitentiary. Sitting there in jail, I got this really bad feeling in the pit of my stomach. I was thinking, "Life isn't supposed to be like this." I'd been living in addiction for six, seven years, had committed all sorts of crimes, and had spent a year living homeless on the street. I didn't have any friends, and my father had told me to never use the family name again.

I'd given up on God, but sitting in that jail cell I was so frightened that I said a little prayer. That prayer went like this: "Dear God, I can't live this way anymore. I need help."

After my preliminary hearing, I was released pending my trial. From an earlier DWI [driving while intoxicated] conviction, I'd been sentenced to go to these ASAP [Alcohol Safety Action Program] meetings. After I got out of jail, I attended my first ASAP meeting, and the instructor asked everybody present to describe how alcohol was affecting their lives emotionally, spiritually, financially, and pro-fessionally. Well, I went on and on for about forty-five minutes, de-scribing the depths to which my life had fallen, and how I was looking at prison when my trial came up. After the meeting the in-structor suggested that I go to an AA meeting. I really wasn't inter-ested in doing that, but he told me that he'd write a letter to the judge saying I'd complied with his request if I'd be willing to give it a try. Well, I needed help in court, so I started going to AA meetings.

At my first meeting there were a bunch of folks there who looked like they were all doing real well. A couple of 'em told me that they'd been as bad as me. Emotionally, I was receptive to these people be-cause I was tired of living the way I was living. I was tired of sticking needles in my veins. I was tired of eating out of trash cans and sleeping in abandoned buildings. Looking around, I could see that none of the folks at this meeting were going back and forth to jail. They all had jobs, and clean clothes, and were eating real food.

My court date was thirty days away, and I made a commitment to go to one AA meeting every day until I went to court, because I needed that letter from my ASAP instructor. Eventually, after listening to these people describe what their lives had been like, I started thinking, "Hey, maybe this will work for me." Hanging around with the people at AA gave me some incentive. They were all clean, so I started to bathe and shave. You know, I didn't want to be the only guy sitting in meetings who smelled bad. Every now and then one of them would buy me coffee or lunch. They took an interest in me, and didn't mind being around me—which was very unusual for a addict living on the street.

I made a commitment to stay clean and sober until my court date. That meant thirty days without booze, cocaine, or pills. In that time, I came to realize that there are a lot of addicts in the world who have experienced what I was feeling then—the loneliness, the fear, the anxiety, the regrets, the remorse. Slowly, I came to understand that there was a way out. That I didn't have to be a drug addict and an alcoholic for the rest of my life.

Fortunately, I wasn't sentenced to the penitentiary, and I didn't have to do any serious time. I got a job working on a construction crew, and kept on going to AA meetings. I'm happy to say that it's been twelve years since my first meeting, and I haven't had a drink or taken an illegal drug since. On the job, I've worked my way up to foreman, and I've earned the respect of my boss as well as of the men who work on my crew.

One of the ironies is that peer pressure had a lot to do with my drinking and drugging. But now, peer pressure is keeping me clean and sober. The folks I hang out with at meetings are all staying straight, and knowing that gives me strength. It helps me resist temptation. Just about every time I leave town I tell myself, "Hey these folks don't know me. I could go out, have a few drinks, and no one would ever know." Or sometimes, when the stress of life is weighing me down, I tell myself, "I need a drink. I need to calm down." But I never do it, because I don't want to be the guy who is sitting there hiding something at a meeting. In addiction, I didn't want to be the only guy who was sober. In sobriety, I don't want to be the only guy who's out there using. I don't want to be the guy that's got to come back in and tell everybody that I screwed up, that I went out and got drunk when I was out of town because I thought I could get away with it. So I stay clean and sober even though there are times when I don't want to. I stay sober because that's what my friends expect of me.

THEODORE ZIEGLER: One of the reasons our treatment success rates are so low is that in working with hard-core addicts from impoverished backgrounds, the problem runs a lot deeper than simply getting them into treatment. Even if you get addicts to really work on their addiction while they're in treatment, you're still not out of the woods.

We have a Job Club run by a guy named Clint, and it's Clint's job to find employment for these hard-core addicts as they come out of treatment. He does "vocational assessments" to find out what they're best suited for. He takes a pencil and he writes "one quarter," and says, "Give me the decimal equivalent." Most of them can't do it. He writes down "one half," and says, "Give me the decimal equivalent." Again, they can't do it. He takes a yardstick and lays it on the table—you and I know the smallest increment is a sixteenth of an inch—he says, "Tell me the smallest increment under one inch." Can't do it. For simple reading comprehension he has them read two paragraphs about the John F. Kennedy assassination that describe the reason Kennedy was in Dallas, the kind of car he was in, the number of shots fired, who was in the car with him, all that. After they read it, Clint closes the book and asks, "Okay, who got shot?" Most of them know it was Kennedy. "What kind of car was he in?" Most can't remember. "Who was in the car with him?" They don't know. "How many shots were fired?" Again, they don't know. They've just read this basic information, but their comprehension is so low they can't answer even the most fundamental questions one minute later.

Clint turns to me and says, "Hey, how am I supposed to get these people jobs when they can't read, they've got no math skills, and they've got very limited comprehension skills? What the hell kind of job am I going to get them?" Now, anybody can leave treatment and go back onto the street and make a couple hundred dollars just by hanging out on the street corner. To do that you don't have to read or be able to do math.

So even if we succeed in getting them off drugs, they've still got to earn a living. How do you think they're going to do that given their "qualifications"? And how long do you think they'll stay off drugs in that environment? Now, there are answers to the problem, but any sane, intelligent person knows that those answers are not cheap. We're talking about a lot more than treatment. We're talking about serious social and political problems that cannot be separated from the drug epidemic in a meaningful way.

RANDY: When I first started going to NA meetings, the people there told me, "We're not about getting good. We're about getting well." That was something I needed to know, otherwise I never would've stayed with it. Nobody was moralizing and telling me that I couldn't steal cars or rob stores. They were telling me, "We're sick and we want to get well. That's all."

Since I got clean, I've been involved in a lot of illegal situations. A lot of wild, bizarre shit has gone down. There are times when I'm still working the street, still living on the edge. Even though I'm not messing with drugs anymore, I haven't given up on fun and excitement. I haven't given up on my criminal life-style.

CHUCK: I've heard some people say that to stop bein' an addict you've got to have some kind of crisis in your life. You've got to hit bottom. But that ain't what happened to me.

What happened to me was somewhere along the line bein' an addict stopped bein' fun. After nineteen years of shootin' heroin, drinkin' alcohol, and smokin' the crack pipe, I woke up one morning and said, "I ain't had me no fun in a long time." I was thirty-four years old, and I felt eighty.

When the opportunity to get into a treatment program came along, I took it. I was thinking, "Man, there's got to be a better life beyond the needle and the crack pipe." I told the treatment counselor, "Man, I been in treatment before, but this is the first time I ever wanted to stop. This is the first time I ever really wanted to come clean."

Since I've been in the program, I've been learning a lot. I was living a criminal life-style for a long time. I was on a violent trip, and I wasn't happy. A lot of it was because I wasn't able to identify—you know, I'd go out on the job market and I wouldn't feel qualified. But I couldn't articulate what I was feeling. I just felt this anger, this rejection, like all of society was against me. I'd go in to apply for a job, and I'd come out sayin', "Them people is prejudiced. They ain't gonna hire me." In my mind it was a black-white thing.

We talk about that stuff in the program. I still believe there's racial prejudice in society, but I've come to understand that destroying myself ain't the way to handle it. I want to build my people up, not tear them down. And that's what the needle does, man. It tears you down. It's a death trip. A motherfucking death trip.

TERRY: After finishing treatment, I got a job and moved out of government housing. I moved out into the suburbs, man, near where my job was. That was a good experience. I stayed drug-free for nine months. That's because I was around positive people—people who was having fun, but wasn't getting high. I couldn't believe that shit. These people was having softball games and barbecues and going camping, and all kinds of stuff. I said, "Man, these people is actually having fun. These people is partying and laughing and carrying on, and ain't nobody getting high."

They was people who was off welfare. They didn't have no trick whores and hustlers hanging around. None of that street shit. They was just having parties and having fun. I'd never been exposed to anything like that before. Where I come from, growing up in government housing, people is always sitting around getting high. The women is selling their bodies for 'caine, and the men is going out robbing and stealing. The hustlers is always on the street right in front of your door.

By living in the suburbs, and associating with these positive people, I stayed clean for nine months. The reason I slipped back into drugs is I started coming around my old neighborhood again. At first, I was just coming to visit my mother. Then I started coming around to see this girl. I wasn't interested in no drugs or nothing. I just wanted to get my dick sucked. Pretty soon, I was staying with this girl two, three nights in a row. I was back in my old environment with my old associates. That environment pulls on you, man. You go to a party and everybody be getting high. Just by being around that shit, man, you gonna get high too. You gonna take a hit on the crack pipe when it gets passed around.

That's what happened to me. I started hitting the crack pipe again. Once I did that, it was all over. My life went straight downhill. I quit going to work, and I lost my apartment. I went back out on the street and was hustling again. I was back in the life, man. I was doing the whole crackhead trip. I was living for the pipe, man.

After I got sent to prison, I was lucky to get into this treatment program here. I'm staying clean again, because the life of an addict ain't no life at all. When I get out, I'm going to be living in a halfway house for a year, and I know I'm going to need that kind of support. I'm going to need to stay away from my old neighborhood, man. I can't be going back there to make whoopee or visit my old associates. This time, you ain't gonna be seeing me on Filmore Street.

ROBERT: When I was messing with hard drugs, my life was a drag. I was robbing drug dealers and ducking bullets. I was kicking in doors and taking drugs and money. On the street, people were afraid of me, because they knew I'd shoot first and ask questions later. When people become afraid, they either kill you or get you locked up. Well, they couldn't kill me, but I've been locked up in prison for these past fifteen years.

I honestly believe that God intervened in my life or I'd be dead. I'm going to be getting out next year, and I think God has a mission for my life. I want to go to the youth and give them a positive role model, a positive example. I want to show them that they don't need to make the same mistakes I made. I want to show them that there's a better way than drugs and guns and murder. The kids coming up in the drug culture today don't know what they're doing to themselves.

I know from experience. There was a time in my life when I prevailed in evil and wrongdoing. I've got these wounds on my body. I got shot in the hip, and right here in the shoulder. These wounds are not from Vietnam. These wounds are from the street war. They're from my own black brothers trying to kill me.

When I go back out, I feel like I can contribute something better than blood and violence. Like I said, I'm going to be on a mission from God.

GERALD: Being in prison has kept me from raising my son. He's eight years old, and I'm scared that he'll get caught up in that drug cesspool the same way I did. I'm scared because he likes gold chains. He likes flashy glamor. And I don't believe my wife can control him. When he comes to visit, he tells me, "Daddy, I ain't going to mess with no drugs." But deep down inside of me there is this fear that when the opportunity comes to him—when that hundred-dollar roll is flashed before his eyes—he'll try hustling. I seriously believe he'll try.

Fortunately, my release date is in June, so I'll be getting out of prison when he's nine years old. When I get out I want to spend time with him—play baseball and basketball. I want him to learn from all the bad things that have happened to me. I've been incarcerated for six years now. That's been six years of doing nothing. My life from the years twenty-four to thirty has been wasted. If I hadn't been a damn fool, I could've spent those years doing a whole lot of good things.

My attitude now is you can never get too much education. I want my son to go to school. I want to instill a dream in him. As long as he has a dream that's positive, I'm going to support him in it. When drugs is offered to him, I want him to be able to say, "Man, I think highly of myself. I'm not going to let you bring me down to that level, because I got a dream. I'm going after my dream, and I can't do it with no drugs."

INDEX